THE MISSING CENTURY

The series Palaestina Antiqua was first published in Dutch by J.H. Kok Publishing House – Kampen. After consultation of the board it was decided to publish in English and German under Kok Pharos Publishing House. The series is now continued by Peeters – Leuven. The editorial board is formed by dr. C.H.J. de Geus (Groningen), prof.dr. Ed Noort (Groningen), and prof.dr. Antoon Schoors (Louvain/Leuven).

The advisory board is formed by:
Dr. G.I. Davies (Cambridge), prof.dr. A. Lemaire (Paris), prof.dr. D. Ussishkin (Tel Aviv), and dr. H. Weippert (Heidelberg).

1. H.J. Franken, Grondstoffen voor de materiële cultuur in Palestina en omliggende gebieden
2. J. Negenman, Een geografie van Palestina
3. C.H.J. de Geus, De Israëlitische stad
4. H.J. Franken, De puinhopen van het verleden
5. Antoon Schoors, Berseba – De opgraving van een bijbelse stad
6. R. van den Broek, J. Derksen, G. Mussies, K. Vriezen (red.), Kerk en kerken in Romeins-Byzantijns Palestina

New Series:

7. Herbert Donner, The Mosaic Map of Madaba
8. Ed Noort, Die Seevölker in Palästina
9. Ze'ev Safrai, The Missing Century

THE MISSING CENTURY

PALESTINE IN THE FIFTH CENTURY: GROWTH AND DECLINE

Ze'ev SAFRAI

PEETERS
1998

ISBN 90-6831-985-X
D. 1998/0602/5

CONTENTS

ACKNOWLEDGMENT

There are many partners and helpers in the writing of a book and it is a great pleasure to thank all those who helped in the research and in the publication of this work.

During the course of the research for this study, I benefited greatly from the advice of many colleagues, more than I can ever name. However, I would especially like to thank Prof. Joshua Schwartz and Prof. Shimon Dar, both of the Martin (Szus) Department of Land of Israel Studies of Bar-Ilan University and Prof. Eric Meyers of Duke University.

Much of this work was written during a stay at the Oxford Centre for Post-Graduate Hebrew and Jewish Studies. The extensive libraries in Oxford provided the materials to base this work on a wide and far-ranging view of the Byzantine Empire.

I should also like to especially thank my family, my wife Dinah and my children, who traveled with me to Oxford and helped me, each according to his or her abilities and individual ways. A special note of thanks is due to my daughter Osnat who helped with certain calculations.

The translation from Hebrew into English was undertaken by Edward Levine. Miriam Waldman prepared the illustrations and Alyta Fitaro the index. They all deserve a hearty vote of thanks. I am especially privileged to thank the staff of Feeters Publishing House and especially Liesbeth Verloove who worked hard on the publication of this book and saved me from many errors.

The research for this book was funded by the Irving and Cherna Moskowitz Chair in the Historic Land of Israel and by the research fund of the Martin (Szus) Department of Land of Israel Studies established through a donation of the Koschitzky Family. To each and all I extend my thanks.

CHAPTER ONE

The Presentation of the Problem

The Theoretical Background and Research Methods

The growth and decline of settlements and societies are, in great measure, quantitative concepts. Population size, economic productive capability, and similar data may, and must, be presented in quantitative terms. The examination of such data from the past presents the historical researcher with an extremely difficult challenge. The historical sources do not, as a general rule, provide quantitative data. We do not know the number of inhabitants of various regions, nor how much they produced, or the quantitative economic importance of each economic branch. Recent research of the Roman Empire has attempted to refine the quantitative research tools, and much effort has been devoted to the search for methods which will enable scholars to deal with issues requiring a comprehensive perception of the processes of expansion and regression. In general, these researchers attempt to examine the disintegration of the Roman Empire and to reveal the beginnings of the degenerative processes within this tremendous empire.

Historical research usually relies upon written sources: works and inscriptions dating from ancient times. Each of the early writers describes his period, and their compositions are of great value in clarifying many historical questions. These sources, however, are problematic when describing the differences between their and earlier periods. These writers had erroneous conceptions regarding previous periods, and they unjustifiably attributed splendor or deterioration to preceding eras. The sources are likely to describe a certain city as prosperous and expanding in a previous period. "Prosperity" in the Roman period, however, does not have the same meaning as was attributed to the term in, e.g., the Middle Ages, and such terms do not add to our understanding when comparing these periods. Furthermore, at times the ancient authors were in thrall to the image they attributed to preceding periods or to their own time. Even though such a conception was patently influenced by the reality, it nevertheless was not totally representative of it[1].

[1] For the difference between image and reality, see, e.g.: I. Morris, *Death-Ritual and Social Structure in Classical Antiquity* (Cambridge, 1992), pp. 6-8.

By the same coin, the tools of literary criticism do not suffice for an examination of economic and demographic decline. It is usually possible to literarily evaluate the nature of various works in comparison with those of preceding periods. Thus, e.g., classical scholars are capable of indicating the degeneration of Greek literature, based on a comparison of the works of Plato or Thucydides with those of later authors. Researchers of Roman literature indicate the qualitative gap between the golden era of Roman literature in the time of the Republic and the late Roman literature. These differences served as a basis, and justification, for determining the decline of the Empire, but such evaluations are unjustified and baseless.

Qualitative differences in literary works are not necessarily a direct consequence of the demographic, economic, or political situation. Creative ability springs from spiritual wellsprings which are necessarily detached from the economic or settlement reality. Thus, e.g., the limited numbers of Jews in the communities of Ashkenaz in the eleventh-twelfth centuries bear no relation to the intensity of the religio-cultural activity in these communities. These small numbers of Jews produced an impressive quantity of books in this period. Moreover, it is difficult to determine and measure qualitative differences, and our understanding of them is totally subjective. There is a natural tendency to portray the "past" as a golden era, aggrandizing the early ones who possessed the "true values," but such evaluations frequently prove to be myth, based solely on the aspirations and wishes of their successors. The ancient warning of Koheleth, "Say not thou, 'How was it that the former days were better than these?' for it is not out of wisdom that you inquirest concerning this,"[2] is still as valid as when it was written.

Slightly more sophisticated is the attempt to measure the quantity of literary output. MacMullen, who has recently devoted a lengthy discussion to this question, presents a quantitative calculation of the numbers of Greek and Roman works in the first centuries CE. His examination indicates a drastic decline after 250 CE.[3] MacMullen correctly expresses the lack of a theoretical basis for the claim that a decrease in the quantity of the cultural product indicates, or at least alludes to, a demographic decline.

Duncan-Jones has recently published a book containing a series of attempts to present quantitative indexes which enable the researcher to

[2] Eccl. 7:10.

[3] R. MacMullen, *Corruption and the Decline of Rome* (New Haven, 1988), pp. 145 ff.

describe and evaluate the decline of the Roman Empire. These indexes include, e.g., an examination and chronological summary of the quantities of inscriptions in general, and especially the quantities of dedicatory inscriptions (Fig. 1); the quantity of public buildings; sunken ships (Fig. 2); and many other indicators (Figs. 3-4).[4] The information is impressive in both quantity and quality, but raises many methodological problems. These questions were raised, in quite sharp fashion, by MacMullen;[5] thus, e.g., the writing of inscriptions is also influenced by a certain social atmosphere, which changes in different societies, as has been demonstrated recently.[6] The motivation to build public buildings also was dependent, inter alia, upon social and religious circumstances. Thus, e.g., the wave of church construction in the fifth and sixth centuries does not attest to economic growth, but rather is explained by a religious transition which entailed new requirements for religious buildings and by the desire of individuals to declare their support, through their contributions, for the new religion which had gained predominance. Such a proclamation had its basis in either religious or utilitarian motives.[7] The research literature cited above constitutes only a part of the material published in the past two-three years, attesting to the intensiveness of the efforts to resolve these historical methodological questions, and indicating that the research in this field is still in its infancy.

This book will attempt to clarify and date the processes of decline in Palestine in the fourth and fifth centuries. Following MacMullen's suggestion, our examination will focus on the archaeological data, making intensive use of the numismatic finds. The utilization of such data is not straightforward, and is dependent upon progress in the clarification of complex methodological questions.

A number of archaeological excavations which were conducted with full scientific rigor have been published in recent years. Their final publication enables us to analyze the finds and to use them as a basis for our investigation. Partially published data has been used sparingly, since experience teaches that there is somewhat of a difference between initial and final conclusions.

4 R. Duncan-Jones, *Structure and Scale in the Roman Economy* (Cambridge, 1990); see also Hopkins (below, n. 12).

5 MacMullen (above, n. 3), loc. cit.

6 A. Meyer, "Explaining the Epigraphic Habit in the Roman Empire: The Evidence of Epitaphs", *JRS* 80 (1990), pp. 74-96.

7 Interesting material about Syria was collected by Liebeschuetz: J. H. W. G. Liebeschuetz, *From Diocletian to the Arab Conquest: Change in the Late Roman Empire* (Variorum, 1990), No. VIII.

The dating of settlement strata from the fourth and fifth centuries is frequently based on the numismatic finds, because the differences between fourth and fifth century pottery have not been sufficiently determined. In many excavations, the pottery has been defined as "Late Roman", "Roman-Byzantine", or "Byzantine". These terms express the inability of the excavators to determine a more precise dating. For our purposes, such reporting is disappointing and prevents our use of such material.

Public buildings, mainly synagogues, have been uncovered in many excavations, including Khirbet Shema', en-Nabratein, Qasrin, and many other sites mentioned below. In such excavations, the establishment of the synagogue may be dated on the basis of the pottery and numismatic finds in its foundation. A portion of the coins apparently were laid in the foundation as a charm or prayer for divine mercy; it may be assumed that they had already ceased to be in circulation. In the absence of supportive material, such an assumption is liable to raise the possibility that the structure was established only 50-100 years after the last coin found in the foundation. Furthermore, the finds pose a difficulty in determining how long the building was in regular use. At times sherds found on the pavement of the structure were swept in from the surrounding area, and sometimes the material collected is insufficient to reconstruct the history of the settlement after the establishment of the building. Similarly, a distinction is to be drawn between the history of the public buildings and that of the settlement as a whole. Only additional excavations of residential structures, and especially of courtyards and streets, are likely to provide the data necessary for a reconstruction of the entire settlement.

Rural or Urban Sectors

Before beginning the clarification of the data, it should be noted that information is to be sought mainly from the rural sector. Most of the large cities continued to be active, in some degree or other, throughout the period under discussion. It is difficult to discern the gradual abandonment of a city in regular archaeological excavations. I.e., any decline in the level of the urban activity or a lessening in the population of the city may not have left traces in the public structures. Furthermore, the religious changes of the fourth and fifth centuries led to a dramatic transformation in the role of the public buildings. The temples, theaters, amphitheaters, and to some degree the forums, were gradually abandoned, and new public structures were built. Consequently, the abandonment or construction of such public structures does not express decline or growth.[8]

Literary sources from the Byzantine period clearly indicate that the number of cities in Palestine did not decrease. To the contrary, the civil administrative lists of Hierocles Synecdemus and Georgius Cyprius and the Christian administrative lists contain more cities than those of any other period (Fig. 5). Still undetermined, however, is whether the population of these cities increased or decreased. A decline in the rural sector is likely to be expressed in the abandonment of a village, and it is highly likely that this will be revealed in excavations. A decline in a large city, in contrast, will be expressed by a decrease in residential density or by the abandonment of structures within the city. The discovery of such data is difficult, and the probability that this will be revealed in excavations is small. Obviously, however, use will be made of data from the excavations of the polis cities in Palestine.

The Quantitative Numismatic Data

One of the central techniques for the measurement of prosperity and decline consists of the effort to integrate the quantitative data of coin assemblages and to use it as a historical source. The underlying assumption is that a large or small average number of coins per year indicates volume of trade, and possibly also population size. The initial efforts were based on a calculation of the number of coin types issued by each emperor. It is assumed that prosperity will be expressed, inter alia, in a larger number of types. This assumption may have a logical basis, but is not to be regarded as an inflexible rule, because the quantity of types is influenced by a group of factors, only one of which is the economic consideration. In any event, Ostrogorsky has shown that the number of types does not constitute reliable testimony,[9] and, consequently, this method has no factual basis. Foss later used the quantitative data in a different fashion. He assembled the data pertaining to quantity of coins found in certain excavations, and assumed that a decrease in the average number of coins per year is indicative of an economic decline (see

[8] The fascinating issue of the church's domination of Palestine and the urban landscape lies beyond the scope of this work; see below, Chap. 4, for a few comments on the topic.

[9] G. Ostrogorsky, "Byzantine Cities in the Early Middle Ages", *DOP* 13 (1959), pp. 45-66.

below, Chap. 5).[10] This attempt did not receive a great deal of attention. Foss's views were accepted by outstanding researchers such as Kennedy and others,[11] but did not generate a methodological discussion, possibly because his research dealt with the Byzantine Empire in the seventh century, a location and period both of which have been relatively overlooked by researchers. Greater interest was aroused by the conclusions of Hopkins, which were based on similar data, but which discuss an entire, central period.[12] Parallel methodological discussions regarding the significance of these data have been conducted by numismatic researchers from the 1970s,[13] and the major elements of this methodological effort will appear in our discussion (see below). Before utilizing this branch of information, we must first resolve the many methodological questions connected with its use:

1. Are the quantities of coins we possess truly representative and constitute a random, but accurate, sampling of the quantities of coins present in the subterranean strata, and what quantity of coins is necessary for the assemblage to serve as a sample?
2. Are the coins found in the subterranean strata genuinely representative of market conditions in all the historical periods?
3. What influenced the quantity of coins present in the market: the volume of trade, or – mainly – the number of inhabitants? How did inflationary factors influence the quantity of coins in the market, and how did monetary legislation affect the quantity of coins in each period?
4. In order to clarify the issues in (3), is it necessary to take into account the differences in coin values and their worth in the market?

The answers to these questions are complex, and entail an examination of the quality of the finds we possess.

[10] C. Foss, "The Persians in Asia Minor and the End of Antiquity", *EHR* 90 (1975), pp. 721-747.

[11] F. Kennedy, "The Last Century of Byzantine Syria. A Reinterpretation", *Byzantinische Forschungen* 10 (1985), pp. 141-183; idem, "The Towns of Bilad al-Sham and the Arab Conquest", in *Bilad al-Sham during the Byzantine Period*, eds. M. A. Bakhit and M. Asfour (Amman, 1986), pp. 88-99.

[12] K. Hopkins, "Taxes and Trade in the Roman Empire (200 B.C. – A.D. 400)", *JRS* 70 (1980), pp. 101-125.

[13] See, e.g.: R. Reece, "Bronze Coinage in Roman Britain and the Western Provinces, A.D. 330-402", in *Scripta Nummaria Romana: Essays Presented to Humphrey Sutherland, eds. R. A. G. Carson and C. M. Kraay* (London, 1978); C. M. King, "The Value of Hoards and Site Finds in Relation to Monetary Circulation in the Late Third and Early Fourth Centuries A.D", in *Studien zu Fuendmuenzen der Antike, Herausgeegeben von M. R. Alföldi* (Berlin, 1979), pp. 79-98; also see below.

1. **Are the quantities of coins we possess truly representative and constitute a random, but accurate, sampling of the quantities of coins present in the subterranean strata, and what quantity of coins is necessary for the assemblage to serve as a sample?**

Excavations, surveys, and chance finds have yielded thousands of ancient coins, all of which may be given a precise chronological definition and which have been given prominence in every scientific publication. At times, however, the publication of the material is extremely deficient, with an inexplicable and serious delay in its publication. Thus, e.g., the assemblages of coins from the excavations in Shiqmona, Beth She'arim, the synagogue in Caesarea, Qasrin, 'Avdat, and many other settlements are still unpublished. Accordingly, all the excavations in Israel (including those as yet unpublished) should be examined and summarized. Notwithstanding this, a quite large number of excavations have been properly published, and accurately represent most parts of the province. Still missing are representative assemblages from the southern Hebron hill country (the assemblage from Susiya is too small) and from the southern Shephelah, which is represented solely by the numismatic finds from Rimmon. During the preparation of this work, many unpublished assemblages also were examined, the most important of which are discussed below.

The extant coin assemblages come from a number of types of finds:[14]

(a) *Excavations*

Needless to say, the assemblage of coins found in excavations accurately reflects the material present in the excavations area. The numismatic finds are likely to teach of the history of the settlement to the same degree that the excavations in their entirety are representative of the settlement. At times, the excavations represent only a special section of the city, but in this respect the numismatic finds are no different from any other archaeological material. The quantity of coins found in each excavation is influenced by a range of factors, some of which are historical (the quantity of coins in circulation in the local markets), while others are technical or random. Thus, e.g., careful excavations and the sifting of the earth, accompanied by the use of modern instrumentation, is likely to

[14] This division is somewhat similar to that proposed by Grierson in 1965, but with some differences: P. Grierson, "The President's Address", *NC* Seventh Series, 5 (1965), pp. i-xiii.

increase the number of coins which are found. Excavations in a paved and built area will yield fewer coins than excavations in an unpaved area; similarly, other such factors also affect the finds.[15] Obviously, the extent of the excavations exerts a decisive influence upon the quantity of finds. Consequently, finds from different excavations should not be combined, and comparisons between the quantity of coins in various excavations are of little value, unless the excavations were conducted under identical conditions. Thus, e.g., more coins were found in Capernaum than in Pergamon, but this datum possesses no real value.

Nevertheless, it may be assumed that all these variables are at work and influence an excavation to an equal degree, and therefore changes in the quantities of coins in given periods of time are significant and must be explained.

Examples and proof of this are provided by the four assemblages from Corinth published at different times[16] or the finds from Carthage.[17] These excavations were conducted in different years, but the chronological distribution is almost identical, thus testifying that these are not incidental finds. The various excavations of Gerasa, on the other hand, yielded results differing from one another to some degree.[18] There are differences between the various excavation areas in Caesarea as well, but these deviations are quite small.

Despite the positive evaluation of the finds from the excavations, it should be emphasized that any excavations which do not encompass an entire settlement are not final. In Sephhoris, e.g., excavations were conducted in the 1930s and in the 1980s, and settlement phases until the late fourth century were uncovered. It is only recently, however, in the excavations of Netzer and Weiss, that settlement phases from the fifth century have begun to be uncovered, a few dozens of meters from the earlier excavations areas. Coin assemblages from different excavations areas frequently yield identical results, while yielding different results in other instances. The coin assemblages from each season (area) in Summaqa were examined separately (see below, appendix a), and the relative results were basically identical. Notwithstanding all these reservations, it

[15] M. Blackborn, "What Factors Govern the Number of Coins Found on an Archaeological Site?" in *Coins and Archaeology Medieval Archaeology Group* (*BAR* 556), eds. H. Clarke and E. Schia (Oxford, 1989), pp. 15-24.

[16] See below, Chap. 5.

[17] See below, the Appendix to Chap. 5; P. Grierson, "The President's Address", *NC* Seventh Series, 6 (1966), pp. i-xv.

[18] See below, appendix a.

is clear that the assemblages of coins from excavations accurately represent the situation in the excavations area, and (in the absence of contradictory finds) that of the entire settlement as well.

The chronological and statistic distribution of the coins is fixed, and therefore a specific explanation is to be sought which is suited to the historical reasons causing such a distribution.

(b) *Hoards*

A hoard is a sort of private purse of an individual or group which was abandoned for whatever reasons. This assemblage represents the circulation of coins in the year in which the hoard was abandoned, but does not reflect the circulation of coins and the monetary situation in the different periods.[19] These finds are of intrinsic interest, but it is dangerous to combine the quantitative finds of hoards with the finds of the excavations. Coins scattered throughout the area represent the circulation of coins over a prolonged period, while a hoard imparts excessive representation to a short period of a few decades and to an individual who thus overshadows the entire public. Furthermore, the number of hoards we possess is dependent upon historical events. Thus, e.g., we possess close to 30 hoards from the time of Hadrian, some of which consist of coins from the Bar Kokhba revolt, while others contain no coins from the uprising. The large number of hoards is unrelated to the volume of trade in the second century, but rather to the destruction and damage inflicted by the war. The hoards from the time of the revolt are likely to show the circulation of coins in the time of the revolt, and possibly a bit before it, but the quantities of Bar Kokhba coins found in hoards are not to be compared with assemblages from other sources. A good example of this rule is provided by a comparison of the assemblages of coins from Rimmon and from Gischala with the composition of the hoards found in these settlements (see below, Appendix a).

The concealment of a large number of hoards is indicative of tension and a wave of destruction, as was proposed by Crawford and Foss,[20] but

[19] M. H. Crawford, "Money and Exchange in the Roman World", *JRS* 60 (1970), pp. 40-48, in contrast to R. Duncan-Jones, *Money and Government in the Roman Empire* (Cambridge, 1994), pp. 78-85, who is of the opinion that a multiplicity of hoards reflects the allocation of money to soldiers. Duncan-Jones, however, discusses a period of relative tranquility. In Palestine, at any rate, there are more hoards in wartime periods, such as the Bar Kokhba revolt, the Great Revolt, and the Persian conquest in 614-17.

[20] Foss (above, n. 10), loc. cit.

this topic belongs to another field of research, one which lies outside the scope of the current work.

Consequently, a hoard is likely to teach only regarding the circulation of coins in a certain place, and in a defined year or period. Interesting testimony regarding the value of a hoard is provided by the Luhe hoard from Sweden. The distribution of coins in this large hoard corresponds to the literary data concerning the quantities of coins minted in Sweden in the period reflected by the hoard,[21] and therefore the hoard reflects the circulation of coins in the market at the time of its concealment. It does not, however, indicate the chronological fluctuations of the quantity of coins in the century or centuries it represents. Consequently, these finds are of no use for our investigation.

synagogue coins – as was stated above, hundreds of worn bronze coins of inferior value were found in the foundations of a number of synagogues, mainly under the pavement in the facade. Their concentration leads us to surmise that they were placed there intentionally, as a charm. It is not inconceivable that coins no longer in circulation were chosen for this. If this is the case, these coins would reflect the coins in circulation at a certain point in time, some decades before the establishment of the synagogue. Accordingly, combining these finds with the other finds is presumably not without its dangers. In practice, however, the differences between the finds in the settlement and those in the foundation of the synagogue are not drastic. E.g., the literature cites the numismatic finds from 'En Nashut and Capernaum (from the foundations as compared to the entire settlement) from the first half of the fourth century to the end of the fifth century. The relative chronological differences in quantity of coins are quite clear, but the overall picture of major developments (growth and decline) indicated by the finds in the foundation of the structure and that evidenced by the finds in the settlement itself are quite similar (see below, Appendix a).

The differences between the finds from the foundation of the synagogue and those from the settlement as a whole cannot be quantified, and therefore these finds have been added to the tables and calculations without further subdivision, even though this comprehensive treatment contains a certain degree of error.

[21] B. Thordeman, "The Luhe Hoard", *NC* Sixth Series, 8 (1948), pp. 188-204.

Many coins were found in the foundations of structures. These assemblages were naturally ended by the establishment of the structure. The latest coin does not attest to the end of the settlement or to a decline in economic activity, but rather the opposite: the initial use of the structure. It is difficult to include this datum in the tables, but it should be taken into consideration by the different theories.

(c) *Incidental Finds and Finds from Surveys*

Incidental finds are of equal value to excavations, provided that the survey was conducted in a methodical manner and that we are assured that all the finds were recorded and that no selection took place (see below). The assemblages of coins from, e.g., Jamnitarum Portus (400 coins) and from Umm Rihan (60 coins) are assemblages from such a survey conducted by the late A. Sadeh (see below, appendix a). The assemblage of coins from Arbel and assemblages from other sites also meet these conditions. At times, however, the assemblage consists of a small number of coins which underwent a process of selection, and not all the material was recorded.

(d) *Museums*

Various museums contain collections, at times large ones, of coins from excavations, from contributions by major collectors, from incidental finds which were donated to the museum, and from acquisitions by the museum's curators in the antiquities market. As a general rule, the place of origin of the coin is not recorded, and the major museums in Israel have received contributions from throughout the world. The acquisition and collection policy of the curators is a dominant factor in the formation of the collection. Every curator has personal priorities, and they all naturally tend to purchase exceptional coins. Consequently, the information to be obtained from such collections is sparse and problematic. Thus, e.g., the Israel Museum collection contains approx. 160 coins from the first half of the fourth century, but only 3 coins from the second half of this century, clearly demonstrating that this collection is random and unrepresentative.[22] It is necessary to understand the acquisitions policy of the specific museum, and only within this context would it be possible to draw any conclusions. Thus,

[22] I was informed of this by Y. Meshorer; I am grateful for his cordial assistance.

e.g., most curators in Israel would probably be eager to acquire coins from the autonomous cities. Accordingly, the assemblage of city coins may possibly be indicative of the quantitative relationship between the coins of the various cities (i.e., which city minted more coins), and of the quantitative chronology of city coins (when greater numbers of coins were issued, when certain denominations were more widely circulated, etc.).

Similar attention may be paid to a defined assemblage of, e.g., fourth century coins, and to ascertain which coins are represented in this assemblage. Although the assemblage is incidental, such an incidental collection of hundreds of coins is both random and reliable.

Small and regional museums and personal collections are a source for the history of the region. A private collector who specializes in local coins functions as a surveyor of the region, and a good local collection is representative of the region, provided that the regional collection has not undergone a selection process. Thus, e.g., most of the coins in the Bet Gordon Museum in Tiberias are from the Arab period, and the curator assumes that the discoverers of the coins kept the earliest ones for themselves. I.e., the collection underwent negative selection, thus becoming in great degree worthless for quantitative analysis.

In general, therefore, within the above-mentioned limitations, it may be assumed that the number of coins discovered in systematic excavations and surveys is representative of the subterranean numismatic inventory. Hoards also represent this inventory, but reflect narrow chronological evidence which is accurate only within a specific period. Accordingly, the following discussion will focus on finds from excavations and regional surveys and from museums containing a dedicated regional collection. This distinction was not maintained for the collection of data from excavations outside Israel, because these are larger assemblages, containing many hoards, and it may therefore be assumed that hoards will not be responsible for statistical deviations.

A significant number of coins is an underlying condition for the entire discussion. Since finds are intrinsically incidental, only a large number of finds will possess scientific worth. It is difficult to determine the necessary minimum which may properly serve as a historical source, but it is obvious that the greater the number of identified coins, the greater the reliability of the research.

2. Are the coins found in the subterranean strata genuinely representative of market conditions in all the historical periods?

In general, this question is to be answered affirmatively, with certain limitations. Naturally, fewer gold than silver coins were found in excavations and in surveys, and many more coins of bronze than of silver or gold. This differential is somewhat reflective of the rarity of precious coins in the market, but also of the better care taken to prevent the loss of the latter.

Coins in use by the inhabitants, and not merely those that they lost, will most likely be found in destruction strata, and it accordingly may be expected that the quantity of silver and gold coins will be slightly higher than normal; this assumption has yet to be methodically examined.

The coins which were discovered constitute incidental finds. In this respect, they are as valid as any other statistical datum, such as the chronological division of pottery vessels, oil-lamps, seals, or any other finds, but with the added advantage of greater ease in handling.

As regards the types of coins, research views coins as a neutral find, like pottery vessels or seals; consequently, the monetary value of the coin is insignificant. In any event, most coins are low denomination bronze coins. The finds of silver coins from Egypt discussed by West and Johnson provide an illustrative example.[23] A table in Chap. 5 lists the quantities of silver coins found in this province, along with the weight of silver in each period. The illustrations accompanying the current study (Figs. 13, 14) provide two calculations: a chronological summation of the quantities of coins, and a chronological summation of the total weight of silver in each period. The two illustrations present the same historical development, of growth and decline. The weight of the material of the coins, i.e., their face value, does not influence the results of the examination, since it does not lead to conclusions different from that provided by the total number of coins in each period.

Consequently, *the real monetary value of the coin and the weight of the raw material from which it was cast may be ignored; the total number of coins may be counted, as integers, and they may be regarded as a representative collection.*

The face value of the coins may serve as the subject of additional examinations, such as a comparison of the composition of the circulation of coins in different periods. Thus a preponderance of heavier coins in

[23] L. C. West and A. C. Johnson, *Currency in Roman and Byzantine Egypt* (Princeton: 1944), pp. 183-184.

period X may possibly reflect an increase in the volume of trade or inflation. While these questions are of undisputed importance, their study requires a very large number of coins. In order to produce significant results, the researchers must possess dozens of coins from each of six or seven values from each period. Such a set of circumstances is rare. It is to be hoped that increasing numbers of quantitative studies will enable the researcher to engage in such questions.

The quantities of coins found in excavations are insufficient to estimate, even approximately, the quantities of coins which were issued. It cannot be determined what percentage of coins in circulation were lost by their owners. Under modern conditions, 2% of the coins in circulation are said to be lost, but it is difficult to establish whether a similar percentage was lost under the conditions in which money was guarded in antiquity. The manner in which money is guarded in a modern wallet bears no resemblance to the "bag" or "pouch" of the ancients, and modern methods of guarding and saving money are inferior to those of our ancestors. Moreover, the quantity of lost coins is to be expressed as a percentage of the coins in circulation, and not of the quantity of coins which were minted.[24] The circulation of coins is expressed in the following equation:

$A = B \times C$

where

A = circulation of coins

B = number of transactions

C = quantity of coins issued

The number of coins which were minted in antiquity cannot be estimated, and consequently, it is difficult to learn from the quantity of coins lost at present (which is measured as a percentage of the quantity issued) and from the quantity of coins lost in antiquity regarding the circulation of coins in ancient times.

Consequently, the quantity of extant coins cannot serve as a basis for estimating the quantity of coins in the past, and therefore, the value of quantitative researches is solely comparative; i.e., whether this quantity is

[24] For the question of the number of coins produced from each die, see: W. W. Esti, "Estimation of the Size of a Coinage: A Survey and Comparison of Methods", *NC* 30 (1986), pp.185-215; J. W. Mueller, Estimation du nombre originel de coin, *Pact* 5 (1979), pp. 157-172. It is highly doubtful, however, if any average formula may be obtained. See: C. Howgego, "The Supply and Use of Money in the Roman World 200 B.C. to A.D. 300", *JRS* 82 (1992), pp. 1-31.

larger or smaller than that in a proximate period. The question arises, is it possible to reveal processes of growth or of decline and depletion? Figuratively speaking, the number of coins per se is not of importance, rather only the relative direction, i.e., an increase or decrease in the number of coins.

Grierson and Howgego raised additional considerations in this context:

(a) it is likely that low denomination coins of small physical size would be lost more frequently, while it would have been easier to keep larger coins;
(b) it is possible that in times of crisis money would be guarded more carefully.[25]

The diameter of coins did not change significantly from the third to the seventh centuries. To the contrary, in the fifth century smaller coins were minted (the "minima"); nevertheless, it will be shown that there are relatively few coins from this century. This consideration as well is of importance when collecting silver coins, but this study deals mainly with the concentration of finds of simple, worthless bronze coins.

Coin "Shelf Life"

Each coin had a characteristic "shelf life", or more accurately, "purse life". I.e., each coin was in circulation for a certain amount of time. The general outlines of the production process are known: the raw material was minted and transported to the mints where the coins were minted, prior to entering circulation as payments to members of the military or civilian officials, and they were used in the market for various transactions. Afterwards, they were returned to the government as tax payments, or perhaps in government-initiated substitutions of coins.[26]

The period of time in which a coin was in common use has not been determined, but is estimated to be decades.[27] In order to provide a full

[25] Howgego (above, n. 24), loc. cit.; Grierson 1965, pp. vi ff.

[26] R. Reece, "Mint, Markets and the Military", in *Military and Civilian in Roman Britain* (*BAR* 136), ed. A. C. King (Oxford 1984), pp. 143-160.

[27] The entire topic has not undergone a fundamental examination. Howgego collected a number of important data. Cities and legions impressed their own countmarks on coins which had been in circulation in a certain year. Howgego demonstrated that in many instances these basic coins were minted within a range spanning several decades, and consequently coins which had been minted several decades previously were in circulation: C. Howgego, *Greek Imperial Countmarks: Studies in the Provincial Coinage of the Roman Empire* (London, 1985).

answer to this question, all the hoards would have to be collected, followed by an examination of the range of years of the coins they represent. It may be assumed that changes occurred in this realm in different periods, and accordingly it may very well be difficult to obtain uniform results. In different periods, the removal from circulation of specific coins was regulated by law. Thus, e.g., the Bar Kokhba coins and the coins of the Great Revolt were clearly removed from circulation and declared illegal ("rebellion coins", in the language of the Mishnah) after thc repression of the revolts.[28] These coins most probably were not in use in the markets, which bore the brunt of direct Roman rule. The force of other laws is less clear. In the fourth century, a number of laws were instituted invalidating certain coins.[29] It cannot be established with certainty, however, that these laws affected activity in the market, and their influence on the simple bronze coins was even more questionable.

Consequently, the discovery of, e.g., coins minted in 300 does not necessarily attest to their use in this year. At best, they indicate activity at the site in the same century or half century. On the other hand, the absence of coins issued in a certain decade, or the presence of numerous coins from another decade, do not necessarily indicate the events of these decades, because the coins were likely to remain in use for a lengthier period of time. Accordingly, any attempted division must be of a general nature, and relate to periods. E.g., *drastic changes in the quantity of coins in Palestine occurred in 363 and in 408. These distinctions are not clear-cut, and are to be regarded as general time frames: ca. the midfourth century and ca. the early fifth century.*

At the same time, however, we cannot generally apply the prevalent claim that a paucity of coins found at a site is due mainly to the use of coins from earlier periods.[30] There were periods in which coins from previous years were used. Thus, e.g., in Egypt coins of Nero were still in use in the third century, and they constituted a majority of the coins in circulation.[31] It may also be assumed that in fifth century Gaul and the entire western Mediterranean use was made of coins from the fourth century,

[28] *Tosefta*, Ma'aser Sheni 1:5-6.

[29] F. M. Hendy, *Studies in the Byzantine Monetary Economy c. 300-1450* (Cambridge, 1985).

[30] See, e.g.: Howgego (above, n. 24); Grierson 1966, p. vi.

[31] E. Christiansen, "On Denarii and Other Coin-Terms in the Papyri", *ZPE* 54 (1984), pp. 271-99; J. G. Milne, "Roman Coinage in Egypt in Relation to the Native Economy", *Aegyptus* 32 (1952), pp. 143-151.

because there were almost no newer coins.[32] A different situation reigned in the eastern part of the Empire. It may be demonstrated that use was made mainly of coins minted in this century, based on a number of proofs:

(a) there are sites which were established or which flourished in the fifth century, in which much use was made of coins from this century. This was the case in, e.g., the church at Resafa (Sergiupolis);[33] the church of Katisma in Ramat Rahel, which was built in 450; the church in Bahan; Horvat Siga; and Scythopolis.[34]
(b) hoards from the fifth century mainly represent this century, e.g., the hoards from Gischala, the synagogue in Rimmon, and Abualanda in Transjordan.[35] The situation in the entire East was similar, thus, e.g., 92% of the coins from a hoard published by Adelson and Kustas are from the fifth century.[36] In the hoard from Corinth, 79% of the coins were minted in the fifth century,[37] with comparable findings from other hoards.[38]
(c) if coins from the fourth century had been in circulation in the fifth century, then we would expect to find hoards from the sixth century containing coins from the sixth century and from the fourth century, while coins from the fifth century would be either lacking or rare. Such hoards were not found, and hoards buried in the sixth century generally begin from the time of Anastasius.[39]

The situation in Egypt may have been somewhat different. In the large hoard from the fifth century published by Milne, the quantity of coins

[32] See, e.g.: R. B. Hitchner, "Meridional Gaul, Trade and the Mediterranean Economy in Late Antiquity", in *Fifth Century Gaul: A Crisis of Identity*, eds. J. Drinkwater and H. Elton (Cambridge, 1992), pp. 122-131.

[33] See below, appendix a n.130.

[34] See below, appendix a n.29

[35] See below, chap., 5. n.44.

[36] H. L. Adelson and G. L. Kustas, "A Bronze Hoard of the Period of Zeno I", *Numismatic Notes and Monographs* (New York, 1962), pp. 36-37; idem, "A Bronze Hoard of the Period of Leo I", *ANMN* 9 (1960), pp. 139-188.

[37] H. Mattingly, "A Late Roman Hoard from Corinth", *NC* Fifth Series, 11 (1931), pp. 229-233.

[38] See below, Chap. 5, n. 61 also see, e.g.: J. W. E. Pearce and M. E. Wood, "A Late Roman Hoard from Dalmatia, *NC* 14 (1934), pp. 269-283; cf. *Coin Hoards* 3 (1977), pp. 82-83, No. 228; No. 231; No. 232; p. 55, Nos. 123-131; p. 69, No. 224; *Coin Horards* 4 (1978), p. 43, Nos. 179-80; p. 44, Nos. 181, 187.

[39] See below, and of appendix a, e.g.: *Coin Hoards* 3 (1977), pp. 82-83, and many other hoards. In contrast, a hoard found in Spain contains coins from the time of Honorius and Arcadius; it does not contain coins from the fifth century, but many sixth-century coins are represented in it: see *Coin Hoards* 6 (1981), p. 50, No. 202.

from the second half of the fourth century greatly exceeds that of coins from the fifth century, thus indicating that most of the coins possessed by the owner of this hoard, who lived in the fifth century, were from the preceding century.[40] This picture is somewhat different from what is known of the other provinces in the East.

Accordingly, in the fifth century in Palestine, Syria, and Asia Minor, mainly coins from this century were in circulation. The fact that such coins are absent or present only in small quantities, indicates the small quantities of coins in circulation in this century. This conclusion leads to the need to discuss the consequences of the phenomenon.

The Quantity of Money: a Function of Supply or Consumption?

Another, similar argument which is raised by Howgego is that the quantity of money in circulation mainly expresses the quantity of money which was issued, and not the quantity of money consumed by the market, based on the assumption that the policy of issuing coins was not an economic one and does not exclusively represent the need of the market.[41] In our opinion, the situation was generally different. The quantity of money in circulation is the product of two factors: (a) the quantity of money issued and (b) circulation (the rate at which coins are used). If the authorities minted fewer coins, then the rate of their use would increase; conversely, if too many coins were issued, they would be used at a slower pace. Consequently, if the government issued fewer coins, the market would compensate for this in one of three ways:

(a) an increased rate of usage of coins, in which case the quantity of coins found in excavations would remain unchanged, in comparison with the preceding quantity of coins;
(b) the utilization of coins from a previous period, which would lead to the discovery of coins from the earlier period in excavations and in hoards;
(c) both (a) and (b).

As was shown regarding hoards from the fifth century, coins of this century are not overrepresented. At least in this period, then, the second solution apparently was not adopted in the market.

[40] J. G. Milne, "The Currency of Egypt in the Fifth Century", *NC* 6, 5th Series (1926), p. 92.
[41] Howgego, loc. cit. not. 24.

Regarding the seventh century (see below, the Appendix to Chap. 5): apparently only some cities experienced the decrease in the number of coins. If, in fact, fewer coins were struck in this period, then all the cities should have been affected to the same approximate degree. In some cities the quantity of coins in 612-641 was no less than, and even exceeded, that in the previous periods. Consequently, the claim that the authorities minted fewer coins is baseless. This claim was raised in addition to the above-mentioned arguments, but is not suitable to the fifth century, in which a decrease in the number of coins was experienced throughout almost the entire East.

3. **What influenced the quantity of coins present in the market: the volume of trade, or – mainly – the number of inhabitants? How did inflationary factors influence the quantity of coins in the market, and how did monetary legislation affect the quantity of coins in each period?**

The major methodological question is: what led to changes in the number of coins in the settlement? The absence or paucity of coins does not attest to the lack of a settlement. It is an undeniable fact that no coins, or only a very few, were found in many rural settlements, and at times also in urban settlements, which flourished or were active in the Hellenistic and Roman periods. In our opinion, the value of the numismatic finds is mainly comparative. The discussion must be limited to a specific settlement and to an examination of the relative changes between one period and another in it, i.e., the profusion or paucity of coins at a certain site. If there were considerable changes in the number of coins in a certain village, then there were economic factors within historical circumstances, which must be clarified.

Three factors most probably fashioned the distribution of coins in the settlement:

(a) the level of national trade: the extent to which the market was open and based on local or regional trade;
(b) the volume of commerce in the specific settlement. The presence, e.g., of a number of artisans, or the bivouac of a military unit, was likely to totally change the quantitative numismatic finds;
(c) growth and increase in the settlement. Logic would dictate that demographic increase directly influenced the nominal extent of trade, as it did the quantities of pottery vessels, or the number of structures in the settlement. Conversely, a decrease of trade in a settlement

which was based on a certain level of commerce would effect a reduction in the revenues of the inhabitants and obviously a lessening of the number of inhabitants, or a decline in the number of inhabitants would be reflected in a reduction in the nominal volume of commerce within the settlement.

It may be assumed that there is a general correlation between changes in the volume of trade and changes in the number of the inhabitants of the settlement. We do not presume to determine which is the cause and which the effect; both processes are seemingly related to each other. This argument presupposes a comprehensive conception concerning the place of trade in Palestine in the Roman and Byzantine periods. The province most likely underwent a process of demographic increase, which created economic pressure (below, Chap. 5). The increase in commerce was not a consequence solely of the desire to improve the standard of living, but mainly of the basic need to provide livelihood for the constantly growing population. Trade, irregardless of its scope, was essential for the economy of the inhabitants of the land; consequently, a decrease in commerce attests, or led, to a demographic decline, while an increase in trade indicates, and made possible, population growth.[42]

The discussion of a connection between a larger or smaller number of coins found at a site and flourishing or declining trade and processes of demographic growth or contraction cannot be divorced from the general historical context. Thus, e.g., Haldon argues that the decrease in the number of coins in the cities of Byzantium in the seventh and eighth centuries does not indicate decline, but rather a change in the economic and administrative character of these centuries.[43] He maintains that the cities ceased to serve as commercial and administrative centers following the Arab conquest, due to the process of centralization that occurred in the Byzantine Empire, i.e., the transferal of functions from the cities to the capital of Constantinople. A discussion of this theory lies outside the scope of the present work, since this process did not begin in the fourth, fifth, and sixth centuries, with which we are concerned.[44]

42 Ibid.

43 J. Haldon, "Some Considerations of Byzantine Society and Economy in the Seventh Century", *BF* 10 (1985), pp. 75-112.

44 Nevertheless, it must be noted that a decrease in the number of coins in the fifth century was discovered also in excavations of a structure in Istanbul itself. See: M. F. Hendy, "The Coins", in *Excavations at Sarachane in Istanbul I*, ed. R. M. Harrison (Princeton, 1986), pp. 278-373. The issue of the influence of the Arab conquest on the reduction in the number of coins is worthy of a separate discussion.

Notwithstanding the above, the quantitative relation between demographic increase and commercial growth (i.e., a rise in the quantities of coins which were found) is not a direct one. It is highly probable that the elimination of commerce in a settlement signifies a decrease in the size of its population, but it may not be concluded that the site was abandoned, for the following three reasons:

(a) the absence of coins from a certain period does not constitute an absolute finding, and presumably as yet undiscovered numismatic material is still present in the depths of the earth. The number of subterranean coins from this period is most probably small, but this does not indicate the total lack of finds of this nature;
(b) an extreme decline in trade signifies that the inhabitants returned to a closed economy and were self-sufficient. The number of inhabitants probably decreased somewhat under these conditions, but the settlement still possessed production resources to maintain a small population;
(c) quite extensive possibilities of barter trade must be considered.

These factors delineate a general model in which changes in the quantity of coins express the direction of changes in the demographic process and its general strength, but do not suffice to accurately quantify these changes (Fig. 6).

Within the context of these limitations, there would be no purpose to compare the quantities of coins in periods distant from each other. Thus, e.g., the fact that more Byzantine than Hellenistic coins were found in Sebaste does not enable us to compare the number of inhabitants of the city in these two different periods. It expresses the difference in the character of the economy in each period, and attests to extensive trade in the Byzantine period and the dependence of the population upon this trade, but is not necessarily indicative of demographic changes. In contrast, the differences between the Ptolemaic and Seleucid periods, and between the Seleucid and Hasmonean periods, are significant and provide the researcher with an additional tool for understanding the city and its history.

The majority of the numismatic finds comes from excavations in cities or villages. These finds, however, are not necessarily indicative of the region as a whole, and a market may possibly have developed in a specific city in a certain period for incidental reasons. The collection of data from many excavations and the fact that the major processes recur in virtually all the excavations teach, however, that such phenomena are not incidental or local, but rather reflect a general process.

4. **In order to clarify the issues in (3), is it necessary to take into account the differences in coin values and their worth in the market?**

In the course of this research, we collected data only from assemblages containing at least dozens of coins. At this stage, it cannot be determined when an assemblage of coins is sufficiently large to permit statistical-chronological analyses.

The Reliability of Numismatic Finds: an Empirical Examination

The information obtained from quantitative numismatic data cannot be treated independently, but must be integrated with additional historical and archaeological data. The coin finds which will be systematically discussed in Appendix a (below) enables us to evaluate the actual reliability of the numismatic testimony. This concentration of data constitutes an empirical test of the proposed methodology. The examination revealed that in most sites in which the numismatic data could be verified, a decrease in the quantity of coins was matched by a corresponding drop in the ceramic finds, and both types of finds are consistent, as is the case, e.g., in the synagogues in Galilee and at additional settlements. At times we possess no coins from the fifth century, while the site contains clear signs of poor settlement activity, as at, e.g., Tel Mevorakh or Khirbet Shema'. Few fifth-century coins were found in Jerusalem, although literary sources attest to the construction of public buildings and churches and the expenditure of money by pilgrims, monks, and government representatives. Thus, e.g., the empress Eudocia was active during this century in the city, in offering assistance to the inhabitants of the city and in constructing churches and a city wall.[45] Consequently, the economic activity in the city was in reality more limited than the representation of such activity in the contemporaneous literature and in the religious and possibly also the political sphere.

MacMullen raises an additional concern, that a large number of coins indicates inflationary processes, and not necessarily the development and growth of the settlement.[46] This consideration may possibly serve as an alternative explanation of the relative increase of coins in the third

[45] For the activities of Eudocia, see: Y. Dan, "Eretz Israel in the Fifth and Sixth Centuries", in *Eretz Israel from the Destruction of the Second Temple to the Muslim Conquest*, eds. Z. Baras et al. (Jerusalem, 1982), pp. 275-78 (Heb.).

[46] MacMullen (above, n. 3), pp. 38 ff.

century, but this hypothesis is not supported by the available testimonies: a period in which inflation came to a halt (the late third century) was not marked by a decrease in the monetary volume. To the contrary, as a survey of the various sites will demonstrate (below), the number of coins increased. Furthermore, the large number of coins corresponds with the pottery and architectural evidence: e.g., in Jalame, Meron, Gischala, and many other sites (see below, Chap. 1). Moreover, inflation was present throughout the Empire, and accordingly cannot explain the type of local and regional phenomena to be discussed in this work.

Inflation influenced the quantities of coins in the market. It may be assumed, however, that the increase in the money supply was expressed mainly in the silver and gold coins. The extant testimonies indicate that the effect of inflation on the bronze coins was of lesser significance.

According to Reece and Grierson,[47] the quantities of bronze coins are not representative of market conditions, because they were not used for the major commercial transactions in the market. While this is true from a purely financial view, this fact enables us to properly utilize the information. A faster tempo of commercial transactions led to the increased use of bronze coins. The number of bronze coins which were lost directly corresponds to the number of commercial transactions, but not to the monetary value of trade. In every commercial action, use was made of bronze coins, either as change or as pocket money for secondary purchases (the wages of porters or payment for a cup of wine in an inn). The quantities of bronze coins found in excavations teach of the number of merchants and the number of commercial transactions, but do not testify to the monetary value of the trade. A merchant who purchased a sack of flour and one who purchased an entire silo were likely to lose the same quantity of bronze coins.[48]

We assume that there is a direct and reasonable relation between the number of commercial transactions and their volume; not inconceivable, however, is the possibility of a large number of commercial transactions but with small monetary value (fewer large merchants and more small tradesmen). This theoretical argument is not supported by the parallel empiric testimonies available to us.

[47] R. Reece, "Coins and Frontier – or Supply and Demand", in J. Fitz, ed. *Limes Herausgegeb*on. (Budapest, 1977), pp. 643-*46*.

[48] D. M. Metcalf, "The Currency of Byzantine Coins in Syrmia and Slavonia", *HBN* (*Hamburg Beiträge zur Numismatik*) 14 (1960), pp. 429-44, and esp. 442-44.

The opinion of Milne should be mentioned in relation to the bronze coins.[49] Milne argues that these coins constituted the main currency in the rural sector, in contrast with the urban sector, which primarily used silver coins and a few gold coins. Milne restricts his discussion to Egypt, and it cannot be determined if he bases his hypothesis on incidental finds; in Palestine, at any rate, silver coins are rare in both city and village, but there is no clear distinction between the two sectors.

Our use of bronze coins is preferable from another aspect, as well. The quantities of silver and gold coins in the market were probably influenced also by government policy, and from the ratio of gold coins to silver coins which were minted. Duncan-Jones has dealt with this extensively.[50] These factors, however, exerted lesser influence upon the bronze coins, whose total worth is estimated by Duncan-Jones as being less than 10 percent of that of all the coins in circulation. Nor was the quantity of bronze coins influenced by inflation, because these coins served as small change under any circumstances.

For the purposes of the current study, the differences between the coins are secondary. Each coin, irregardless of its worth, represents a single transaction, as did lamps or any other single pottery vessel. Most of the numismatic finds from excavations are obviously bronze coins, with a minority of silver and gold coins; this distinction is not represented in the tables, because the coins of precious metals are extremely few in number.

The collected data in the following chapter comprise an empirical attempt and a method of examining the nature of the data. One would expect that reliable data would depict a fairly uniform picture, with local characteristics and exceptions. It stands to reason that if there was a general decline in the land, a few settlements would nevertheless continue to flourish, and the converse: if the entire land enjoyed prosperity, there would probably be some settlements not as fortunate. If the quantitative finds were purely incidental, we would obtain a chaotic picture. The finds collected in appendix a will be analyzed in the following chapters, especially in Chaps. 2 and 4. The concentration of data does indeed indicate a uniform picture and clear regional characteristics. Furthermore,

[49] J. G. Milne, "Roman Coinage" (above, n. 31), loc. cit. Duncan-Jones (above, n. 19), pp. 181-94 argues that bronze coins were used three times as much as silver ones. He admits, however, that his examination, which is based on wear and loss of weight of the coins, does not take into account differences in the nature of the metal. Nevertheless, bronze coins were clearly used a great deal.

[50] Duncan-Jones (above, n. 19), pp. 122-24; for the value of the bronze coins, see: op. cit., p. 169.

this picture corresponds to the data of the surveys, the excavations results, and the ethnodemographic situation.

Another empiric proof is obtained from a comparison of the quantitative analysis of the coins found in African cities and that of the pottery vessels examined in these excavations. The quantity of coins in Carthage increased in the fifth century (see below, Chap. 5).[51] Corresponding to this datum, much more imported ware from the East arrived in Carthage in this century. These amphorae contained various goods, such as oil, wine, and fish. In Benghazi, in contrast, no coins from the fifth century were found, and the quantity of pottery vessels, and especially the quantity of amphorae, are extremely low, in comparison with other centuries.[52]

Consequently, the quantitative numismatic data serve as a reasonable and reliable indicator corresponding to the entirety of the extant information. This conclusion is correct for fifth-century coins. Further clarification is necessary to determine if the quantity of coins in other centuries as well reflects the economic and/or demographic situation, for the prevailing circumstances in one century do not automatically represent the reality in another century.

The Historical Sources

The dearth of studies of everyday life in the Byzantine period obligates us to relate in some degree to the nature of the sources, in order to clarify a number of prior methodological questions.

Researchers of the period of the Mishnah and Talmud enjoy a plethora of sources for a description of rural life in Palestine. In Israel

[51] J. H. Humphrey, ed., *Excavations at Carthage I* (Tunis, 1976), pp. 151-98; idem, ed., *Excavations at Carthage IV* (Ann Arbor, 1978), pp. 99-163; idem, ed., *Excavations at Carthage V* (New Delhi, 1980), pp. 185-290; idem, ed., Excavations at Carthage VII (Ann Arbor, 1982), pp. 63-168; W. E. Metcalf, "The Coins – 1982", in *The Circus and a Byzantine Cemetery at Carthage I*, ed. J. H. Humphrey (Ann Arbor, Michigan, 1988), pp. 337-82; P. Visona, "The Coins – 1983", in ibid., pp. 383-422; R. Reece, "Coins", in *Excavations at Carthage: The British Mission I*, 1, eds. H. R. Hurst and S. P. Roskams (Sheffield, 1984), pp. 171-81.

[52] M. G. Fulford, "Carthage: Overseas Trade and the Political Economy, c. A.D. 400-700", *Reading Medieval Studies* 6 (1980), pp. 68-70; idem, "The Long Distance Trade and Communications of Carthage, c. A.D. 400 to c. A.D. 650", in *Excavations at Carthage: The British Mission I, 2*, eds. M. G. Fulford and D. P. S. Peacock (Sheffield, 1984), pp. 255-61; J. A. Lloyd, ed., *Excavations at Sidi Khrebish Benghazi (Bernice) II (Tripoli*, 1979), pp. 194, 229-33. For an analysis of the pottery vessels, see: ibid., III (Tripoli, 1985), pp. 106 ff.

only a few inscriptions were found resembling those in, e.g., northern Africa, which provide detailed descriptions of the laws of sharecropping in a number of agricultural estates. There is a surfeit of Talmudic references and discussions reflective of rural life from the viewpoint of the "natives", i.e., the inhabitants of the villages and farm workers. This situation changes regarding the Byzantine period. There are many extant Christian Byzantine treatises, but these provide us with very limited knowledge of the villages. The researcher interested in the life of the village in Syria or in Egypt finds a wealth of information in the hagiographical material. Thus, e.g., Vita Theodorosi contains many details regarding the villages of Galatia,[53] or the heartwarming story about the monk Abraham (early fifth century) who became the patron of an independent village in the hills of Lebanon that grew nuts; the author emphasizes that this monk did not know Greek. [54] A different situation prevails regarding Palestine. Even the stories about the saints and monks in Palestine contain sparse information regarding rural life, and for a simple reason: most of the ecclesiastics and authors in Palestine were of nonlocal origin. They came from the cities of the East and the West, most of them spoke only Greek, and their contacts with villagers was naturally limited. It may further be assumed that their contacts with the wealthy villagers, who spoke Greek, were more numerous than with the masses of the rural population. Furthermore, in most instances the locally born monks and those who were closer to the rural population were not fortunate in having an author interesting in documenting this aspect of their activity. Thus, e.g., the life of Hilarion, a native of the village of Thabatha, near Gaza, was described by Hieronymus. This author prided himself on the great interest he took in the local 'natives', and that he spoke their language after a fashion. Notwithstanding this, in his writings he was not successful in completely bridging the gap between his mentality and theirs. The Life of Hilaron which was written by Hieronymous nevertheless contains a few important details regarding this monk's contacts with the villagers.

Generally speaking, four geographic groups of monks and holy men were active in Palestine:

(1) the monks of the Judean Desert, who were extensively documented, thanks mainly to Cyril of Scythopolis;

[53] A. J. Festugiere, *Vie de Theodore de Sykeo* (Bruxelles, 1970).
[54] See: Theodoretus of Cyrus, XVII.

(2) the monks of the Gaza and southern Palestine region, whose lives were documented less extensively. Some of the monks in the Gaza region were native born, and the works dealing with them provide a few interesting details. Especially noteworthy is the collection of responsum composed by Barsanuphius.[55] We obviously shall attempt to make full use of the information contained in this material;
(3) the monks of Jerusalem. There were dozens of monasteries within the city itself, fragmentary information regarding which is scattered throughout the Christian literature and hagiographies, and mainly in dedicatory and burial inscriptions found in the city;
(4) monks in various monasteries throughout the land; the archaeological remains of these monasteries constitute the primary source of our knowledge of them.

The Reliability of the Hagiographic Literature

The research literature dealing with the Byzantine period generally makes intensive use of the hagiographic literature. These testimonies are usually thought to be highly reliable, without critical study or doubts concerning their accuracy. Every legend is accepted as authentic testimony by reliable witnesses; at times it would seem that naturally skeptical researchers even believe the stories telling of miracles.[56] In our opinion, the historical material concealed in this literature is to be divided into two types:

(1) geographical, chronological, and technical details – in this realm the hagiographic literature generally maintains historical accuracy.[57] Thus. e.g., Cyril of Scythopolis tells of the establishment of the Euthymius Monastery, and of the settlement in the vicinity of the monastery by an Arab tribe that converted to Christianity. This story is fully confirmed by the archaeological evidence.[58] In another pas-

[55] *Barsanuphius and Ioannes, Biblos...*, ed. S. N. Schoinas (Volos 1960); *Barsaunphe et Jean de Gaza: Correspondance, trans. Regnault* (Lemaire et Outier, 1972).

[56] See, e.g.: J. Binnes, "The Distinctiveness of Palestinian Monasticism 450-550 AD", in *Monastic Studies*, ed. J. Loades (Bangor, 1990), pp. 11-20.

[57] See, e.g.: J. Gould, "Early Egyptian Monasticism and the Church", in *Monastic Studies* (above, n. 56), pp. 1-10; E. A. Judge, "The Earliest Use of Monachos for 'Monk' (P. Coll. Youtie 77) and the Origins of Monasticism", in *Jahrbuch für Antike und Christentum* 20 (1977), pp. 72-89.

[58] Y. Hirschfeld, "St. Euthimius' Monastery", *Hadashot Arkheologiyot* 84 (1984), pp. 42-44 (Heb.); O. Sion, "A Monastic Precinct in Khirbet Handumah", *LA* 42 (1992), pp. 279-87.

sage, Cyril relates the miraculous story of a lion that – obviously, at the command of the saint – helped to draw water from a spring to water the garden of the monastery. Even if the miraculous event itself is doubtful, the geographical details are highly probable, and appear to be accurate.[59]

(2) testimonies regarding the religious nature of the society and the degree to which the monks were successful in disseminating Christianity, and, consequently, regarding the status of the holy men in the society and their place in the ecclesiastical hierarchy. The hagiographic literature was written by different authors within the monastic society. The writings of these holy men provides a historical picture of a campaign continually blessed by success, of triumphant struggles against heretics, within the camp or from the surrounding environment, and of universally venerated holy men who fill a central role in the rural society as miracle workers, physicians, and spiritual guides.[60] It would appear that the testimony of the holy men about themselves should be treated with some degree of skepticism. The authors of the hagiographic literature came from within the circle of the holy men, with the goal of persuading both the convinced and the unconvinced. The "convinced" were the hundreds of monks, mainly those of lower rank; the literature extolling the holy men was intended to raise their spirits and console them in time of crisis or doubt. The "unconvinced" were the masses, the heretics, and, obviously, the non-Christians: Jews and pagans. The hagiographic literature served as one of the leading weapons in the struggle to convert the local population. The stories of success in this battle filled a basic need of the literature, and any search for balanced and realistic evaluations or for self-criticism will prove to be fruitless.

The literature of the holy men contains recurring literary themes such as: the "miracle of the lion"; the healing of the son of the tribal leader, village chief, or other local leader which is followed by the conversion of the entire tribe; the monk who is attacked but is miraculously saved, at times followed by the conversion of the attackers; important rulers who come to the holy man, who receives them only following special supplications, etc. Thus, e.g., the above-mentioned story of the lion who

[59] Cyril of Scythopolis, *Lives*, ed. E. Schwartz, *Vita Euthymii*, chap. 49.

[60] For the place of the holy men in society, see the well-known article by Brown: P. Brown, "The Rise and Function of the Holy Man in Late Antiquity", *JRS* 61 (1971), pp. 80-101. Many articles have recently been published on this topic.

aids in the watering of the monastery garden also appears in the hagiography of John of Nhel.[61] In another narrative about Euthymius, Cyril of Scythopolis relates that the monk urged Anastasius, the archbishop of Jerusalem, not to visit him, for if he were to receive this cleric, he would have to waste his time in the future by receiving other visitors.[62] The reasoning is touching, but somewhat strange, because Euthymius received many people, and drew his public support from this practice. A similar story is attributed to Antony, the founder of Egyptian monasticism.[63] This should correctly be regarded as a recurrent literary motif, and not as reliable testimony; it may also be possible to deduce from the story that the distinguished archbishop did not visit the holy man, and the story was intended to provide an explanation which not only would not disparage the monk, but would even raise his esteem in the eyes of his followers. Similar motifs reappear in the literature of Christian holy men which is currently produced in Palestine, but this topic exceeds the scope of the present work.

Several leaders of the monastic movement were active in Jerusalem and its environs in the midfifth century: Euthymius, Peter the Iberian, and Bar Zoma. The works about them were written by different authors; each one, however, hardly mentions the other individuals, and there is insufficient peripheral mention of the greatness and fame of the others. Many pilgrims visited Jerusalem during this period, but they too do not devote a great deal of attention to the desert monasteries.

It therefore may be concluded that the literature of the holy men contains many exaggerations; the descriptions of their splendid success in propagating the faith are greatly embellished and cannot be accepted as accurate testimony, or as a reliable source regarding the society in Palestine or the place of the holy men in it. These conclusions will be pertinent for our discussion of the pace of the Christianization of Palestine, a subject which is discussed extensively in this literature.[64]

This work will not concern itself with testimonies regarding the Christian society in the city, village, and monasteries, but mainly with information regarding the degree to which the Christian monastic propaganda was successful, and the rate of Christianization in the various parts of the land.

[61] J. Brock, "John of Nhel, an Episode in Early Seventh-Century Monastic History", *Orientalia Lovaniensia Periodica* 9, pp. 95-101.

[62] *Vita Euthemii*, chap. 52.

[63] Arsenius, *Apophthegmata Patrum* 8.

[64] See below, Chap. 4.

The Jewish Literature

Additional, albeit scanty, material is contained in the Jewish literature from this period. This is not the place to survey this literature or to evaluate its literary and historical value, [65] but two major points must be emphasized:

(a) the majority of the midrashic literature, especially its later portions, was edited in the late Byzantine period, but most of this literature consists of earlier material which was collected and edited. It mentions only sages who lived and were active in the period of the Mishnah and Talmud, while documenting only a very few problems, events, and conditions from the late Byzantine period. Works such as *Pirkei de-Rabbi Eliezer*, *Midrash Tehillim* and others relate to some degree to later events as well, but it cannot be demonstrated with certainty that a specific midrash reflects a post-Talmudic reality. Such a claim can be proved only in exceptional cases in which the midrash alludes to a known event. Consequently, despite the importance of this halakhic material, it cannot serve as a historical source for the late Byzantine period in Palestine; this thesis will be restated below, in the course of the discussion itself.

(b) a rich Palestinian legal literature was generated in the fifth-seventh centuries, only fragments of which are extant. The collection and discovery of these fragments in the treasures of the Genizah and the riches of the Geonic literature are an adventure in themselves. This literature contains two types of works: halakhic collections and private law books. The halakhic collections made an effort to systematically arrange all the laws by topic, such the laws of forbidden sexual relations appearing in MS. *Kaufman* at the end of *Tractate Kiddushin*, the *laws of kashrut* in manuscripts from the *Genizah*, and in *Halakhot Kezuvot* (MS. Sassoon, fol. 193 ff). The collection of laws inscribed in the synagogue mosaic in Rehob also belongs to this category. These halakhic collections contain Talmudic material and additional elements. This material is not dated, because the laws, especially those not explicitly mentioned in the Talmud, are not attributed, and it is difficult to determine the reality they reflect. In this case, the selection of the material and the rules governing the collection are not indicative of the reality during the time of the redactor, since they are not dependent solely on this reality, but are

[65] See below, Chap. 4.

also dependent upon the nature of the sources of the collector. Consequently, these works are of little value for this study and for the research of the Byzantine period in general, and only information of secondary importance may be obtained from them. The selection of the subject of the compilation, however, obviously attests to the importance of the subject.

The private law books (The *Ma'asim* literatuer) are different in nature. These works contain a selection of laws which were chosen by a certain rabbi, and which give expression to his sphere of interest. The claim that the list of topics and laws reflects the areas of public interest exhibited by the redactor and his disciples apparently is well-founded. Thus the many laws concerning adultery, e.g., attest to serious problems in this realm within the Jewish society. This argument was advanced by Herr, probably with a great deal of justification.[66]

The Reliability of the Written Sources

As noted above, the second, third, and fourth centuries, and to a lesser degree the fifth century as well, are rich in literary sources, which provide information about many events, but which do not provide data regarding settlement or demographic processes. Thus, e.g., the third century, following the time of R. Judah ha-Nasi II (222-284), is depicted in the Talmudic sources as a period of regression and decline. Leading researchers have developed this concept; Sperber has quite skillfully collected many Talmudic sources bemoaning this state of affairs.[67]

The archaeological finds from this century, however, indicate the reverse process, that of a strengthening of the settlement. There is a simple reason for this seeming contradiction: contemporaneous literary sources reflect the situation in their period and the mood of the time, but do not contain valid evidence regarding long-term processes. Our ancestors possessed a very low capability for evaluating processes of change over a chronological range of decades. Such a conclusion was reached by MacMullen in his collection of various literary data from the Roman

[66] M. D. Herr, "Hellenistic Influences in the Jewish City in Eretz-Israel in the Fourth and Sixth Centuries C.E"., *Cathedra* 8 (1978), pp. 90-94 (Heb.).

[67] D. Sperber, *Roman Palestine 200-400: The Land. Crisis and Change in Agrarian Society as Reflected in Rabbinic Sources* (Ramat Gan, 1978), pp. 11-29; G. Alon, *The History of the Jews in Eretz Israel in the Period of the Mishnah and Talmud* (Jerusalem, 1971), pp. 182-91 (Heb.).

period, with which we concur after comparing the Rabbinic sources with the archaeological evidence. Accordingly, the following discussion will impart decisive importance to the archaeological evidence, and especially to the numismatic finds.

CHAPTER TWO

Settlement Processes in Palestine in the Byzantine Period

Appendix A summarized a considerable portion of the archaeological excavations in which settlement strata from the Byzantine period were uncovered and dated. A number of conclusions clearly may be drawn from the excavations in this list and from many others not mentioned whose dating is more problematic, while taking into account the methodological considerations discussed in the Introduction:

1. The first half of the fourth century was the period of maximal activity and growth in all areas of Palestine, excluding the central Negev area which was part of Palestina Tertia. This conclusion, which is indicated by both the numismatic finds (five times as many coins as in the preceding period) and the pottery finds, breaks no new ground, and the concentration of finds merely provides additional confirmation. The main importance of the collection of this data consists of the possibility it affords to determine with greater accuracy, and on a truly scientific basis, the date of the settlement turning point.

Earlier studies and regional surveys in Israel indicated the "Byzantine" period as that of peak activity in the history of the land, and hundreds of sites in the country were dated to this period.[1] It may be assumed that this "Byzantine" period refers mainly to the fourth century, as is indicated by the finds from various excavations. We will not address the issue of the causes of the settlement growth in the fourth century, and will state merely that this process occurred throughout the East, as is clearly indicated from an analysis of the quantitative numismatic finds in many cities in the East, such as Antioch, Sardis, Gerasa, Apamea, Tarsus, Corinth, Carium, and other cities.[2]

[1] Z. Safrai, *The Economy of Roman Palestine*, London 1994, pp. 436-457; Y. Tsafrir, Some Notes on the Settlement and Demography of Palestine in the Byzantine Period: The Archaeological Evidence, *Retrieving the Past*, ed. J.D. Seger (Winona Lake) 1996, pp. 269-281.

[2] Above chap., 5; Safrai, Ibid, pp. 412-413.

The process of settlement development apparently had already begun in the third century and reached and maintained its highest level, at the latest, from 305 on. It is difficult to determine if this prosperity already reigned in the time of Diocletian (284-305). Coins from this short period are common at some sites, including Mambre, Khirbet Jalame, Meron, and Meroth, while in a small number of additional sites, such as Horvat Kanaf, Jerusalem, and'En Nashut, there either very few or no coins of Diocletian.

Furthermore, only conclusions of a general nature, and not those presenting an exact chronology, may be drawn from the numismatic evidence. Obviously, coins of Diocletian remained in circulation for decades after his time; conversely, their scarcity may be a quite random phenomenon.

2. The settlement picture in the country during the course of the Byzantine period is less clear, with indications of two regional processes:

(a) a process of decline and regression began in the midfourth century, and characterized almost all the settlements of western Galilee (excluding Jalma), e.g.: Beth She'arim, Sepphoris, Meron, Qedesh, Kefar Hananyah,'Ammudim, Summaqa in the Carmel, and additional settlements, as well as other regions and sites such as Mambre, Jerusalem, Samaria, and possibly also Antipatris and additional settlements.[3]

The damage is almost completely clear and uniform in rural western Galilee; the coastal plain; in Samaria and in Judea the damage is clear but less severe and less consistent in nature.

These regions suffered a devastating blow in the early fifth century. The pottery finds also indicate decline, severe deterioration, or even the abandonment of settlements. It may be assumed that a large city such as Sepphoris or Scythopolis was not totally abandoned, and it is still mentioned in the literary sources; nevertheless, this urban center suffered severe damage.

(b) a different settlement process took place in the Golan, eastern Upper Galilee (the basaltic region), the Sea of Galilee valley, the Beth Shean Valley, the southern Philistine Shephelah, the southern Hebron hill country, and Transjordan. These regions continued to flourish

[3] See also D. Adan-Bayewitz, *Common Pottery in Roman Galilee*, (Ramat-Gan 1993), pp. 148-150.

and even exhibited settlement growth in the second half of the fourth century. The extent of the settlement decreased in the fifth century, but this decline is more moderate than that experienced by the preceding group. Thus, e.g., the Golan settlements, Meroth, Chorazin, and Capernaum witnessed the establishment (or at the very least, fundamental renovation) of synagogues at the beginning of this century, each of which was active for at least several decades. Nevertheless, the quantity of coins in these Settlements is much lower than in the fourth century, both in the settlement itself and under the synagogue foundations.

There may have been a population transfer in the midfourth century from Galilee to the Golan, and possibly also from the coastal plain and from Judea towards the southern Hebron hill country. This process cannot be proved, but is strongly indicated by the different fates of the fertile mountain settlement as opposed to that of the ecologically inferior fringes.

3. The fifth century was generally marked by decline, which was expressed in an extremely drastic reduction of commerce (few coins) and a comprehensive demographic drop. Galilee reveals the most severe damage. This region played a 'pioneering' role: processes which began to develop in Galilee in the second half of the fourth century would later emerge in other regions. Moreover, the collapse of the settlement in rural Galilee in the fifth century was more severe and intensive than that experienced in the other regions of the land. This collapse is evidenced both by the numismatic finds and the ceramic material. This is only an interim conclusion, since the condition of the extant evidence sharpens the conclusions, but without providing a sufficient factual basis. A relatively large number of excavations have been conducted in Galilee in comparison with other regions. They are characterized by their well-founded dating, rich numismatic finds, and the fact that a relatively large number of rural settlements have been excavated. Consequently, it is not inconceivable that the collapse of the settlements in the Golan, Samaria, and Judea was even more severe than is presently imagined.

4. All regions of the land participated in the general recovery in the sixth century. Abandoned sites such as Beth She'arim, Tel Keisan, Ma'on in the southern Shephelah, and many others were resettled. Many settlements continue to grow, and a large number of coins

appear in this century, as is attested by a number of Byzantine hoards which begin in the early sixth century and end during the course of the seventh century. New synagogues are established in this period, mainly in Judea and in the Beth Shean Valley and the eastern (basaltic) Galilee; this is also the main period in which churches are established throughout Palestine, chiefly in the rural sector. This settlement cycle of growth and recovery, development, and decline is worthy of a detailed discussion, which would exceed the scope of this work.

It presumably could be argued that the paucity of fifth century coins ensued from the use in this century of coins minted in the fourth century. Based on an analysis of hoards from the fifth and sixth centuries, this thesis was rejected in Chap. 1, above.

Based on the data we currently possess, the Beth Shean Valley did not suffer damage to the same degree as did the other parts of the country, and thereby constitutes a local or regional exception.

CHAPTER THREE

The Land Question in Palestine between the Roman and Byzantine Periods

The Background

Agriculture was the most important branch of production and livelihood in antiquity in Palestine. Most of the gross national product was derived directly from labor in the fields. The products which reached the markets consisted mainly of raw or processed agricultural products (oil, wool, flax), and the inventory of foods was based almost exclusively on agricultural produce, with the exception of fish; although the latter originate in the sea and not in the earth, they too may be defined as agricultural produce.

The modern world speaks of the control of six means of production: land, water, quarries, manpower, (technological) knowledge, and capital. In the ancient world, land was the prime means of production. Water was the gift of heaven, and was free to all, and agriculture in most parts of Palestine relied on rainwater. Technology also was freely available to all, problems of financing were immediately translated into wages, i.e., manpower, and thus land and manpower remained the chief means of production. Consequently, control of land and of manpower will occupy center stage in our discussion of the economy and the society in this period.

Roman and Byzantine law recognized a number of types of land ownership. Only the economic agrarian aspects are germane to this discussion, and the ensuing legal problems lie beyond the scope of the current work. Land ownership may be divided into three main categories:

1. state land and the property of the emperor: the Roman fiscus;
2. private estates belonging to the wealthy;
3. private lands.

There were also three parallel conditions of personal status relating to possession of manpower resources:

1. free agricultural laborers who worked their property;

2. sharecroppers or tenants, i.e., people personally free, but who used means of production belonging to others, with the consequent mortgaging of property;
3. slaves lacking both personal status and property.

The social stratum constituting the backbone of Palestine in the Roman period (that of the Mishnah and the Talmud) was that of small farmers, who were freemen. They appear in the Rabbinic literature as the buyers and sellers of land, as taxpayers, and as sellers of property. They decided when to uproot an orchard and when to plant it, and they invested surplus income from agriculture in the purchase of goods and services. They are to be credited with the growth of the villages and the impressive cultural achievements of the Jews of Palestine, which were a consequence of this free society which earned its livelihood from working the land with honor, but not necessarily with great profits.

This is paralleled in the Rabbinic literature by the phenomenon of sharecroppers and renters of private or state lands. The area of state lands and the number of private estates clearly began to rise at the end of the Second Temple period.[1] The percentage of lands in the province held by the owners of private estates cannot be determined. At any rate, the phenomenon of state lands and private estates was not marginal. The Rabbinic sources give the impression that the lands of Palestine within the bounds of the Jewish settlement were overwhelmingly in private hands, but this generalization cannot be confirmed in the absence of quantitative data.

The private estates and state lands were operated in a quite similar manner. The owner (the "master") generally lived in a polis and paid supervisory visits to his estate. The day-to-day affairs of the estate were administered by an overseer who supervised the work of the slaves, workers, or sharecroppers who labored in the fields and in who processed the crops. The estate house generally stood in the center of the estate. This was a quite large structure, usually standing by itself, which housed the workers or slaves, and (under slightly better conditions) the overseer. The master would reside in a special, opulent wing during his visits to the estate. This wing contained luxurious installations such as a bathhouse, and at times additional installations as well.

[1] Z. Safrai, *The Economy of Roman Palestine* (London, 1994), pp. 82-99; S. Appelbaum, "The Problem of the Roman Villa in Eretz-Israel", *Eretz-Israel* 19 (1987), pp. 1-5 (Heb.); D. Sperber, *Roman Palestine 200-400: The Land. Crisis and Change in Agrarian Society as Reflected in Rabbinic Sources* (Ramat Gan, 1978), pp. 177-86.

The estate house also contained storerooms and workshops, an olive-press, etc.

The Rabbinic sources and the Byzantine literature also teach of the existence of a different type of estate, which employed the *emphyteusis* method, which the Jewish sources apparently call "*hakirei beit avot*" (hereditary sharecroppers) or "*arisei beit avot*" (hereditary tenants). Such an estate was worked by sharecroppers or tenants, upon whose death the right of tenancy was passed on to their heirs. The sharecroppers or tenants lived in villages as freemen, while their lands belonged to a non-resident wealthy person, the "master of the village." The agricultural produce was processed either individually or communally. This last issue, of importance in its own right, lies beyond the scope of the present work.

Also noteworthy was the *ktema*, a Byzantine term for area belonging to a private individual; this was not an estate, but rather a large settlement with many structures, including churches. Tekoa, e.g., with an area of more than 70 dunams, including two churches and public buildings, was termed a ktema. We are of the opinion that the ktema was a private villageestate of "hakirei beit avot."[2]

These agrarian distinctions are of cardinal social and economic importance. Small-scale farming produced a landscape of villages of different sizes and a free and active community which was free to fashion its way of life, religious nature, and institutions. The estate system generated a landscape of scattered patrician houses ("*villae*") and large work installations. At the same time, this method led to the growth of the cities, in which the wealthy resided, and channeled resources from the village to the city. The landscape produced by the "hakirei beit avot" method consisted of villages, but it too inaugurated a massive flow of resources from the village to the city. The community in the villages was probably of limited activity and degree of autonomy. The profits of the villagers were lower: they enjoyed a certain degree of economic security, but they did not possess surplus economic resources.

In purely economic terms, the system of private farming enjoyed a certain advantage, since the conditions in antiquity bestowed no advantage to large-scale operations, while private ownership ensured closer

[2] For this system in the late Byzantine Empire, see: J. F. Haldon, *Byzantium in the Seventh Century: The Transformation of a Culture* (Cambridge, 1990), pp. 125 ff.; P. Lamerle, *The Agrarian History of Byzantium from the Origins to the Twelfth Century* (Galway, Ireland, 1979), pp. 27-35; see also S. Dar and Z. Safrai, "Horvat Birah", (Heb.), *Hikrei Eretz. Studies in the History of the Land of Israel*, ed. Y. Friedman et al. (Ramat-Gan 1997), pp. 57-108.

supervision of the land, careful and correct working, and the long-term considerations of the landowners to maintain the quality of their land. The method of sharecropping or tenancy evolved in response to the fear of careless maintenance of the fields, and was intended to guarantee the interest of the farmer in his work, the land, and the preservation of its fertility.

The Purpose of the Discussion

We are of the opinion that a change occurred in the Byzantine period which may possibly be defined as a revolution in the agrarian structure in Palestine. The following discussion will attempt to demonstrate that the system of estates expanded in this period, becoming the dominant element in the agrarian landscape.

The Agrarian Situation in the Byzantine Period

We should first mention the well-known Byzantine law, that of the "Colonatus." This law, which was enacted in the early fourth century, forbade landowners and sharecroppers from abandoning their lands. It also stated explicitly that the sharecropper must remain subservient to his former master.

Ca. 386 the Colonatus was extended to Palestine, about 80 years after the law was initially enacted and put into effect throughout the Empire.[3] The enactment of special legislation for Palestine teaches of a tangible change in the agrarian structure in the land. The actual economic significance of the law has not been determined; this issue has been researched by many scholars, and need not be discussed here.

The version of the law dealing with Palestine explicitly mentions land owners, and it implies that a sizable portion of the agricultural work force were already considered to be sharecroppers. The text of the law per se does not require the elimination of private farming (and as will be shown below, it was not wholly eradicated), but does indicate the widespread nature of the system of sharecropping. Moreover, the law stands in the breach against attempts by sharecroppers to move to other regions.

[3] CJ 11.51.

[4] E. g: A. H. M. Jones, "The Roman Colonate", *Past and Present* 13 (1958), pp. 1-13; W. Goffart, *"Caput" and Colonate: Towards a History of Late Roman Taxation* (Toronto, 1974), pp. 84-86.

Y. Dan, who has dealt extensively with the Colonatus law, searched for a special reason for the application of the law to Palestine in the year in which it was enacted.[5] In our opinion, the law was not intended to change the existing legislative system, but rather, to the contrary, to adapt the legal system to the existing conditions. The law was not applied before 386, as long as there still were many small landowners. The change in the agrarian system caused, or enabled, the authorities to apply this law to Palestine.

It may be assumed that the enactment of the Colonatus law is also indicative of the mass abandonment of lands, a phenomenon which the law sought to prevent. Furthermore, the law encouraged farmers who had difficulty in meeting tax payments to subordinate themselves to the rich landowners (the "patronage" system). Therefore, the enactment of the law dovetailed with the strengthening of the landowners class and attests to the widespread nature of this phenomenon.

The inscription on the aqueduct leading to Jerusalem also reflects the general state of agriculture in Palestine. In this text, the governor warns the agricultural workers not to approach the aqueduct. The inscription is addressed to the *ktatores*, the rich landowners; the tenants; and the farmers (*georgoi*).[6] The last term may possibly refer to the private landowners, but it also appears frequently as an accepted translation for "sharecropper" (see below), thereby leading to the conclusion that the decisive majority, or possibly even all, of the lands in the Jerusalem region were held by the wealthy. They operated their estates either directly, by themselves, or through the medium of the sharecroppers. The legislator does not address himself to the small-scale farmers; at most, they appear as one of the three categories of those working the land.

Samaria experienced a similar phenomenon: the description of the Samaritan revolts in the late fifth century implies that the rebellion in 484 was in large extent an agrarian uprising by Samaritan sharecroppers (*georgoi*) against the wealthy landowners, most of whom by this time were Christians,[7] thus leading to the conclusion that sharecropping already occupied a central position in Samaria as well.

Many episodic testimonies relate to the Gaza region. Kfar Tota, which apparently was an independent village in the time of Hilarion,[8] and which

[5] Y. Dan, "*Social Life in Eretz Israel in Byzantine Period*", Ph.D. diss., Hebrew University, Jerusalem, 1976, pp. 234-44 (Heb.).

[6] *SEG* 8 (1937), p. 179.

[7] Procopius, *Anecdota*, XI, 29; this is also implicit in Justinian, Novellae 144.

[8] Hieronymus, *Vita Hilarionis* 2-3; Sozomenos, *HE* III, 14.

is depicted in the Madaba map as a small village, became an estate or private village belonging to a wealthy individual by the name of Dionysius.[9] The village apparently returned to the small farmers in the sixth century.[10] This clearly attests to the agrarian process of the transformation of a regular village to a private one. This process is also implied in the Mishnah: "A town of an individual which became of many... and of many which became of an individual."[11] The Mishnah mentions members of the generation of Usha; such processes apparently also occurred in the Roman period, and especially following the Bar Kokhba revolt.

Vita Hilarionis, about the monk who was active in the region of his birth, to the south of Gaza,[12] mentions additional villas,[13], along with a farm called "Pacida" in the Rhinocorura area, which was already under Egyptian control.[14] The hagiography of Porphyrius of Gaza speaks of one of the wealthy inhabitants of Gaza, and of a noblewoman who owned lands in the area.[15] Aneas, one of the heads of the academy for rhetoric in Gaza, owned a garden with a sophisticated irrigation mechanism.[16] Noteworthy within this context is an inscription attesting to such an advanced installation which was found "in southern Palestine".[17] There obviously are no grounds to claim that this mechanism was the irrigation installation of Aneas, but this irrigation installation either also belonged to an estate, or was an urban installation. The inventor of the mechanism is called "the extolled father", which is a common urban appellation. Similarly, Burni (the present-day Beror Hayil) also had the status of ktema.[18] The anecdotes of John Moschus frequently mention estates. Since he lived and was active in the south and in the Gaza region, the anecdotes without geographical designation most probably represent this area. Thus, e.g., he relates of a landowner who was dispossessed by the provincial governor.[19] Aneas of Gaza relates of an

[9] Dan, p. 192

[10] John Moschus (chap., 1, n. 55), responsa 571, 595; Dan, loc. cit.

[11] .Mishnah Erubin 5:6.

[12] See above, chap. 1.

[13] Moschus, 14, 25.

[14] Ibid., 15.

[15] *Vita Porphyrii* 22.

[16] Aeneas of Gaza, *Epistulae*, ed. L. M. Positano (Rome, 1950), no. 25.

[17] M. Schwabe, "A Greek Inscription on a Water-Supply Installation from Southern Palestine", *Yediot* (Bulletin of the Jewish Palestine Exploration Society) 9 (1942), pp. 89-93.

[18] *Vita Sabae* 79.

[19] Th. Nissen, "Unbekannte Erzaelungen aus dem Pratum Spirituale", *BZ* 38 (1938), pp. 351-376, No. 2.

additional dignitary, Alphius, who was a landowner.[20] In another anecdote, John Moschus describes individuals who sought protection (*prostetia*), but does not explicitly state that they were agricultural workers. In another letter, mention is made of an "*epitropos*", a title given to the individual in charge of the estate. [22] On the other hand, there also is evidence of a small private farmer from the Gaza region in the village of Betakabea (Beit'Eqev) in the vicinity of Gaza.[23]

The remains of a number of estates have been discovered in the Gaza region, such as the estate houses near Ashkelon,[24] the mosaic in Erez,[25] as well as additional estates of which we possess only preliminary reports.[26]

The abundance of information in the literary sources regarding estates in the south is not necessarily indicative of relatively large numbers of estates in other regions. This plethora of reports is related to the general abundance of urban and monastic literary sources from the Gaza region (see above, Introduction).

In Eleutheropolis area Kfar Zechariah was a private village,[27] and there was an estate in Beth Zedek (Besandouke).[28]. Socho contained a ktema,[29] Agla in the western Shephelah contained a large estate at the beginning of the Islamic conquest which was expropriated by Amr b. al As for his own use, thereby indicating that its existence predated the Muslim ruler.[30] There also was a large private estate in Kefar Torban.[31]

A number of estate houses in this region have been excavated, such as the estate house in Khirbet el-Maqerqesh near Beit Guvrin,[32] and the estate house in Horvat Hazzan.[33]

[20] Aeneas, *Epistulae* 20.
[21] Moschus, responsum 785.
[22] Ibid, responsum 154.
[23] *Vita Euthymii* 57.
[24] *Hadashot Arkheologiyot* 16 (1966), pp. 17-18 (Heb.).
[25] L. Y. Rahmani, "The Erez Mosaic", *Eretz-Israel* 11 (1973), 263-64 (Heb.).
[26] E. g., *Hadashot Arkheologiyot* 7 (1963), p. 23 (Heb.); idem, 34-35 (1970), p. 26 (Heb.).
[27] Sozomenos, *HE* IX, 17.
[28] *Vita Epiphanii* 1.2. Epiphanius himself, however, came from a family of small-scale farmers from this village.
[29] Moschus, responsa 180, 181.
[30] For a clarification of this issue, see: M. Lecker, "The Estate of Amr b. al As in Palestine – Note on a New Negev Inscription", *BSOAS* 52 (1989), pp. 24-37.
[31] M. Avi-Yonah, *Historical Geography of Palestine from the End of the Babylonian Exile up to the Arab Conquest* (Jerusalem, 1966 Heb.), p. 112
[32] See: *NEAEHL* (1993), pp. 197-98.
[33] G. Avni et al., "Ahuzat Hazzan", (below appendix a.n. 97).

Additional reports of estate houses in various regions appear within various sources, such as Porphyreon on the Carmel, which was a private village belonging to a wealthy individual from Caesarea;[34] Tafsha, near Jerusalem, also was a private village.[35] The number of examples cited above, from the many episodes contained in the literary sources, create the general impression that agriculture and the rural landscape were based on the estates and lands of the wealthy.[36] Noteworthy within this context are two marginal testimonies which demonstrate the problematic nature of the sources. A Coptic text on the life of Mary, the mother of Jesus, relates that she was born in the small village of Magdala in the vicinity of Jerusalem. According to the text, the village belonged to a certain family before it was given to Jehoiakim.[37] This narrative does not belong with the above-mentioned testimonies, since there is no certainty that the story is based on the reality in Palestine, and it is more probable that the author wrote it under the inspiration of the reality with which he was familiar.

Another story in this text, which is attributed to Epiphanes, describes the punishment imposed on the Jews by Vespasian: that they were not to engage in the processing of agricultural produce (olive-presses, granaries, threshing-floors). The story seems to indicate that restrictions were also imposed upon their freedom.[38] The background of this narrative as well is unclear.

The Palestinian Halakhic Literature

The Palestinian halakhic literature (the "*ma'asim*" literature) contains responsa on various agricultural topics, which is only natural. There are various testimonies regarding the poor state of security, such as the narrative about "stratelates" who spread over the Jewish community and disturbed the wedding ceremony of a young couple;[39] or another episode about a couple who were captured by Ishmaelites.[40] Falling into Ishmaelite captivity was likely to have occurred mainly in the fringe regions before the Muslim conquest; obviously, such raids are characteristic only of a

[34] Procophius, *Anecdota* XXX, 18.

[35] R. Raabe, ed., *Petrus der Iberer* (Leipzig, 1895), p. 98.

[36] For additional sources, see: Dan, pp. 171-276; Safrai, *Economy* (above, n. 1), loc. cit.

[37] E. A. W. Budge, *Coptic Texts* (London, 1916), p. 630.

[38] Budge, p. 786.

[39] B. M. Lewin, "Ma'asim le-bne Erez Israel (Palestinian Halachic Practice)", *Tarbiz* 1, no. 1 (1929), p. 87 (Heb.).

[40] M. Margoliot, *Palestinian Halakhot from the Genizah* (Jerusalem, 1973), p. 46 (Heb.).

rural community. This literature contains a series of discussions pertaining to "one who went to an *akhsaniya* [lodging]", i.e., someone who set out on a journey and some event befell him on the way. Levin regards this term as a usage unique to the *ma'asim* literature, i.e., a linguistic innovation of the period.[41] The fact that a new Greek term was created to describe such trips teaches of their frequency, and of the fact that they had become a frequent occurrence.

Another halakhah speaks of Reuben who was lodged "in an inn (*pundak*)", with an additional discussion devoted to "a woman whose husband went to 'beyond the sea' ".[42] This passage contains a number of additional queries, one of which emphasizes that the Roman Empire is not a just government, and it also includes a number of laws applicable only in the Land of Israel. All this demonstrates that the passage is of Palestinian origin, at least originally, and predates the Muslim conquest. Another halakhah speaks of "an Is[raelite] who came in a ship from [beyond the sea]... which entered the harbor."[43] These halakhot attest to the intensive occupation by the rabbis with matters pertaining to large-scale commerce. Land, however, was still the most important and significant property, as is evidenced by the multitude of laws pertaining to agricultural topics. Another important testimony appears in a halakhah limiting land inheritance by a wife, so that the holding would not leave the "clan",[44] thereby teaching of the economic importance of land in the Jewish society.

Talmudic law also deals with the rules governing the collection of a debt from lands,[45] based on the assumption that cash was extremely rare. This law reappears in a Geonic responsum from Palestine.[46] A study of this halakhah reveals that the respondent established a new law, which is of interest for its determination of the relative worth of

[41] Lewin, pp. 87-88; N. N. Coronel, *Teshuvot ha-Geonim* (The responsa of the Geonim) (Jerusalem, 1961), p. 13.

[42] *Ginze Kedem* I (1922), pp. 7-8 ((Heb.); Lewin loc. cit. already demonstrated the linguistic connection between this passage and the Palestinian halakhot.

[43] J. Mann, "Sefer ha-Ma'asim le-bne Erez Israel (Book of Palestinian Halachic Practice)", Tarbiz 1, no. 3 (1930), p. 14 (Heb.); *Teshuvot ha-Geonim ha-Ketzarot* 83. The passage contains a number of Greek words, which confirm its attribution to Palestine.

[44] .Margoliot, p. 88. This halakhah is connected with additional testimonies of a society constructed of family systems of extended families; also see: Lewin, p. 29; *Teshuvot ha-Geonim ha-Ketzarot* 60, 67; J. N. Epstein, "On the Sefer ha-Ma'asim", Tarbiz 1, no. 3 (1930), p. 144 (Heb.); and additional responsa of unclear origin, such as Coronel, Teshuvot ha-Geonim 33 and others. For the process of the natural division of the ancestral house in this period, see Epstein, p. 151.

[45] Mishnah Gittin 5:1.

[46] *Sha'arei Tzedek* (*Teshuvot ha-Ge'onim*) (Salonika, 1792) IV:4:78.

average land in comparison with land of inferior quality. This ruling teaches that the collection of debts from land was a prevalent phenomenon. Consequently, agriculture was still a major source of livelihood, but there was a considerable rise in the percentage of the urban Jewish population and that of large-scale trade in the sum total of income. Additional halakhot portray the leasing of land from a Gentile.[47]

The subject of slaves appears frequently in the Palestinian halakhot. Jews buy and sell slaves, and a relatively large number of testimonies teach of the large numbers of wealthy slave owners, in contrast with the Jewish society in the Talmudic period, in which slaves were only a marginal economic factor.[48]

Agriculture was the main source of livelihood, and these slaves worked the land; consequently, the system of estates was widespread, and Jews were among the estate owners.

Landowners and farmers appear in many halakhot and in both Jewish and Christian narratives. Narratives in which it could not be determined if the subject was a wealthy farmer, an estate owner, or a small farmer have not been cited. Approx. thirty of all the Christian and Jewish literary testimonies which can be clearly understood undoubtedly deal with the wealthy, while ordinary farmers appear in only approximately four stories.

The Archaeological Testimony

Many estates from the Byzantine period in Palestine have been uncovered in archaeological excavations. The recent discoveries include, inter alia: two estate houses in Ramat ha-Nadiv, on the Carmel, not far from

[47] Margoliot, p. 44.

[48] J. N. Epstein, "Ma'asim le-bne Erez Israel (Palestinian Halachic Practice) (Ant. 35), *Tarbiz* 1, no. 2 (1930), p. 39 (Heb.); Mann, p. 14; *Sha'arei Tzedek* (*Teshuvot ha-Ge'onim*) III:6:13 (this halakhah concludes with the wording "and thus is the halakhah", which is characteristic of the Palestinian responsa); Coronel, *Teshuvot ha-Geonim* 24 (which uses the wording "and thus is the din [law]"); idem, 77 (in which the wording "thus we have seen" appears); and idem, responsum 78, which speaks explicitly of the sale of Edomite slaves in Palestine; Halakhot Gedolot, Ketubot 68c (according to Epstein, Tarbiz 1, no. 3, p. 150); B. M. Lewin, "Geniza Fragments", *Tarbiz* 2 (1931), p. 408 (Heb.); Margoliot, Palestinian Halakhot, pp. 64, 80, 88; E. E. Urbach, "The Laws regarding Slavery as a Source for the Social History of the Mishna and Talmud", in *Papers of the Institute of Jewish Studies*, ed. J. G. Weiss (London, 1964), pp. 1-94.

[49] For a partial count, see: Safrai, *Economy* (above, n. 1), loc. cit.

Caesarea;[50] a large estate house in Tel'Ofer, near Giv'at Olga;[51] near Hofit;[52] near Beth Shean (Scythopolis);[53] and two estates in the vicinity of Mishmar ha-'Emeq.[54] Based solely on the archaeological results, it is not possible to determine when there were more estate houses in Palestine, and when the settlement phenomenon reached its peak, because of the insufficient quantity of the finds, and the influence exerted on the finds by incidental and local factors.

Regular villages were also found, such as the villages in the southern part of Palestine: Eshtemoa, Susiya, Ma'on, Anim, Jattir, Rimmon; and many other settlements in Samaria, Judea, and Galilee. The archaeological evidence cannot conclusively establish if a certain settlement was a regular village of private individuals, or whether it belonged to a private master or to the emperor, which also was a common phenomenon. A special type are the villages with a large structure which is located in their center or which towers over them. Such villages probably belonged to the "master" (the village owner) whose residence dominated the settlement. This was the interpretation given by the excavators of the structure in Khirbet el-Bire,[55] as may also be the case regarding the plan of the settlement in Horvat Najar.[56]

Large wine-presses, capable of processing the harvest of vineyards extending over hundreds of dunams, were found in proximity to many villages. They may have been communal institutions of the entire community, although there are no literary proofs of the existence of such communal installations. Conversely, the press may have belonged to the estate owner; this issue requires further study. The wine-press in Hulda may possibly belong to this category.[57]

The Regional Surveys

It is difficult to isolate the archaeological material from the Byzantine period from that of other periods in antiquity in order to depict the

[50] Y. Hirschfeld and R. Birger-Calderon, "Early Roman and Byzantine Estates near Caesarea", *IEJ* 41 (1991), pp. 81-111.

[51] *Hadashot Arkheologiyot* 92 (1988), pp. 26-28.

[52] *Hadashot Arkheologiyot* 74-75 (1980), p. 56.

[53] *Hadashot Arkheologiyot* 50 (1974), pp. 6-7.

[54] Z. Safrai and M. Linn, "Excavations and Surveys in the Mishmar Ha-'Emeq Area", in *Geva: Archaeological Discoveries at Tell Abu-Shusha, Mishmar Ha-'Emeq*, ed. B. Mazar (Jerusalem, 1988), pp. 172 (Heb.).

[55] Dar and Safrai, "Horvat Birah". Op. cit. note 2.

[56] According to this interpretation, structure A was the manor house. See: S. Dar, *Landscape and Pattern* (*BAR* 308) (Oxford, 1986), Fig. 3.5.

[57] A. Kloner, "The Structure at Hulda and Its Use as a Wine Press, in *Man and Land in Eretz-Israel in Antiquity*, eds. A. Kasher et al., (Jerusalem, 1986), pp. 197-208 (Heb.).

settlement landscape of Byzantine Palestine. The number of cities clearly increased, and their area expanded considerably beyond that of the Roman period. The data in the rural sector is less clear.

Some surveys conducted in Israel have uncovered many dozens of extremely small single-phase sites which are characteristic mainly of the Byzantine period. Portugali reached this conclusion on the basis of surveys in the Jezreel Valley.[58] The Land of Ephraim survey revealed a decline in the number of large and small villages in the Byzantine period; however, the survey also revealed in this area 110 isolated structures or small satellite settlements from this period. The excavator regarded the latter to be a new phenomenon, since there are no sites of this type from the Roman period (or possibly, small Roman sites became slightly larger in the Byzantine period?).[59]

Other surveys present a less distinct or different picture. The Golan almost totally lacks small villages or isolated structures. Structures of this sort are rare in southern Judea, while in other regions, such as the northern Samaria hill country or'Emeq Hefer, there is a clear increase in the number of small Byzantine sites, but this cannot be defined as a "new" phenomenon, as in the Ephraim hill country. Superficial examinations conducted in other surveys did not distinguish different settlement sizes in the various site types.

Such small sites are likely to be field structures, small satellite settlements, monasteries, or estate houses. In many instances, only excavations will enable us to distinguish between these settlement types. Different processes led to the spread of satellite settlements or to that of estates. There are still too few good surveys which clearly differentiate between Roman and Byzantine sites. Furthermore, we surmise that a change occurred in the agrarian situation between the fourth century and the sixth-seventh centuries. Needless to say, surveys encounter difficulty in separating the early Byzantine ceramic material from that of the late Roman period. Generally speaking, finds from the various surveys are likely to support the hypothesis regarding the increase of estates in the Byzantine period, but such support cannot be said to be well-founded at the present time. The object of the current discussion is to suggest a new perspective and working guidelines for surveyors. It is to be hoped that the very presentation of the question may spark the search for suitable answers.

[58] Y. Portugali, "The Settlement Pattern in the Western Jezreel Valley from the 6th Century B.C.E. to the Arab Conquest", in *Man and Land in Eretz-Israel*, pp. 7-19.

[59] I. Finkelstein, "The Land of Ephraim Survey", *Tel-Aviv* 15-16 (1988-89), p. 159.

Based mainly on the Christian and Jewish literary testimonies, it may be stated that a concrete change took place in the agrarian structure in Palestine. The evidence points to a lengthy process in which private agriculture declined. This process began in the late Second Temple period, intensified in the early Byzantine period (the end of the Amoraitic period – fourth century), and became substantive in the late Byzantine period. In the period under discussion, most of the lands in Palestine were already in the hands of the rich, city-dwelling landowners.

This was a slow process, extending over 300-500 years. The aggregate of estates gradually reached a critical mass, and the new situation was acknowledged by the imperial legal system in the late fourth century. This recognition patently served to further accelerate the process. The process in itself is not surprising, because the system of estates was common in the Roman world, and its domination of Palestine was a function of the process of the Romanization of Palestine.[60] Two essential questions must be asked, the answer to which is likely to alter in great degree our understanding of the Byzantine period, and to shed light on the central settlement processes in this period:

1. was fourth-century Palestine witness to additional processes which assisted and expedited the agrarian processes?
2. how did the change in the agrarian structure affect other processes in the land?

These questions will be discussed in the following chapter.

[60] The phenomenon of the estates already began in the Biblical period. The connection between the Biblical roots and the Hellenistic-Roman reality is important and of interest in its own right, but it lies beyond the scope of the present work.

CHAPTER FOUR

The Ethnographic History:

The Decline of the Jewish Community in the Byzantine Period and the Rise of Christianity

In the period of the Mishnah and Talmud, the Jewish community was a central factor in the province and constituted a decisive majority in Galilee. This public thrived culturally, produced the Talmudic literature, and left archaeological remains and a cultural heritage of the greatest importance. It is well known that a major change occurred in the Byzantine period. The Jewish community became a minority, albeit a vigorous and prominent one. This was matched by a serious weakening of its literary output, which began to assume a completely different nature (see below), thus bringing to a close the period of the Mishnah and Talmud, which is regarded as a golden age in Jewish history. Of great significance is the question, what caused this drastic change in the situation of the Jewish community, and is this to be regarded as an internal Jewish occurrence, or was it possibly related to processes and events of a more general nature?

This chapter will resume our study of the settlement and cultural processes in the fourth and fifth centuries, and attempt to propose an amended chronology of the main happenings in the Jewish community in Palestine, based on a reexamination of the literary sources, while also utilizing the excavation results which were summarized in the preceding chapter. This will enable us to propose an explanation for these processes of change in Jewish history within the broader context in which they took place.

1. The Literary Data – the Decline in Talmudic Creativity

The PT (Palestinian Talmud) was "completed" ca. the midfourth century, but was never redacted. The arranger of the Talmud collected dicta and portions of discussions and edited the material in only rudimentary fashion, in contrast to the Babylonian Talmud, which was collected and edited over the course of many years. The last events mentioned in the PT are the revolt of Gallus in 351-2 CE, and possibly also the Julian wars in Persia. The "revolt of Gallus" and Orsicinus, Gallus' war commander, are mentioned in approx. five passages.[1] The attempt to rebuild the Temple during the time of Julian, which occurred ca. a decade later (363), is not explicitly mentioned in the Talmud, which does speak of the emperor's invasion of Persia.[2]

The halakhic and midrashic product did not cease upon the completion of the PT. An extensive literature of aggadic midrashim was edited and consolidated during this period, which extended until the eighth or ninth century. These aggadic midrashim may be divided into at last three categories, based on internal literary and historical criteria: early aggadic midrashim contemporaneous with the PT such as *Genesis Rabbah*, *Leviticus Rabbah*, and others; intermediate *midrashim*; and later midrashim (including *Midrash Tehillim*, *Pirkei de-Rabbi Eliezer*, and other works).

In addition to the literature of aggadic midrashim, an extensive literature was written in Palestine, and new literary genres were developed. Many *piyyutim* were composed in this period, and basic values and frameworks of the Palestinian piyyutical literature were developed. Prayer books were written, prayers were stylized, halakhic works were written (the "*ma'asim* literature"), and a portion of the "*minor tractates*," which were arranged by topic. These works constitute the first systematic attempt to establish halakhic rulings on topics which were still undecided, and to arrange the rulings in the Talmudic literature in a certain order by subject. This period, or possibly only from the eighth century on, witnessed the development of the format of responsa, which would become one of the major types of the halakhic literature.[3] Works such as *Pirkei*

[1] For a discussion of these dicta, see: Y. Geiger, "The Revolt in the Time of Gallus and the Rebuilding of the Temple in the Time of Julian", in *Eretz Israel from the Destruction of the Second Temple to the Muslim Conquest* (in Baras et al., above, chap., 1, n. 45), vol. 1, pp. 202-208 (Heb.). Also see: B. G. Nathanson, *The Fourth Century Jewish Revolt during the Reign of Gallus*, Ph.D. diss., Ann Arbor, 1981; M. Mor, "The Events of 351-352 in Palestine – the Last Revolt against Rome?" in *The Eastern Frontier of the Roman Empire*, eds. D. H. French and C. S. Lightfoot (*BAR* 553), (Oxford, 1989) pp. 335-53: G. Stemberger, Juden und Christen, (München 1994), pp. 132-150. The extent of the "revolt" is of secondary importance for the current discussion; at any rate, the numismatic finds cited below prove that the revolt was quite significant – also see below, Chap. 5.

[2] PT Nedarim 3:37:d: "When the emperor Julian went down there, 120 myriads went down with him".

[3] The Christian literature also developed the responsa style from the sixth century onward. An attempt should be made to clarify where this literary genre first appeared and to determine the realistic background for this development.

Zeraim were written, which deal with life sciences, on the border between science and folklore; also written and redacted during this period were a number of esoteric works on various levels, popular literature such as *Harba de-Moshe* (*The Sword of Moshe*) and literature of a more intellectual nature such as Pirkei Heikhalot. It may be assumed that a part or the majority of the *Targumim* were composed in this period.[4]

It is difficult to determine if all these literary types were first developed in Palestine or in Babylon. At any rate, the extant fragments of works from Palestine of each of these literary types suffice to attest to continued activity in the *batei midrash*, indicating that the religious wellsprings had not run dry.

Nevertheless, the nature of the post-Talmudic literature differs from that of the Talmudic works. Most of the halakhic and midrashic compositions are not independent works, but rather consist of editing and ordering of early halakhic material. There is hardly any new material in this literary corpus. Post-Talmudic sages are not mentioned, and there is only the slightest of references to later events. The enemy is usually still pagan Rome, and not Christian Byzantium, and the "fourth kingdom" which will be followed by the redeemer is the Byzantine Empire. Researchers have struggled to identify isolated passages which reflect facts or social situations postdating the Talmudic period, and a number of such efforts appear to have been successful, but this cannot change the general picture. Thus, e.g., *Pirkei de-Rabbi Eliezer* contains evidence of the Arab conquest,[5] and the "*redemption midrashim*"[6] allude to the Persian and Arab conquests of the seventh century, but these are exceptional, and are characteristic of only a portion of these works.

The PT and the Palestinian midrashim do not contain teachings by the Babylonian Amoraim of the last two generations such as R. Ashi, Merimar, Ravina, and their colleagues. Taken together with the above-mentioned testimonies, this proves that the redactors of these works added little new material to their midrashim.[7]

[4] For a review of the literature of the period and its accomplishments, see, e.g.: M. B. Lerner, "The External Tractates", in *The Literature of the Sages* I, ed. S. Safrai (Assen, 1987), pp. 367-403; Z. Safrai, "Post-Talmudic Halakhic Literature", in *idem*, pp. 404-409; Y. Dan, "Byzantine Rule", in *The History of Eretz Israel: The Roman Byzantine Period*, ed. M. D. Herr (Jerusalem: 1985), pp. 338-49.

[5] See, e.g.: *Pirkei de-Rabbi Eliezer* 30.

[6] Y. Ibn-Shmuel, *Midrashei Ge'ulah* (Midrashim of redemption) (Jerusalem and Tel Aviv, 1954).

[7] The later Babylonian Amoraim presumably are mentioned in a number of rulings, but these are all late or distorted. Thus, e.g., the sentence in Midrash Tehillim 103:7, ed. Buber (p. 218): "Meremar said..". does not appear in MS Buber; the statement by

The *ma'asim* literature, which is concerned with halakhic subjects, is slightly different. It does not contain discussions between scholars of the period, but rather relates to contemporary issues, thereby enabling us to learn of the social background in the late Byzantine period (see above, Introduction and Chap. 3). Also relevant in this context is the Rehob inscription, whose literary and stylistic nature is close to that of the *ma'asim* literature, and which contains a compilation of halakhot and rulings on a well-defined halakhic subject.[8] The inscription contains a decision exempting the Samaria region from the laws applicable only in Eretz Israel, which was issued in the sixth or seventh century.[9] This decree attests to the ability of the scholars of the time or of the halakhic institutions to deliver rulings. Such a decision could almost certainly have been taken only in a formal session of the Sanhedrin, as were similar decisions which had been made in the time of the Amoraim.

The institution of the Nasi was abolished sometime between 415 and 429. In 415 the Nasi was reduced in rank, his powers were limited, and he was censured,[10] and by May 429 the legislator already discussed the expropriation of the "coronarii" tax which had been collected for the Nasi,[11] while the Sanhedrin itself was not abrogated. One version of the law imposes upon the Sanhedrin the duty to collect the coronarii for transferal to the Roman authorities,[12] while in a second version the Sanhedrin was empowered to collect these funds, possibly for its own use.[13] In any event, the Sanhedrin appears as an existing body; there probably were two Sanhedrins, one in Tiberias, in the province of Palestina Secunda, and the other in Diospolis, in Palestina Prima.

There is a later report in the sixth century about Mar Zutra, who fled from Babylonia and was appointed *Rosh Perek* head of the court) in

R. Ashi in *Midrash Tehillim* 126:4, ed. Buber (p. 406), and the statement by R. Ashi to Ameimar in Tanhuma, Mishpatim 6:1 similarly are absent from MS Buber; and the pronouncement of Meremar in Tanhuma, Hukat 2:1 (both in the printed edition and in MS Buber) is taken from the She'iltot, as Buber already noted in his edition of *Midrash Tanhuma*.

8 See: Y. Sussman, "A Halakhic Inscription from the Beth-Shean Valley", *Tarbiz* 43 (1973), pp. 90-158 (Heb.).

9 Z. Safrai, "Marginal Notes on the Rehob Inscription", *Zion* 42 (1977), pp. 7-12 (Heb.). This dating has recently been proved, since the synagogue building itself is from *the* seventh century. See below, appendix A, the discussion on the Beth Shean Valley sites.

10 See: *CJ* 1, 9, 15; *CTH* 16, 8, 22.

11 *CTH* 16, 8, 29; *CJ* 1, 9, 17.

12 *CTH* 16, 8, 29.

13 *CJ* 1, 9, 17.

Palestine. The narrative is a bit vague, and the term "*Rosh Perek*" may be a Babylonian term adopted to describe the different reality of the Palestinian *batei midrash*. Despite its Babylonian association, the narrative apparently alludes to the continued activity of educational institutions and the rendering of legal decisions in Palestine.[14]

Evidence of the greatest importance for our discussionis contained in a conclusion reached by Epstein, incidental to a discussion of the laws of *kashrut* by the Palestinian scholars. One expression of the superiority of Palestine and of the cultural-religious hegemony enjoyed by its scholars consisted of the dispatch of rulings, directives, and instructions to the Babylonian scholars. The Talmudic terminology for this is "they sent from there" or "they sent from the West." Slightly less formal is the expression "they said in the West." Such directives continued to reach Babylonia even after the sealing of the PT. Tractate Hullin relates that "they sent word from there, saying: 'The law is in accordance with R. Samuel b. R. Abbahu; nevertheless, pay heed to the opinion of R. Ahai, for he enlightens the eyes of the exile.'"[15] This R. Samuel b. R. Abahu is mentioned in Iggeret de-Rav Sherira Gaon as a Savorai who died in the early sixth century.[16] R. Ahai is not identified, although several Savoraim bore this name.[17] According to Albeck, the passage refers to two Babylonian Amoraim of the last generation, from the midfifth century,[18] but even according to this interpretation, rulings would have been sent to Babylon after the sealing of the PT.

In the discussion of another topic, R. Nahuniah (Rahumi) relates "I enquired of all those who decide questions of *terefot* [improperly slaughtered animals] in the West, and they informed me that the law is in accordance with the ruling of Rabbi Rakish son of Papa, and the law do not follow the ruling of R.'Awira."[19] The time in which rabi Rakish son of Papa was active cannot be determined, but R. Nahuniah (or Rahumi)

[14] A. Grossman, *The Babylonian Exilarchate in the Gaonic Period* (Jerusalem, 1984), pp. 15-44 (Heb.).

[15] BT Hullin 59b; J. N. Epstein, "The Lore of Erez Israel", *Tarbiz* 2, no. 3 (1931), p. 310 (Heb.); idem, *Introduction to Amoraitic Literature: Babylonian Talmud and Yerushalmi* (Jerusalem, 1962), pp. 273-76 (Heb.); see also: Judah b. Kalonymus, *Yihusei Tanna'im ve-Amoraim (The genealogy of the Tannaim and Amoraim)*, ed. I. L. Maimon (Jerusalem, 1963), pp.100-101.

[16] *Iggeret Rav Sherira Gaon*, ed. B. M. Lewin (Haifa, 1921), p. 98 and n. 16 (French version).

[17] Epstein, Introduction, loc. cit.

[18] Ch. Albeck, *Introduction to the Talmud: Bavli and Yerushalmi* (Tel Aviv, 1969), p. 451 (Heb.).

[19] BT Hullin 55b.

apparently was a well-known Savorai who died in 506.[20] This discussion uses the term terofaei de-ma'arava – scholars from the West expert in the laws of improperly slaughtered animals. R. Nahuniah apparently went up to Palestine and asked this question of the rabbis there. It should be noted that the Palestinian halakhah regarding *terefot* was widely at variance with the law as promulgated by the Babylonian rabbis, and the Palestinian halakhic literature of the period discusses this topic extensively.

Another report mentions that "in the West it was said in the name of Rabina."[21] Rabina I lived in the second half of the fourth century, at the same time as R. Ashi, and a teaching attributed to him could have been transmitted only following his death.

Consequently, a central *bet midrash* was still active in Palestine in this period (the last quarter of the fourth century), and the teachings of Rabina returned to Babylonia through the medium of the Palestinian rabbis. Another tradition relates "in the West they said thusly: 'R. Jacob son of Aha said in R. Ashi's name.'"[22] According to Iggeret [Letter] de-Rav Sherira Gaon, R. Ashi died in 426, and a teaching could have been related by his pupil no earlier than the second quarter of the fifth century.

In the time of R. Hamma (d. ca. 317),[23] one of the pupils brought "a letter from the West that the law is not in accordance with R. Eliezer."[24] Thus in the Spanish version of *Iggeret de-Rav Sherira Gaon*; according, however, to the French version of the *Iggeret*[25] and another Geonic responsum, this refers to the bringing of a letter "from the metivta [the college],"[26] and therefore is not a certain proof. If so, the Palestinian rabbis continued to study, teach, and disseminate their teachings in the Diaspora, and their authority and prestige were not questioned by their Babylonian counterparts.

The Sanhedrin also continued to be active. Thus, e.g., the Sanhedrin continued to intercalate years and declare the New Moons. A detailed

[20] J. E. Ephrathi, *The Sevoraic Period and Its Literature in Babylonia and in Eretz Israel (500-684)* (Petah Tikvah, 1973), pp. 123-24 (Heb.); B. M. Lewin, "The Savoraim and Their Teachings", *Azkarah le-Nishmat... A. I. Kook, ed I.L. Fischman, 4* (Jerusalem, 1937), pp. 157-58 (Heb.).

[21] BT Bekhorot 33b.

[22] BT Zevahim 55b.

[23] *Iggeret Rav Sherira Gaon*, p. 89.

[24] BT Shevuot 48b.

[25] *Iggeret Rav Sherira Gaon*, p. 90.

[26] *Teshuvot Ge'onei Mizrah u-Ma'arav* (Responsa of Eastern and Western Geonim), ed. J. Müller (Berlin, 1888), end of responsum 2.

discussion of this topic lies beyond the scope of this work, and only the main points can be considered. In the period of the Tannaim and Amoraim, these two responsibilities devolved upon the Nasi and the Sanhedrin, with many testimonies attesting to the discharge of these duties. This right was perceived as one of the clearest expressions of the hegemony of Palestine and its scholars. This prerogative was contested, but all these challenges were defeated, and the Palestinian sages and the Nasi consolidated their authority in these matters and established it as a religious principle.

R. Hai Gaon relates regarding the situation in the post-Talmudic period that R. Hillel b. R. Judah established the fixed order of incalation in 358, since he was witness to the diminution of scholarship in successive generations. The fixing of the calendar put an end to the need for calculations and discussions on the subject, and thereby (either indirectly or directly) ended the prerogatives of Palestine. It seemingly is strange that at this early date the Nasi already feared the collapse of the authoritative institutions in Palestine and instituted a fixed calendar. If this tradition were reliable, it would constitute importance proof of the initial acknowledgement of the "image" of the process of decline within the Jewish community in Palestine.[27] This tradition, however, is thoroughly refuted.

The testimony attributing this tradition to R. Hai Gaon is a later one, and appears only in *Sefer ha-Ibbur* by R. Abraham b. Hiyya;[28] in *Yesod Olam* 4:9, where it is attributed to the "*Geonim*" who stated it in the name of "*the Sages*"; and in the *responsum* of R. Eliezer b. Jacob of Narbonne.[29] This great innovation is absent, however, from other responsa by R. Hai Gaon himself on the same topic.[30] Furthermore, it is well-known that a serious disagreement and confrontation erupted over the right to intercalate between R. Saadiah, the Gaon of Babylonia, and Ben Meir, the Gaon of Palestine. The former presented various arguments in support of his demand for Babylonian independence and superiority, the chief claim being that the Babylonian scholars had already learned the principle of intercalation He does not, however, mention the presumably decisive argument that R. Hillel b. Judah had established the

[27] For "image", see chap., 1, n. 1.

[28] Ed. London (1851), Article 3, Gate 7, p. 97.

[29] S. Assaf, *Sifran sel Risonim: Responsa, Dicisiones atque Minhagot* (Jerusalem, 1935), para. 36, p. 39, and also other Rishonim, such as the author of *Ha-Me'or, Nahmanides*, etc.; see also: M. M. Kasher, *Torah Shelemah* 13 (New York, 1954), pp. 24 ff. (Heb.).

[30] See: B. M. Lewin, *Otzar ha-Gaonim, Rosh-Hashana* (Jerusalem, 1932), pp. 40 ff.

order of the Festivals.[31] This "regulation" is similarly ignored by additional *Geonim* who were occupied with the history of the intercalation of years, such as the author of *Megillat Avitar*;[32] additional *Rishonim*, especially the early ones, such as R. Tobias, the author of *Lekah Tov*;[33] R. Menahem, the author of *Sekhel Tov*;[34] R. Meshullam b. Kalonymus;[35] R. Samuel b. Eli,[36] and others.

Accordingly, all the testimonies regarding the regulation of the Nasi R. Hillel b. Judah are of late origin. Its attribution to R. Hai Gaon is suspect and problematical; even if this was stated in the name of R. Hai Gaon, there still is room to doubt if this is an original tradition. It was not mentioned by the contemporaries of R. Hai Gaon and the members of the succeeding generations, even though it could have justified and legitimized their halakhic method. Additionally, the tradition well serves the body of Babylonian arguments in the controversy with the Palestinian scholars, and therefore should be questioned as being of late origin. Its absence from the polemic literature of the early Geonim on this issue leads us to distrust the tradition. It is clear from Palestinian sources that the Sanhedrin continued to convene for the purpose of declaring the New Moon and intercalating the year. An explicit description of the ceremonies appears in *Tractate Soferim* 19:9-10:

> "The associations of elders, leaders, and students were assembled in session (on the first day) from the time of *Minhah* onwards until the sun had set. It is necessary to recite in the blessing over the wine: "Blessed are You..." One concludes with: "Blessed are You, O Lord, Who sanctifies Israel and the New Moons. Give thanks to the Lord, for He is good; on this day, we all in Jerusalem rejoice and are happy in the Omnipresent. May Elijah the prophet soon come to us; may the king Messiah cause to spring forth in our days... Consecrated is the New Moon, consecrated at the beginning of the month, consecrated in its proper time, consecrated in its intercalation... consecrated in all the habitations of Israel, consecrated by our Rabbis, consecrated *in the house of assembly [beit va'ad]*. Give thanks to the Lord, for He is good."...

The text of the declaration is preserved in a *Genizah* fragment: [...] Sanhedrin [...]

[31] For the method of R. Saadiah Gaon, see: Kasher, pp. 40-66.
[32] *Ibid.*, pp. 50-52.
[33] *Ibid.*, pp. 67-70.
[34] *Ibid.*, pp. 70-71.
[35] *Ibid.*, pp. 71-72.
[36] *Ibid.*, p. 75.

> Blessed are You, Lord, the God of Israel. The *head of the Court* says, "C[ons]ecrated", and they reply [after him], "Consecrated, this month is consecrated, consecrated, consecrated. Blessed are You, O Lord, King of the universe..."[37]

This apparently is evidenced in additional *piyyutim* as well.[38] *Pirkei de-Rabbi Eliezer* 8 preserves an additional depiction of the intercalation ceremony as it apparently was conducted at a later time, after the final collapse of the Jewish community following the earthquake in the eighth century:

> "Likewise, in the future [the intercalations] will be diminished at the end of the fourth kingdom until the king Messiah shall come. Just as the Holy One, blessed be He, was revealed to Moses and Aaron in Egypt, so too in the future He will be revealed to us at the end of the fourth kingdom... The intercalation is effected in the presence of three; R. Eliezer says, In the presence of ten, as it is said, "God stands in the congregation of God" [Ps. 82:1]. And if they become less, they bring a Torah scroll and open it before them, and they sit in a circle; the greatest sits first, and the least, last; they direct their gaze downwards to the ground; then they spread out their hands to their Father in heaven. The rosh yeshivah pronounces the [Divine] Name, and they hear a heavenly voice cry out the following words: "And the Lord spoke to Moses and Aaron in the land of Egypt, saying: 'This month shall be for you.'" If, due to the iniquity of the generation, they hear nothing, then, as it were, He is not able to let the Divine Presence dwell among them..."

Thus the ceremony continued to be held, albeit without a community, but with faith in the role of the leadership in Palestine and a sense of national destiny.

This passage in the midrash is likely to be later, from the eighth century, since it is already reflective of a weak, sparsely populated community. Consequently, it would seem that the "tradition" attributed to R. Sherira Gaon regarding the determination of a fixed calendar was more of a wish or commentary. The practice of intercalating the year and of declaring the New Moon on the basis of observation continued in Palestine, and the Sanhedrin continued to bear the burden of this task, deriving from it prerogatives and power.

If this is the case, then the institutions of Torah remained active in disseminating their teachings in the fifth and sixth centuries, and were the

[37] E. Fleischer, "Clarifications in the Problem of the Liturgical Function of the Piyyutim in Honour of the New Moon", *Tarbiz* 42 (1973), p. 348 (Heb.).

[38] Z. A. Steinfeld, "The Sounding of the Shofar on the New Moon", *Tarbiz* 54 (1985), pp. 347-65 (Heb.); see also M. D. Herr, "Matters of Palestinian Halakha during the Sixth and Seventh Centuries C.E"., *Tarbiz* 49 (1980), p. 62-80 (Heb.).

venue for the composition of halakhic works. These works contain virtually no realistic details concerning the contemporaneous *batei midrash*: the names of individuals, places, and similar identifying details are missing, and they contain no testimonies about the life of the bet midrash and the methods of study followed in it. The only name to appear in the *ma'asim* literature is that of R. Jonathan, whose death marked the "end of the *ma'aseh*" and the end of the *ma'asim* literature.[39]

In conclusion: the Palestinian post-Talmudic literature differs in character, quality, and possibly also in quantity from the Talmudic literature, but the *batei midrash* in Palestine clearly did not close their doors, and the sound of Torah study was not stilled. The change in the nature of the written work is expressed in the paucity of Talmudic discussions, and in the abstention from mentioning the names of the scholars active at the time these sources were produced. The literary product of the period consisted of the collection and redaction of the teachings of earlier scholars, while ordering them by halakhic or midrashic topic, and with the clear intent of providing halakhic rulings. This was accompanied by the development of new literary genres such as responsa, piyyut, the Targumim, and other ventures into new literary realms.

This definition compels us to reexamine the completion of the PT in order to understand and date the editing process which this work underwent.

The last generation of Palestinian Amoraim lived and was active in the midfourth century. R. Jonah and R. Jose are involved in rulings which refer to the events of the revolt of Gallus (352/3), and R. Mana is mentioned as studying before his father in a ruling connected with this episode, evidencing that at this time R. Mana was a young scholar who sat before his teacher\father, who was still in the prime of his activity.[40]

Another tradition tells of the action taken by R. Mana when a three-year-old child died in Caesarea.[41] If the reference is to R. Mana II, then the event occurred in his old age, at least two or three decades after the Gallus rebellion, which had erupted in his youth. The sources also relate of the death of R. Mana's nephews[42] and of a number of rulings of the

[39] J. Mann, "*Sefer ha-Ma'asim*", (above, Chap. 3, n. 43), p. 2.
[40] PT Shevuot 4:35:a.
[41] PT Moed Katan 3:82:c.
[42] PT Moed Katan 3:82:d.

entourage of the 'Nasi'(the president), which were issued by a pupil of R. Mana.[43]

All these events occurred in the generation following the revolt of Gallus. R. Mana also had other pupils, such as R. Zeira, and possibly also R. Azariah and R. Nahman. It is not possible, however, to isolate the events which took place in their time or traditions regarding their activity with no connection to their teacher. Partly responsible for this confusion is the profusion of scholars bearing the same name.[44]

R. Jonah's colleague was R. Jose b. R. Bonn, who issued joint rulings with him regarding the revolt of Gallus. R. Jose's son, R. Samuel, who is called "R. Samuel, the son of R. Jose (Joseph) son of Bonn," is mentioned in several topics, and in one story together with an additional scholar, R. Mataniah.[45]

R. Mana is mentioned in many topics, while R. Samuel and R. Mataniah appear only in isolated topics, thereby attesting to the process of diminishing creativity from dozens of Amoraim in the generation of R. Jonah and R. Jose to only three Amoraim in the succeeding generation. The most active of the latter (R. Mana) is already mentioned in the context of the revolt of Gallus, and he is to be regarded as constituting a sort of interim generation. The two other scholars are mentioned in only a few topics.

The methods of transmission of Talmudic traditions are well-known. Since the sage's words are generally reported by his pupils, the teachings of the last Amoraim were transmitted by the scholars of the next generation. Consequently, the PT was compiled approx. two generations after the revolt of Gallus, ca. the end of the fourth century. This hypothesis seems logical and has been proposed by various scholars, including Epstein, Gafni, and others, based on a portion of the above-mentioned proofs.[46]

According to the chronology we have proposed, the editing of the PT belongs to the phase in which the nature of the rabbinic literature had already undergone change, i.e., the editing itself was conducted in the post-Talmudic phase. This period of the rabbinic literature is characterized by the collection and editing of early teachings, which in itself

[43] PT Yoma 7:44:d; Taanit 1:64:c; Sukkah 2:53:b; Moed Katan 3:83:a.

[44] W. Bacher, *Aggadat Amora'i Eretz Yisrael* (The aggadah of the Palestinian Amoraim) 3, 3 (Tel Aviv, 1938), p. 43 (Heb.).

[45] PT Gittin 5:46:d; in PT Ketubot 4:28:d, however, the text is fragmentary and the name of R. Samuel is missing.

[46] See: I. Gafni, "The Spiritual-Literary Product", in Eretz Israel from the Destruction (in Baras et al., above, chap., 1 n. 45), p. 489.

constituted a form of creative endeavor, but which did not incorporate new, independent material. The PT was edited in such a manner. It is certain that the *batei midrash* did not cease their activity, neither in the second half of the fourth century in which the pupils of R. Samuel, R. Mana, and R. Mataniah were active; nor after this time (see above). These scholars, however, limited themselves to editing and ordering, and left very little evidence of independent teachings or of their attitude to contemporary events.

A decline in spiritual production is generally a protracted process, and not a one-time event, unless the cultural spiritual activity is forcefully and traumatically disrupted by an external element. This process had already begun in the midfourth century, and it intensified ca. two generations later. This change in the Talmudic literary product presumably should not serve as the basis for conclusions regarding the collapse or decline of the Jewish community. As was shown above, a decline in creative output may be caused by a settlement decline, but may also be due to internal processes divorced from the demographic or economic reality. Furthermore, the principal change in the post Talmudic period is essentially qualitative, relating to the ability to create and renew, and not quantitative. Such change is also characteristic of the entire Christian literary product in the Byzantine period, and does not necessarily express demographic change.

The post-Talmudic literature does not supply geographical-historical data and details. The paucity of information regarding Jewish settlements should not in itself lead to conclusions concerning a settlement decline, because the lack of details is merely a central characteristic in the nature of this literature, but implies nothing beyond this.

2. The Organization of Palestinian Jewry

Only limited material concerning the organization of Palestinian Jewry in this obscure period may be gleaned from the post-Talmudic literature, contemporary inscriptions, and non-Jewish sources. This fragmentary information teaches of the vitality of the community and of several of its centers. As was shown above, the Sanhedrin continued to be active, and the hegemony over Diaspora Jewry continued at least in the fifth century. The inscriptions and the *ma'asim* literature indicate that the communal structure and the public institutions of the community continued to function. Thus, e.g., an inscription in the synagogue in Nevoraiah (=

en-Nabratein) indicates that the method of rule by a pair of leaders continued in the sixth century as well.[47] The Susiya inscription attests to a school at the site and of scholars bearing the title "*Rabbi.*" Evidence of the orderly activity of a local court is provided by the presence of a person calling himself "*sahada* – witness.[48] Important additional testimonies teach of the continuous functioning of the rural community in Palestine.[49]

On the other hand, the literature of the period also contains evidence of the collapse of the community. Thus, e.g., mention is made of the judgment of adultery by the entire community, which almost certainly is indicative of the weakness of the court and the organized community, since judgment by the entire community apparently reflects the breakdown of the normal judicial procedures of the community; and also the shocking description in *Pirkei de-Rabbi Eliezer* cited above, of the difficulties encountered by the heads of the community in mustering a quorum of people for a ceremony.[51] As was shown above, however, this testimony may be dated to a later period, the late eighth century.

Interim Summary

The writing of the PT stopped in the beginning of the fifth century, which was paralleled by the concurrent collapse of the rural settlement in Galilee. This occurred within the context of the general settlement process throughout Palestine, but the process in Galilee was extreme, acute, comprehensive, and methodical to a greater degree. From the fifth century on, the Jewish community was concentrated in the cities, in the western Upper Galilee, in the Golan, and in southern Judea, but these communities apparently no longer maintained institutions of Torah study; if such bodies were still in existence, they certainly were not of the same nature as the Galilean *batei midrash* of the Talmudic period. Of interest within this context is the inscription appearing on the lintel of a structure in Dabbura in the Golan: "This building is the bet midrash of Rabbi *Eliezer ha-Kappar.*"[52] This lintel may possibly have stood in the

[47] J. Naveh, *On Stone and Mosaic: The Aramaic and Hebrew Inscriptions from Ancient Synagogues* (Jerusalem, 1978), pp. 31-33 (Heb.).

[48] Naveh, pp. 115-24.

[49] See: Z. Safrai, *The Jewish Community in the Talmudic Period* (Jerusalem, 1995), pp. 337-346 (Heb.).

[50] Safrai, op. cit., Chap. 6.

[51] *Pirkei de-Rabbi Eliezer* 30.

[52] Naveh, p. 25.

entrance of the bet midrash in which this scholar was active in the late second-early third century. All the known synagogues in the Golan, however, were built in the fifth century, and all the pottery finds uncovered in the survey of Dabbura are solely from the "Late Roman" and "Byzantine" periods.[53] This leads to the interpretation that the builders of the structure regarded themselves as the disciples of R. Eliezer ha-Kappar, and as belonging to "his *bet midrash*", i.e., as following his system and teachings.[54] In other words, the inhabitants of the Golan regarded themselves as the maintainers of the normative Talmudic study tradition.

It was argued above that the cultural and demographic changes were not necessarily related. In this case, however, both processes occurred at the same time, and it is difficult not to connect them, and there apparently is a correlation between the "internal" processes and the general events in Palestine, especially in Galilee.

In the midfourth century, after 352-363, a process of decline began in several regions in Palestine, mainly in Galilee.[55] In this period the Galilean settlements diminished, the extent of trade and activity in them was reduced, and the process of change in the character and quantity of the Talmudic product began just at this time. The process of the decline of the *bet midrash* was more drastic and speedier than that of the settlements. The ratio between the number of scholars of the fifth generation and the quantity of teachings attributed to them is considerably lower than that of the preceding generation, while the difference in the quantity of coins and pottery vessels is smaller. Such a picture is natural and can easily be understood. The decline in the settlement led to a crisis in cultural activity. The community, under pressure and suffering, concentrated on its essential efforts to survive, and was incapable of channeling spiritual and intellectual resources to presumed "luxuries".

The process of decline occurred in many regions, and was not restricted to Galilee, but the Jewish community was concentrated in this region, and loss in this area apparently led to changes in the nature of the batei midrash. Furthermore, the repression of the rebellion of Gallus may also have had negative effects for the Jewish community (see

[53] M. Hartal, *The Northern Golan* (Katzrin, 1989), pp. 112-13 (Heb.).

[54] The term beit midrash frequently refers, not to the actual building, but rather to the act of study; see Z. Safrai, "The Nature of the Beit Hamidrash", *Cathedra* 24 (1982), pp. 112-13 (Heb.).

[55] For the question of the exact dating, see below.

below). The communities in Caesarea[56] and in Lydda[57] incurred damage during the uprising, and the synagogues in en-Nabratein, Beth She'arim, and Caesarea were destroyed.[58] These compounded woes apparently were responsible for a special weakening of the Jewish community in general, and particularly of its *batei midrash*.

The Jewish community participated to some degree in the general recovery of the settlement in Palestine in the sixth century, as is attested by the construction and renovation of synagogues in Hammath Tiberias, en-Nabratein, Scythopolis, Rehob, Beit Alpha, Jericho, Na'aran, Ma'on in the Besor region, Ma'on in the southern Hebron hill country (the second phase of the synagogue), and others. Notwithstanding this construction, the Jewish community did not restore the previous nature of Talmudic literary activity, nor did it resume its previous position in the settlement network in Palestine, thus attesting that the blow suffered by the Jewish settlement in the fifth century had been so severe as to have prevented the community in Palestine from flourishing from anew. The strength of the Christian community may also have contributed to impede the recuperative ability of the Jewish community. The sixth century lies outside the scope of this work, and this brief mention of major trends must suffice.

3. The Jewish Community and the Penetration of Christianity in Palestine

The Byzantine period, beginning in the fifth century, is rich in archaeological finds. More than 300 churches and monasteries have been uncovered, along with many score of finds of a Christian nature, mainly stone crosses, imprints, etc. Excavators have also discovered dozens of synagogues, some of which have been dated with certainty to the late Byzantine period, as in Beit Alpha, Hammath Tiberias, Rimmon, and additional settlements.[59] The proposed map (Fig. 6) includes recently discovered finds which have been

[56] This is indicated by the finds in the synagogue in Caesarea and from the literary reports (below, appendix a., n, 78.

[57] According to the literary sources alone.

[58] See below, appendix a, nn. 25, 47.

[59] For the list of churches, see: A. Ovadiah, *Corpus of the Byzantine Churches in the Holy Land* (Bonn, 1970); A. Ovadiah and C. G. de Silva, "Supplement to the Corpus of the Byzantine Churches in the Holy Land Part I. Newly Discovered Churches", *Levant* 13 (1981), pp. 200-61; idem, "Supplement... II. Appendices", *Levant* 16 (1984), pp. 129-65. For a list of synagogues, see: Z. Ilan, *Ancient Synagogues in Israel*, (Tel-Aviv, 1991) (Heb.).

published either in detail, or only in preliminary fashion in *Hadashot Arkheologiyot* (the offical journal for archaeological news).

There are no quantitative totals of finds of different nature, such as a summation of the Jewish inscriptions in comparison with the Gentile ones. The general impression gained from the finds, however, is that most of the tomb inscriptions from the Byzantine period are not Jewish, although it frequently is impossible to determine if a specific inscription is Jewish or not. The many non-Jewish finds are indicative of the expansion of the Christian community, albeit without providing statistical data. Furthermore, the finds are incidental and are influenced by episodic factors, such as the practices of the inscription writers or the degree of opulence of the structures, the nature of their construction, the character of the post-Byzantine settlement in the specific location, and other incidental factors. At most, the finds tend to generally indicate that the non-Jewish population grew, while the Jewish community contracted and its public strength waned. While there is no doubt that Christianity took root in Palestine, the conclusion that the Jewish community was weakened still requires further proofs. In order to further this examination, an attempt must be made to define, clarify, and date the process of Christian domination of the land.

4. Christian Domination of Palestine

Christianity in Palestine obviously began in the first century CE. The activity of the apostles led to the creation of the first Christian community in Jerusalem, but this was a small community whose members regarded its comprising 120 souls as an achievement.[60] There were small Christian communities in Palestine in the second and third centuries, but Christian propaganda and proselytizing efforts were directed mainly at the outlying lands. Until the fourth century, the Christian population was not a significant factor in Palestine. In this period Christianity was still a small religion, which exerted only limited and insignificant influence within the total settlement.[61]

[60] *Acts of the Apostles* 1:15.

[61] For a description of Christianity in Palestine until the fourth century, see: B. Bagatti, *The Church from the Gentiles in Palestine: History and Archaeology* (Jerusalem, 1971), pp. 5-54; Y. Geiger, "The Spread of Christianity in Eretz Israel, from Its Beginnings to the Time of Julian", in *Eretz Israel from the Destruction of the Second Temple to the Muslim Conquest* (Baras et al., above, chap., 1, n. 45), pp. 218-24 (Heb.); J. A. Taylor, *Christians and the Holy Places* (Oxford, 1993), pp. 56-64.

The Roman Empire experienced important religious change in the fourth century. Constantine I declared religious freedom and ended the persecutions of the Christians, shortly followed by Christianity becoming the official religion of the Empire. These changes in the status of Christianity: its emergence from the underground and its transformation into the state religion, greatly expedited the spread of the new religion. The growth of Christianity is attested by the Council of Nicaea, which was attended by many representatives from Palestine (Fig. 8). A number of central churches were built in the land in the second third of the fourth century, mainly in the holy sites in Jerusalem, Bethlehem, and Mambre. Pilgrims and immigrants streamed into Palestine, as is copiously attested in the sources.[62]

In contrast, Christianity spread more slowly in the rural sector in Palestine. Only the general picture will be presented here, as it is indicated by the extant sources. Most of our historical knowledge of the period is drawn from the writings of the Church fathers. A superficial study of this literature portrays the period as an uninterrupted victorious march of Christianity against the pagans, the Jews, and the Samaritans. This literature is tendentious in great degree, and some of the writings were produced as propagandistic works, in order to encourage the Christianizing movement in the Empire; all were written from the viewpoint of the Christian leadership.[63] Nonetheless, a number of hidden testimonies emerge to teach of the slow penetration of Christianity into Palestine. Thus, e.g., in the midfourth century, the Christians were frustrated in their efforts to build churches in the central holy sites in Galilee: in Tiberias, Sepphoris, Nazareth, and Capernaum.[64] Epiphanius speaks of this in an anecdote one of whose purposes is to portray the degeneration of Judaism as it is presented by a convert of Jewish origin. In the late fourth century Hilarion is active in the Gaza region and the southern section of Palestine, among a completely pagan population. He succeeds in converting many idolaters, but in the end is compelled to leave the country.[65] Ca. 400, Bar Zoma, a fanatical monk born in Nesibin, arrived in Palestine. The author of his hagiography related that the land was inhabited by many pagans and few Christians, "and Jews and Samaritans persecute the Christians."[66]

[62] See the survey by Geiger (above, n. 61), pp. 224-51.

[63] For the problems raised by the usage of the hagiographic literature to resolve these issues, see above, chap., 1.

[64] Epiphanius *Panarion, Haer*. 30, 3, 4-30.

[65] Hieronymus, *Vita Hilarionis*.

[66] F. Nau, "Résume de monographies Syriaques", *ROC* 8 (1913), p. 272.

In the fifth century, Porphyrius struggles with the inhabitants of Gaza, worshipers of the god Marna. When he arrived in 394, the Christian community consisted of 127 souls,[67] an obviously symbolic number, but which attests to the smallness of the community. The reports by his disciple the deacon Mark, as do the descriptions of Porphyrius' life and activity, indicate that Christians drew their main strength from the masses of Syrian-speaking natives, while the leadership and the wealthy of the city were predominantly pagan. One narrative relates of anti-Christian riots in which Porphyrius was pursued and required the assistance of military units from Caesarea to forcefully impose his rule. He required imperial confirmation to close the temples and destroy the central temple of Marna. All these details teach of the weakness of the local Christian population.

Sozomenus tells of a pagan center in the late fourth century in Gaza, in Anthedon and Bitulion.[68] As he relates the events, the first churches in the area of Ascalon and Gaza were established only in the early fifth century, and in the time of Honorius, Raphia and Gaza were considered to be pagan centers.[69] In contrast, Majumasa Gaza Maritima, a residential suburb of the fisherman and harbor workers of Gaza, was proclaimed a polis in the midfourth century in order to afford its Christian inhabitants protection from persecution by the idolaters of Gaza.[70] In another passage, Sozomenus relates of pagans from Galilee who participated in the struggle between religions in Aphamea and prevented the closure of temples in the city.[71]

The literature of the Church fathers contains many narratives about individual and mass conversions to Christianity. Most of these stories concern the conversion of Saracens in the south and in the Judean Desert. These include the encounter tales of Euthymius in the wilderness, the story of the monk Moses in the Negeb, and other testimonies. A few of the stories deal with the conversion of idolaters, such as the narrative of the conversion of the Manicheans of the village of Ziph in Judea,[72] or the narrative of that of the family of Sozomenus.[73] The conversion of Jews is mentioned only in isolated instances, as a special and

[67] Marcus Diaconus, *Vita Prophyrii episcopi Gazensis*, ed. Teubner (Lipsiae, 1985), p. 20.
[68] Sozomenos, *HE*, V, 9.
[69] *Ibid*., V, 14; VII, 15.
[70] *Ibid*., II, 5.
[71] *Ibid*., VII, 15.
[72] Cyril of Scythopolis, *Vita Euthymii*, chap. 12.
[73] HE V, 15.

exceptional Christian achievement. Thus, e.g., it is related that Peter the Iberian succeeded in converting a fisherman from the port of Jamanea On-the-Sea,[74] or a series of general testimonies of miraculous acts of salvation which led to the conversion of many Jews.[75] These episodes are discussed extensively in the research literature, and need not be discussed in detail here.[76]

The slow pace of the Christian penetration of Palestine may also be learned from the list of bishops in the land. It is commonly assumed that a bishop was appointed in a polis, or administrative center, in which a Christian community had been established. We possess a number of reliable lists of Palestinian bishops who participated in the Christian Councils. The first list, from the Council of Nicaea in 325, comprises 17 bishops. Bishops were not appointed in Galilee and the Golan, neither in cities such as Tiberias and Diocaesarea, nor for rural administrative centers such as Gischala and Ittabarion. The only representative from Galilee resided in Zabulon (Cabul), a small village on the fringe of Galilee. This village apparently was selected so that Galilee, the cradle of Christianity, would not be bereft of Christian representation. The number of bishops slowly grew afterward, due to both the increase in the number of cities in Palestine (see above, Fig. 5), and the strengthening of the Christian communities in additional cities (Figs. 9,10).

The Council of Nicaea was attended, inter alia, by the bishops of Gaza and of Ascalon, which contained impressive Christian minorities. Bishops were also appointed as early as the beginning of the fourth century in the Samaritan cities: Sebastea, Neapolis and in Lydda, which remained primarily Jewish. Consequently, the appointment of a bishop does not attest that the city was mainly Christian, but only to the existence of an early Christian community. Two conclusions arise from the above:

1. the Christian penetration of Galilee was relatively late, only in the midfifth century.
2. by the end of the Byzantine period, Christian communities had still not firmly established themselves in Ono, in eastern Upper Galilee, and in the lower Golan (Fig.10). This map corresponds to additional data (see below).

[74] *Petrus der Iberer* (above, Chap. 3, n. 35), p. 126.

[75] E.g., *Chronica ad. an. 419 Chronica Minora* II, 74 *MGH*, xi, p. 74, containing testimonies of the "mass" Christianization in the wake of the earthquake of 363; see: S. P. Brock, "A Letter Attributed to Cyril of Jerusalem on the Rebuilding of the Temple", *BSOAS* 40 (1977), pp. 267-86.

[76] See: Geiger, pp. 234-51.

The archaeological finds, mainly the ruins of churches, enable us to date and map the penetration of Christianity in Palestine. The dating of the remains of churches constitutes a methodical problem which in many instances cannot be resolved. A large portion of the churches have not been excavated, and their dating is based exclusively on surveys. Some were excavated years ago, before the ceramic distinctions were clear. The dating of churches based on their style is extremely problematic. Thus, e.g., the dating of a number of churches to the fourth-early fifth centuries was based on a cross found in the pavement of the church. This is based on the reported enactment in 429 of iconoclastic legislation prohibiting the depiction of crosses in pavements, including those of churches. Accordingly, every pavement of this sort would presumably have to have preceded 429. It has recently become clear, however, that this law was honored mainly in the breach, and therefore cannot serve as the basis for the dating of churches.[77]

We will not discuss the churches in detail, but the data regarding them leads to a number of extremely clear conclusions:

1. churches were established in the fourth century only in central holy sites, such as Jerusalem, Bethlehem, the Mount of Olives, and Mambre.
2. few churches were built in the fifth century, mainly at sacred sites and the tombs of prophets, such as the tomb of Zechariah[78] and that of Habakkuk.[79] Churches were also established at Shiloh, Bethel, and Ramat Rahel. They were joined by a number of "regular" churches in cites and even in villages, such as those in Magen, Scythopolis,[80] Beth Yerah, and possibly also the church in Bahan.[81] The construction of the first monasteries in the Judean Desert also began in the early fifth century.
3. Many churches also began to appear in the rural sector in Palestine only in the second half of the fifth and the first half of the sixth centuries. Most of the churches in the land date to this period, and probably a majority of the Christian remains in the land belong to this period.

[77] Z. Safrai and M. Linn, "Excavations and Surveys in the Mishmar Ha-'Emeq Area", in *Geva: Archaeological Discoveries at Tell Abu-Shusha, Mishmar Ha-'Emeq*, ed. B. Mazar (Jerusalem, 1988), p. 213 n. 5 (Heb.).
[78] Sozomenos, *HE* IX, 17.
[79] *Ibid.*, HE VII, 29.
[80] Ovadiah, No. 24; ibid., No. 26.
[81] See below, appendix a, n. 61.

4. from the sixth century to the end of the Byzantine period, the churches became a central feature in the urban and rural landscape in most regions of Palestine, while there remained regions with sparce Christian communities which contained only few churches, namely (Fig. 7):

(a) Samaria – only three churches have been uncovered in the rural sector (in Horvat Buraq, Boberiye, and Balah),[82] along with a few additional Christian remains.
(b) eastern Upper Galilee (only a single church, in Safed).[83]
(c) the lower Golan.

This geographic and chronological review, based on more than 340 remains of churches, leads to two chief conclusions:

1. the Christian penetration of Palestine was a slow process, and it encountered many obstacles that hindered its progress. Christianity became the religion of the masses only in the late fifth or early sixth century. This process was accompanied by delays in the establishment of the centers of the Christian administration and in the appointment of bishops, as can be seen from a comparison of Figs. 8 and 9).

The finds unequivocally indicate general delays in the spread of Christianity throughout Palestine, especially in the rural sector, and the weakness of the Palestinian Christian communities in the fourth and early fifth centuries. This conclusion corresponds to those of Liebeschuetz,[84] who argues that Christianity spread in Syria from the north to the south, and it was embraced by the masses in southern Syria only in the late fifth century. The reasons for these setbacks are worthy of a separate discussion.

2. the fifth century, between ca. 408-491, was a period of regression and decline (see above, Chap. 2). It may be assumed that the economic and general weakness of the settlement in Palestine was an additional reason for the small number of churches in the land, but it was not the sole factor; the above-mentioned literary testimonies teach of the difficulties hindering the spread of the new religion in Palestine.

82 The church in el-Boberye is to be added to this list: H. Vincet, "Bulletin", *RB* 35 (1926), p. 471; Y. E. Meimaris, *Sacred Names, Saints, Martyrs, and Church Officials...* (Athens, 1986), No. 308; idem, No. 112. Z. Safrai, "The History of the Settlement in the Samaria Hill Country in the Roman-Byzantine Period", in *Samaria Studies*, eds. S. Dar and Z. Safrai (Tel Aviv, 1984), p. 167 (Heb.).

83 Above, note 138.

84 J. H. G. W. Liebeschuetz, "*From Diocletian to the Arab Conquest: Change in the Late Roman Empire*", (Variorum, 1990), No. VIII.

Bishops were not appointed for eastern Upper Galilee and the lower Golan (with one exception in Deir Orukh) (Fig. 10), which corresponds to the deployment of churches and synagogues. Only synagogues, and not churches, were discovered in these areas from the fifth century on. This correspondence seems to prove that Christianity was frustrated in its attempts to penetrate the lower Golan and the basaltic Upper Galilee (see below).

5. The Destruction of the Pagan Temples

The Christianization of the land is also evidenced by the fate of the pagan temples. The fourth-century emperors generally refrained from adopting harsh measures enforced by imperial might against the centers of the pagan cult. Thus, e.g., police measures were usually not taken against temples, theaters, and other pagan centers.[85]

In contrast, a different policy was implemented in Jerusalem, Bethlehem, and Mambre (near Hebron). According to Sozomenus, Constantinus II decided to destroy the fairgrounds and temple and build a church in their stead. The numismatic finds from the excavations of the church indicate a major decrease in the number of coins after this upheaval (see below appendix A). All three churches were established as central sacred sites, and it is not surprising that they were constructed over existing temples, which had been of only local importance.

Additional temples in Tel Qadesh and possibly also the altar in Tel Dan apparently were destroyed or abandoned in the midfourth century,[86] but it has not been determined if this was caused by an earthquake or was due to religious reasons. Furthermore, it is also possible that the structure in Tel Qadesh was in fact destroyed in the earthquake of 362-3, but its rebuilding was prevented by Christian pressure, and the structure may even have been abandoned before it was harmed by the earthquake.

In Tiberias, the Romans attempted to build a church on the ruins of the Hadrianeum, the temple that had been abandoned in the early fourth century,[87] and in Jerusalem, the temple of Hadrian that stood on the Temple Mount also apparently was abandoned. The temple in Shuni

[85] There is extensive research literature dealing with the attitude of the Christian Empire to the pagan world and its centers. See, e.g.: R. MacMullen, *Christianizing the Roman Empire* (New Haven, 1984); B. Ward-Perkins, *From Classical Antiquity to the Middle Ages: Urban Public Building in Northern and Central Italy AD 300-850* (Oxford, 1984), pp. 85 ff.; Taylor (above, n. 61), pp. 296-306; and many additional studies.

[86] See below, appendix a.

[87] See above, n. 64.

probably suffered damage in the midfourth century, but remained in use until the fifth century.[88]

The Samaritan sacred precinct on Mount Gerizim had been seized in the late fifth century and turned into a church, while in Gaza, Porphyrius' vigorous activity had led to the destruction of the temple and its transformation into a church already at the beginning of the century. The temple in Paneas remained active until the late fifth century,[89] and the temples on the Hermon until the sixth century.[90]

This list is by no means exhaustive, but nevertheless is indicative of the pace of the religious change that occurred in Palestine, which had begun in the fourth century but accelerated only in the late fifth and early sixth centuries.

6. The Sources of Growth of the Christian Community in Palestine

The slow growth of the Christian community was likely to have been nourished by a number of possible sources of growth:

a) the conversion of Jews
b) the conversion of Samaritans
c) added population (immigration)
d) the conversion of pagans.

(a) The conversion of Jews – the literature of the church fathers contains anecdotes of the conversion of Jews, such as the narrative about the fisherman who was converted by Peter the Iberian; the proselyte Joseph who was appointed comes;[91] and other accounts. Each of these incidents is depicted as a great accomplishment, thereby implying that it was a quite uncommon occurrence. On the other hand, a number of laws in the post-Talmudic ma'asim literature deal with halakhic problems posed by Jews who had converted:

"And you asked [regarding] a woman whose husband had died and had left her a daughter; the mother of the girl converted and went and married a non-Jew..."[92] "If someone betroths a woman and left for his

[88] I was so informed by A. Shinhav, the excavator of the site, for which I am grateful.
[89] See below, appendix a, n, 21.
[90] S. Dar, *Settlements and Cult Sites on Mount Hermon, Israel: Ituraean Culture in the Hellenistic and Roman Periods* (Oxford, 1993).
[91] See above, nn. 64; 74-75.
[92] N. N. Coronel, *Teshuvot ha-Geonim (The responsa of the Geonim)* (Vienna, 1871), para. 16; Lewin, "*Ma'asim le-bne Erez Israel*" (above, Chap. 3, n. 39), p. 84.

world";[93] "It once happened that a person had a wife, and he had a brother... and his brother left for his world";[94] and a second incident recorded in the continuation of the same passage. The expression yatza' le-'olamo, lit., "left for his world," which is used as a euphemism for conversion, is a new halakhic term first appearing in the Post-Amoraitic literature.[95]

A total of four incidents are described. This is a relatively large number from among the limited number of extant halakhot, and indicates that the phenomenon existed. It is not sufficient, however, to teach of a mass movement of conversion. The multiplicity of testimonies ensues from the fact that the problem of conversion created complicated halakhic issues, and therefore was fully documented. In each instance, family members remained Jews and the conversion was regarded, and judged, as the act of an individual, presumably teaching that conversion was a phenomenon of limited scope. This understanding, however, would be erroneous, since a conversion would have halakhic repercussions only in an instance in which the family as a whole remained Jewish. If the entire family converted, there would be no one to pose a query, nor reason to do so. Generally speaking, conversions by Jews were a quite common occurrence, but it is highly doubtful if they constituted a mass movement.

If there had been a large wave of conversions to Christianity, then it should have taken place between the midfifth century and the midsixth century, the period of expansion in which Christianity became the religion of the masses. In this period, however, the Jewish community was concentrated in eastern Lower Galilee, the Sea of Galilee Valley and eastern Upper Galilee, southern Judea, and the coastal cities, but only eastern Upper Galilee and the Golan were wholly Jewish (see above). As was shown above, the Jewish areas did not become Christian, nor did the southern Judean hill country, in which the Jewish community remained stable (see below). Consequently, the Jewish community was not harmed by the wave of conversions, for if such a phenomenon had occurred, churches would have been constructed and bishops appointed in the Jewish regions. In marked contrast to such a scenario, churches were not discovered in the regions which were Jewish in the fifth and

93 Ibid., p. 97.
94 J. N. Epstein, "The Lore of Erez Israel: (B) Maasim le-bne Israel", *Tarbiz* 2 (1931), p. 320 (Heb.).
95 S. Lieberman, "Yaza le-Olamo, on Maasim le-Bnei Eretz Yisrael", *Ginze Kedem* 5 (1934), pp. 177-78.

sixth centuries, but rather in areas which were no longer clearly Jewish in this period. These finds clearly attest that the penetration and growth of this new religious population did not come at the expense of the Jewish public.

Therefore, two processes took place in Palestine: the decline of the Jewish community and the spread of Christianity, but they were not closely causally related, because they occurred separately, each in a different time and different geographic expanse. The weakening of the Jewish community took place ca. a century before the spread of Christianity and its transformation into a religion of the masses, while the expansion of the new religion into the regions in which the Jewish community remained strong was either checked or considerably retarded.

(b) The conversion of Samaritans – contemporaneous private Samaritan works contain complaints against the conversion to Christianity of Samaritans: "Cursed be the Hebrew who abandons the faith of the righteous."[96] The Christian writer Procopius also complains of Samaritans who convert only for appearance's sake in order to advance in the Byzantine hierarchy,[97] and the *Chronicle of Paschales* tells of Samaritans who converted out of fear after the Samaritan revolt in the time of Justinian.[98] The religious decrees of this emperor probably led Samaritans to convert. The degree to which this was a mass movement cannot be determined; at any rate, Christianity did not gain a strong footing in the rural sector in the Samaria hill country (see above), and it therefore may be assumed that the phenomenon of conversion, to the extent that it existed, was concentrated in the "diaspora" in Caesarea, Scythopolis, and the coastal plain, and possibly also in the cities of Samaria: Neapolis and Sebaste.

The Talmudic literature contains allusions to the assimilation of Samaritans into the Gentile environment in fourth-century Caesarea.[99] The fact that only three churches were discovered throughout the bounds of the rural sector in Samaria demonstrates that conversion was not a mass phenomenon in Samaria as well.

[96] Z. Ben-Hayyim, *The Literary and Oral Tradition of Hebrew and Aramaic amongst the Samaritans*, vol. III, part II (Jerusalem, 1967), pp. 47, 52 (Heb.).

[97] Procopius, *Anecdota* II, OR XXVII, 2]

[98] Paschales, *Chronicle*, para. 530.

[99] PT Avodah Zarah 4:44:d.

Settlements in Samaria and its environs were damaged or destroyed in the wake of the Samaritan revolts in the late fifth and early sixth centuries.[100] Within this context, Christian farmers may possibly have seized Samaritan settlements. In Tel Hefer, e.g., excavations have uncovered a late fifth century destruction stratum, while the later settlement layer contains traces of a pig-eating Christian population.[101] The construction of the church in Buraq in Samaria, in contrast, antedated the destruction of the settlement in the sixth century.[102] The extent of this phenomenon requires further clarification.

(c) Added population (immigration) – two types of Christian immigration to Palestina are reported in the Byzantine period:

(1) pilgrims, monks, and religious functionaries who arrived in Palestine by the hundreds. As many scholars have remarked, the Christian leadership in the land was composed mainly of immigrants who had moved to Palestine for religious reasons, coming from Syria, Egypt, Asia Minor, and even from the west. This immigration was impressively represented in the ecclesiastical hierarchy and in the monastic movement, but it is doubtful if it was of great demographic significance. This was complemented by the additional peoples who established communities and monasteries, such as the Armenians, the Copts, he Syrians, the Georgians, and others, many of whom were concentrated in Jerusalem and its environs and in the Judean Desert centers. The total numbers of the monastic and ecclesiastic population were not great, and their deomgraphic significance was secondary. Furthermore, they did not reproduce, or so the church leaders proudly proclaimed.

(2) the immigration of Christian Saracens, such as, e.g.,[103] Asuebtus, the head of a tribe who migrated to the Judean Desert where, under the influence of Euthymius, he and his entire tribe converted to Christianity,[104] A generation later, Thalabas, one of the leaders of the tribe, is described as a resident of Lazarium (the present-day el-Azariyah, a village in the suburbs of Jerusalem).[105] The tribe, in

[100] S. Dar, "Archaeological Evidence on the Samaritan Revolts of the Byzantine Period", in *Jews, Samaritans and Christians*, ed. D. Jacoby and Y. Tsafrir (Jerusalem 1988), pp. 228-38 (Heb.).

[101] See below, appendix a, n. 77.

[102] Dar, op. cit., pp. 235-37.

[103] *Vita Euthymii*, chap. 10, and other passages.

[104] Ibid., chap. 51.

[105] Ibid, chap. 52.

full or in part, moved from the desert, ceased to be nomadic, and settled in a village on the desert fringe. In the time of Justinian, an additional Christian tribe, headed by one Arethas, moved to Palestine.[106]

Another group of Christian Saracens established the martyrium of St. Salome in the Judean Shephelah.[107] An additional Christian Saracen tribe lived in the Golan, between "Mount Harib" (the present-day Kefar Harub) and Jabiye.[108] These migrations occurred mainly in the sixth and seventh centuries. The imperial edict contained in the Beersheva inscriptions mentions the head of a tribe, apparently in reference to the Gerar region.[109] Support for the claim of Arab penetration to this region is provided by an inscription in a church in Kisufin containing the name of a Christian notable called "Abba," thereby attesting to his Semitic origin.[110] Military units from the Limes detachments encamped in this region; it is known that some were of Arab origin. These soldiers may have been responsible for the appearance of an Arab tribe in the region. The name of a donor of Arab origin appears in an inscription in the church in Beit Loya, more to the north, in the Eleutheropolis area.[111]

These tribes were concentrated in the periphery of the provinces of Palestina Prima and Palestina Secunda, and in the Negeb, which formed a part of Palestina Tertia. It would therefore seem that they were of relatively limited importance in the demographic structure of Palestine.

(4) The conversion of pagans – it may naturally be assumed that the pagan converts constituted the primary source of recruits to the Christian communities in Palestine. A number of testimonies regarding the slow process of Christianization were cited above, and allusions were made to others. The "Christianization" of Palestine took place primarily in the areas of pagan settlement, and not in the clearly and exclusively Jewish and Samaritan centers. Thus Christianity spread in the Negeb, in the polis cities, in the coastal plain, in

[106] I. Shahid, "Procopius and Arethas", *BZ* 50 (1957), pp. 39-67; 362-82.

[107] A. Kloner, "The Cave Chapel of Horvat Qasra", *'Atiqot* Hebrew Series 10 (1990), pp. 129-36; also see idem, the series of articles about this site.

[108] I. Shahid, *Byzantium and the Arabs in the Fifth Century* (Washington, D.C., 1989), pp. 258-62.

[109] A. Alt, *Die Griechischen Inschriften der Palaestina Tertia Westlich der Araba* (Leipzig, 1921), p. 12.

[110] Meimaris, No. 869.

[111] J. Patrich and Y. Tsafrir, "A Byzantine Church and Agricultural Installations at Khirbet Beit Loya", *Qadmoniot* 71-72 (1985), pp. 106-116 (Heb.).

the Judean hill country (between Samaria and the Hebron hill country),[112] in western Upper Galilee, and in Lower Galilee.

It may consequently be concluded that the pagan settlement did indeed serve as the main source augmenting the Christian communities. A secondary contribution to this process was made by the Christian immigration and the conversion of Jews and of Samaritans.

7. The Demographic and Ethnic Changes in Palestine – An Overview

The data and considerations cited above enable us to propose a probable reconstruction of the settlement history in the various regions of Palestine in the fourth and fifth centuries. The regional division is based on the regional data presented in Appendix A.

1) *Western Galilee* (Including the Lower Galilee, the Carmel, and Possibly also the Jezreel Valley)

Until the midfourth century the Jewish community constituted a decisive majority in Galilee. The population in the cities was mixed, while the villages were predominantly Jewish. Alon collected much evidence of this.[113] The sources assume that a majority of the region's inhabitants were Jewish. Moreover, the Talmud assumes, incidentally, that there are no non-Jews in the villages. Thus the Mishnah determines that the milk of an unidentified beast in the villages is not regarded as "fit for consumption," since the Jews refrain from consuming it.

Similarly, the carcass of a fowl in the villages is not regarded as food at all. In the cities or the markets, in contrast, in which the milk or the carcass could be sold to Gentiles, they are regarded as fit for consumption.[114] Many other halakhot pertaining to the laws of tithes, impurity, and eruvei hatzerot (the formal joining together of courtyards to permit carrying on the Sabbath) simply assume that at least in the villages Jewish life is undisturbed. There were also, however, a number of mixed

[112] The Hebron hill country and the Sea of Galilee Valley shared a unique historical fate (see below).

[113] G. Alon, *Toledot ha-Yehudim be-Eretz Yisrael* II (Tel Aviv, 1971), pp. 256-58 (a condensed version appears in the English edition: *The Jews in Their Land in the Talmudic Age (70-640 C.E.)* [Jerusalem, 1984], pp. 750-51); also see: Safrai, *Galilee Studies* (Jerusalem, 1985), pp. 14-15 (Heb.).

[114] Mishnah Uktzin 3:2-3.

villages, mainly in the fringe of Galilee. Thus, e.g., Biri is mentioned as a mixed village.[115] The reference apparently is to Baram, on the northwest boundary of Jewish Galilee.[116] Another such mixed village was Beit Anat, apparently Be'einah in the Beth-cherem Valley, on the northern border of Jewish Galilee.[117] Another narrative, relating of Johanan Haqoqa'ah (from Huqoq) who sold hametz (leavened food, prohibited on Passover) to a Gentile, apparently took place in Sepphoris, where Rabbi Judah the Nasi had his residence.[118]

This area within Galilee apparently was harmed in the midfourth century, and suffered a crisis of extreme severity in the early fifth century (see above, Chap. 2). The area was not abandoned, but the population suffered grievous damage. The Jewish settlement in the region was not completely uprooted, thus, e.g. there are later reports in the sixth century of a community and synagogue in Nazareth, where Antoninus of Placentia (Piacenza) met comely Jewish maidens.[119]

Eutychius makes mention of the aid extended by the Jews of Nazareth to the Persian conqueror at the end of this period.[120] As was mentioned above, Sozomenus tells of the pagan inhabitants of Galilee in the fifth century,[121] which may be regarded as an allusion to the strengthening of the pagan settlement in the region, also he does not specify in which portion of Galilee they dwelt.

The settlement in Galilee recovered in the sixth century. It apparently had become predominantly Christian by this time, as is attested by the many churches which were built in Galilee; in marked contrast, not a single Galilean synagogue from this century has been discovered. Many settlements which were known to be Jewish in the Talmudic period now contained churches or other evidence of a Christian settlement, including:

Beth She'arim evidence of a Christian settlement was found in the sixth century settlement phase (see bellow appebdix A).

[115] PT Avodah Zarah 2:40:c.

[116] Safrai, *Galilee Studies*, pp. 97-99.

[117] Ibid., p. 62; S. and Z. Safrai, "Beit Anath", *Sinai* 78 (1976), pp. 18-34. E. Damati has recently proposed identifying Beit Anath with Beina in the Netophah Valley (oral lecture). This proposal is worthy of study, but it implies that Beit Anath was a mixed village in central Lower Galilee. Such a phenomenon is possible, of course, but it would be more likely that such a mixed village would be situated on the fringe of Galilee.

[118] PT Pesahim 1:27:c; BT Pesahim 13a.

[119] See: J. Wilkinson, *Jerusalem Pilgrims before the Crusades* (Jerusalem, 1977), p. 79.

[120] Eutychius, p. 1083, but the historical value of this work is doubtful.

[121] Sozomenos, *HE* VII, 15.

Summaqa – pig bones from the settlement phase of the fifth-sixth centuries were discovered in the previously Jewish settlement of Summaqa. The synagogue was in secondary usage of an undetermined nature.[122]

A church was found in Daburiah,[123] which Eusebius had listed as a Jewish village in the Onomasticon.[124]

In Kafer Kanah, a church was built on the ruins of the synagogue.[125]

In the Galilean Bethlehem, which was known as a Jewish settlement and the residence of the priestly extended family,[126] a church was discovered.[127]

In'Araba, one of the centers of the Jewish settlement in Galilee and a residence of the priestly extended family, a church was uncovered.[128]

We know of only a few mixed settlements, such as Nazareth or Shiqmona, which is also called "the City of the Jews,"[129] but in which a church and monastery were also unearthed.[130]

The ruins of a synagogue and of a church were discovered in Danna.[131]

Ramah – a synagogue and a church were uncovered.[132]

Sarona – Jewish and Christian remains.[133]

Gebath – Jewish and Christian remains.[134]

Beit Gan – Jewish and Christian remains.[135]

These testimonies come in addition to other churches found in settlements not known to be Jewish but which were located within the Jewish sphere. As I have shown elsewhere, the Gentile penetration of Galilee began in the Tabor (Ittabarion) and Issachar ridge region.[136] Most of the Christian remains are undated, and the assumption that they are of late origin is based on the fact that the majority of churches which have been dated are relatively late.

122 I was informed of this by S. Dar, for which I am grateful.
123 Ovadiah, No. 29.
124 Eusebius, *Onomasticon*, No. 375, p. 56.
125 Ilan, *Ancient Synagogues*, pp. 216-19.
126 See: S. Klein, *Sefer ha-Yishuv*, vol. I (Tel Aviv, 1939), p. 115 (Heb.).
127 Ovadiah, No. 190.
128 Ibid., No. 183.
129 See: *Sefer ha-Yishuv*, p. 156.
130 Ovadiah, Nos. 165, 166.
131 Ilan, *Ancient Synagogues*, p. 121; N. Zori, *The Land of Issachar: Archaeological Survey* (Jerusalem, 1977), p. 95 (Heb.).
132 Naveh, pp. 33-34; V. Tsaferis and T. Shai, "Excavations at Kafr er-Rameh", *Qadmoniot* 34-35 (1976), pp. 83-85 (Heb.); see below, appendix a, n. 15.
133 Ilan, *Ancient Synagogues*, pp. 167-68.
134 Ibid., p. 202.
135 Ibid., p. 119.
136 Safrai, *Galilee Studies*, p. 18.

2) *The Golan and Eastern Galilee*

There was a strengthening of the settlement in the Golan in the early fourth century, and this trend intensified in the second half of the century. Synagogues were established only in the fifth century (see above, Appebdix A), and they and the Jewish settlement as a whole remained in existence until the late fifth or early sixth centuries. A Christian settlement did not take hold in the Golan. Only a single monastery was discovered, in Deir Qrukh, and no bishop was appointed for the region.

A similar situation reigned in eastern Upper Galilee. Some of the synagogues may have been established in an earlier time, but, as in the Golan, they remained active until the sixth century, and some even later. The Christian community apparently did not set down roots in the area, and no bishop was appointed.

A Christian tomb discovered in Gush Halav (Gischala) in the fringe of the region[137] and a fragmentary Christian inscription from Safed[138] are the only Christian testimonies from the region. A later sixth-century living stratum from Khirbet Shema' contains pig bones, thereby attesting to an at least partially Christian (or Gentile) population.[139]

3) *Eastern Upper Galilee*

This region, which was administratively subordinate to Phoenicia, already had a Gentile majority in the period of the Talmud, and naturally became Christian.[140]

4) *The Southern Hebron Hill Country*

There is little information regarding this area. Eusebius lists seven Jewish and two Christian settlements. This listing is incomplete, and there probably were additional Jewish settlements in the region that were not mentioned in the Onomasticon, or that were listed but without reference to their Jewish character.[141] Of the settlements in this list, churches were

[137] See below, appendix a, n. 58.

[138] The inscription may possibly be a memorial inscription for a contributor to the church; see: G. Hoelscher, "Drei Griechische Inschriften", *Mitt. u. Nach D. D. Pal. Ver*. 1910, p. 83.

[139] E. M. Meyers et al., *Khirbet Shema'* (above, Chap. 1, n. 5), pp. 99-101.

[140] Safrai, *Galilee Studies*, pp. 4-5.

[141] Thus, e.g., Ma'on is depicted as a regular settlement, but a synagogue from the fourth century was discovered in it (see below).

found in the two Christian settlements of Jethira and Upper Anaea, and synagogues or other remains of a Jewish nature were found in the seven settlements described as being "of Jews". Thus in Rimmon, Thala, Eshtemoa, Lower Anaea, En Gedi, Na'aran, and Jotta. In addition to a synagogue, a church inscription was also found in the latter settlement, and in Carmel, which is described as a village of Jews, churches were uncovered. A synagogue was recently discovered in Ma'on, [142] which was depicted as a regular village.

All these finds indicate that ethnic stability generally prevailed in the southern Hebron hill country. Most of the villages that had been Jewish at the beginning of the fourth century remained so in the fifth-seventh centuries as well, and mass conversions to Christianity apparently occurred only in the pagan villages. Ziph is an example of such a village whose pagan inhabitants assumed the Christian faith.[143] An Aramaic and Greek bilingual inscription was discovered in the village. The writer of the inscription may have been a Jew living in a mainly Gentile village, or this may possibly have been a Jewish village whose inhabitants abandoned it or left their religion, first in favor of idolatry and afterwards Christianity. At any rate, the date of the inscription is unclear, nor has it been determined if its author was a Jew, or an Aramaic-Syrian speaking Gentile.[144]

[142] For a discussion of these finds, see: J. Schwartz, *Jewish Settlement in Judaea after the Bar Kokhba War until the Arab Conquest 135 C.E.-640 C.E.* (Jerusalem, 1986), pp. 98-109 (Heb.).

[143] *Vita Euthymii*, chap. 12.

[144] L. Y. Rahmani, "A Bilingual Ossuary-Inscription from Khirbet Zif", *IEJ* 22 (1972), pp. 113-16.

CHAPTER FIVE

Why the Land Was Laid Waste

The discovery and mapping of the settlement processes in the fourth and fifth centuries and the examination of their scope constitute a necessary preliminary step to examining the possible factors which caused, aided, and fashioned such processes. Historical research has naturally focused on the reasons which are likely to explain the decline of the Jewish settlement, while at the same time providing localized explanations of destruction in specific sites. Four fundamental explanations have been proposed:[1]

1) the decline of the Jewish settlement was caused by the revolt of Gallus and its aftermath. The extent and circumstances of the revolt, which erupted in 352-3, are unclear. The degree to which this event proved traumatic for Palestine in general and especially the life of the Jews cannot be determined from the historical sources.[2]
2) the settlement in Palestine was harmed by the earthquake that struck the land in 363. Past research knew of this natural disaster from various sources, but did not attribute great importance to it. In 1977 Brock published a letter written by Cyril of Scythopolis describing the earthquake. The letter paints a picture of widespread destruction. Following the publication of this document, a number of researchers began to emphasize the role of the earthquake in the destruction of settlements in Palestine.[3]
3) according to Meyers et al. the synagogues in Khirbet Shema', Meron, and Gischala were totally destroyed, or severely damaged, in the earthquake in 408. Dothan similarly attributes the destruction of the synagogue in Hammath Tiberias to the earthquake in 419.[4]

[1] For a theoretical discussion of the possible reasons for the waves of destruction in the rural settlement, see: C. M. Cameron, "Structure Abandonment in Villages", *Archaeological Method and Theory* 3 (1991), pp. 173-82.

[2] For discussions of the revolt of Gallus, see: Geiger, Nathanson, and Mor (above, Chap. 4, n. 1)

[3] Geiger, pp. 208-211; G. Stemberger, Juden und Christen im Heiligem Land, Munchen 1993, pp 132-150; Brock (above, Chap., 4, n. 75), pp. 267-86.

[4] See the conclusions and explanations by Meyers and others on the excavations at Meiron, Khirbet Shema', and Gush Halav (below, Appendix A nn. 5, 56); E. M. Meyers et al.,

4) the Jewish settlement was damaged and weakened by the social and religious pressure exerted by the Christian empire and by the anti-Jewish legislation which the latter enacted.[5]

In addition, several, or all, of these factors may have joined together with deleterious effect upon the Jewish community.[6]

These reasons must be examined to determine which is likely to provide a fuller explanation of the various phenomena and description of their scope. The first question in this context is the precise time of the settlement shift of the midfourth century. Should the year 352-3 be established as the exact time of the damage inflicted upon the settlements, in which case the revolt of Gallus would be the likely cause; or did this change take place only in 363, with this settlement process beginning after the earthquake of that year?

1) *The Revolt of Gallus – the Archaeological Evidence*

The archaeological and numismatic finds cannot provide an unequivocal answer to the question of time. Pottery vessels cannot be defined so precisely, nor does numismatic science offer the necessary accuracy. The number of coins decreased in the midfourth century, but did not actually stop, thereby hindering a precise determination of the time of the change. Furthermore, prominent among the numismatic assemblage are the coins of Constantius II, who ruled during the years 337-361. It cannot be determined if his coins precede or follow the revolt of Gallus. These factors, together with the fact that coins remain in circulation for decades, prevents an accurate determination of the date of the settlement change.

The reports state that a number of sites were either destroyed or became inactive ca. 350: there is such information regarding the synagogue in Caesarea, the settlement in Beth She'arim, and the synagogue in en-Nabratein.[7] The finds from Caesarea are of interest because they presumably prove that the Jewish settlement, or at the least its synagogue, was damaged while the city as a whole continued to exist and

Excavations at Ancient Meiron, Upper Galilee, Israel, 1971-1972, 1974-75, 1977 (Cambridge, Mass., 1981), pp. 160-61; and also K. W. Russell, "The Earthquake of May 19 A.D. 363", *BASOR* 238 (1980), pp. 47-64.

5 This explanation lies, e.g., at the center of the thesis of Yaron: D. Yaron, "Byzantine Rule", in The History of Eretz Israel (above, Chap. 4, n. 4), pp. 323-38.

6 Safrai, *Galilee Studies*, (Jerusalem 1985) (Heb.), pp. 15-19.

7 See above, Appendix A, nn. 25, 47, 78

flourish. Meshorer reports of a gap in the continuity of coins in Chorazin in 340-380. The final and complete report, however, makes no mention of such a gap.[8] The report published by Kloetzli is similar, as is the situation in additional sites in Galilee such as Jalame, Meron, and others. A report from Transjordan lists a few coins from these years,[10] and this apparently was the case in Summaqa in the Carmel. These data do not constitute an unequivocal finding, because coins from 353-363 remained in circulation for decades afterward, and they could have been buried in the settlement in 370 or 380.

Generally speaking, the finds we possess do not indicate that the revolt of Gallus led directly and immediately to the severe and general destruction in Galilee or in other regions, but it was responsible for instances of extensive localized damage. The uprising may also have served, however, as the catalyst for another settlement process (see below). Incidentally, *it may be concluded that the revolt did in fact occur, with severe consequences, but was of modest geographic extent.*

2) *The Earthquake in 363*

The earthquake struck all Palestine, and according to Cyril, inflicted severe damage everywhere. Cyril distinguishes between regions which were totally destroyed and those which were only "half" or partially devastated. This division does not indicate any common regional factor.[11] An anonymous chronicle from 724, in contrast, specifically mentions the area of the south, "Teimana," as the center of the earthquake.[12]

The excavators attribute to this earthquake the destruction of the synagogues in Meron, Gischala, and Khirbet Shema', along with many other structure which were destroyed in the midfourth century.[13] This interpretation is based both on a historical consideration and on an analysis of the direction of breakage and destruction of the structures. Although we will not examine the archaeological-architectural considerations, we must make a number of historical comments:

[8] D. T. Ariel (unpublished); my thanks to the author for showing me the manuscript of his article.
[9] Kloetzli 1970 (above, Appendix A, n. 52).
[10] Kirkbride 1939 (below n. 39)
[11] Brock (above, Chap. 4, n. 75).
[12] E. W. Brooks and J. B. Chabot, eds., Chronicon Miscellaneum ad Annum Domini 724 (CSCO Ser. III), p. 133.
[13] Russell (above, n. 4).

The numismatic finds portray the period 361-363 as a turning point in the history of the region, albeit one that is difficult to date with precision. This acute change attests to a traumatic event. Based on the numismatic evidence, the damage may have been due, not only to the earthquake, but also as a result of the pro-Christian, and possibly also anti-Jewish riots that followed the death of Julian the Apostate.

The devastation wreaked by the earthquake was limited to certain regions in Palestine. Galilee, the Shephelah region (including Antipatris), Jerusalem, and possibly also Mambre and Petra in Transjordan were damaged in the midfourth century, while there is no evidence of destruction in the southern Hebron hill country, which is described in the anonymous chronicle as being the epicenter of the earthquake. No effects of the earthquake are felt in the Golan, eastern Upper Galilee, Meroth, Capernaum, and the Tiberias basin, even though Cyril states that the latter region suffered severe damage. It therefore may be presumed that the earthquake was not the critical factor, and certainly not the only one, responsible for this change. Fig. 11 shows the levels of severity of the earthquake, as described in the letter by Cyril. This map does not correspond to that of the regions which experienced economic decline in the fourth-fifth centuries. Moreover, if the settlement was on a sound footing, it would have recovered shortly after the earthquake. Since such a revival did not take place, an additional factor must be sought, which will prove to have been of critical importance in the degeneration of the settlement.

3) *The Earthquake in 408*

Little is known about this earthquake. According to the literary sources, it did not play a central role in the life of the settlement in Palestine.[14] According to Meyers et al., the synagogues were destroyed and abandoned in the early fifth century in the wake of an earthquake. There is no basis for this claim, however, and the earthquake may have occurred some time after the abandonment of the settlement.

Furthermore, the conclusion that a structure was destroyed by an earthquake is based on an analysis of the pattern of destruction. This analytical tool is not sophisticated, and such a proposal must be regarded as no more than mere conjecture. Such an explanation for the settlement collapse seems to be too simple and partial. There is settlement damage

[14] Meyers (above, Appendix A, n. 5).

in all regions of Palestine, and throughout the entire East – Transjordan, Syria, and Egypt (see below), and therefore an additional reason, one which is more fundamental and essential, must be sought. It is our contention that the settlement had entered a process of decline, and the earthquake was, at the most, the final blow which exposed the process and transformed it into a crisis.

4) *The Influence of Christianity*

The subject of the influence exerted by the assumption of power by Christianity, with the Empire adopting the new religion and the ensuing promulgation of anti-Jewish legislation, has been discussed extensively in the scholarly literature. The anti-Jewish laws appear in *CTh*, and they have been analyzed and explained in earlier works.[15] Additional evidence of attacks by the Christian population against Jews is present in various ecclesiastical sources, and there are extant testimonies of pogroms and riots in different cities, mainly in the eastern part of the Empire. Thus, e.g., Bar Zoma attacked various settlements, and under his inspiration, pogroms were launched against Jews and Samaritans. Nevertheless, the historical significance of these laws and attacks has not been clarified, and the degree to which they actually disturbed the daily life of the Jewish settlement in Palestine has not been determined. In another work, I raised doubts regarding the extent to which this legislation was of significance for the simple villager in Palestine.[16] Thus, e.g., the ban on holding Christian slaves was of no concern to the unpretentious villager who had never owned slaves. The prohibitions against the building of synagogues were honored only very partially, and the fear of assaults by their Christian neighbors was limited, since the latter constituted only a small minority in the main Jewish centers (Galilee, the Golan, and the Shephelah of Lydda).

Moreover, Christian pressure may have led to the undermining of the Galilean Jewish settlement in the midfourth century, but cannot serve as the sole explanation for the fact that no harm came to the Jews of the Golan and southern Judea, for whom this was a period of recovery and growth.

The anti-Jewish legislation of the fourth century was quite moderate, and increased in severity only in the following century. The entire

[15] For a summation, see: A. Linder, ed. and trans., *Roman Imperial Legislation on the Jews* (Jerusalem, 1983) (Hebr.); see above, Chap. 4.

[16] Safrai, *Galilee Studies*, (Jerusalem 1985) (Heb.), p. 18.

settlement throughout Palestine, and not just the Jewish community, generally underwent a process of decline in the fifth century (see above). Consequently, a general explanation must be found for the decline and regression of the settlement in Palestine. It may be argued in this context that the Jews, who had been weakened by the pressure from the authorities, were more vulnerable to attacks by other ethnic groups. Government pressure cannot, however, fully explain this process, nor could it have been the primary reason for the decline of the settlement as a whole.

It presumably could be argued that the large Christian population exerted pressure on the Jewish community, and that this was the main reason for the destruction of the Jewish centers. This possible connection between the rise of Christianity and the demographic and ethnographic developments in Palestine in the fourth and sixth centuries has been discussed relatively extensively in another context (see above, Chap. 4), where it was shown that there was no close causal relationship between the decline of the Jewish community and the ascent of Christianity.

The synagogues in Galilee were not supplanted by churches. The synagogues were destroyed in the late fourth or early fifth century, while the churches in these regions were built only in the late fifth or the sixth century. The gap of 80-100 years teaches of the separation between these two processes; furthermore, there was minimal Christian penetration in the areas in which synagogues were active in the fifth century.

Excavations have revealed the intriguing fact that the churches in Galilee were not built over synagogues, in contrast with the usual practice of constructing churches on the ruins of temples, or in the courtyard of the destroyed temple. In, e.g., Shechem, churches were built on the ruins of Samaritan synagogues. The church on Mt. Gerizim was erected on the remains of the Samaritan sacred precinct, as was probably the case with the church in the center of Shechem (which would later become the chief mosque in the city);[17] a monastery which apparently caused at least partial damage to a Samaritan synagogue was uncovered near Zur Natan.[18] The only Byzantine church under which a Jewish synagogue was discovered is that in Kanah, and the church in Nazareth may also rest on the ruins of a synagogue.

[17] See: C. R. Conder and H. H. Kitchener, *The Survey of Western Palestine* II (London, 1882), p. 203.

[18] These finds are unpublished. I am grateful to E. Ayalon for showing me the structure.

The anti-Jewish legislation and Christian social pressure may have been oppressive to the Jewish community, but they cannot explain either the settlement collapse in the villages of Galilee in the early fifth century, or the calamitous change in the midfourth century which presaged this ruin. The earthquake in 363 was likely to have served as a catalyst, but it too cannot bear full responsibility for the wide-sweeping change that affected Palestine.

The Demographic and Economic Decline in the Eastern Empire

All the explanations cited above appear in the scholarly literature as possible causes, and they have been used by different researchers (including this author), but they are not sufficient, mainly because they do not provide a precise or comprehensive definition of the problem. The question which must be clarified is of much wider scope than the destruction of a specific site or group of sites, or even the possible "cause" of the collapse of the Jewish settlement. All the questions which have been raised above are merely partial aspects of a broader process. Without exception, the explanations dealing with the causes of the collapse of the Jewish community ignore the fact that non-Jewish settlements in other parts of Palestine suffered damage in the same period in which signs of decline began to appear in Galilee, while the Jewish settlement in the Golan and in the southern Hebron hill country embarked on a period of growth. The collapse of the Jewish settlement in Galilee was not the result of a regional phenomenon in Galilee or of any other internal Jewish event, but rather followed an event or process that affected all Palestine, including non-Jewish areas.

In order to understand what happened in Palestine in the early fifth century, we must search for a cause the effects of which were likely to disrupt the entire settlement fabric in Palestine. We should accordingly examine the situation in the entire Eastern Empire. An analysis of various excavations in the region, and especially of the numismatic finds at different sites, indicates that the fifth century was marked by general decline and weakness throughout the East.

Egypt

The agricultural system in Egypt suffered an extremely severe collapse in the late fourth century. Bagnall indicates a decrease of 95 percent (!) in tax revenues in Karanis and in Horiodiktia from the fourth to the sixth centuries, and an almost identical population drop (90 percent).[19]

There are not a great deal of numismatic finds from Egypt, and many excavations conducted in the past neglected this material. Nonetheless, the sparse information we possess teaches of a decrease in the quantity of coins in the fifth century (408-491).

The coin finds from Karanis (Fig. 12) indicate a steep reduction in the quantity of coins in the fifth century.[20] This data is of interest for resolving the different sources of information, and for validation of the numismatic testimony used for the purposes of the current discussion. This also demonstrates the degree to which early writers were unaware of demographic fluctuations, for the writings of contemporaneous authors make no mention of the demographic collapse in Egypt. Irregardless of the cause of the upheaval in Egypt, the Egyptian market was eradicated or at the very least greatly reduced.

General data regarding the circulation of coins in Egypt were collected and analyzed by West and Johnson,[21] who also end their discussion in 450 and indicate a major collapse in this period.

In the table which appears an appendix to their work,[22] West and Johnson summarize the quantity of silver coins by weight (Figs. 13,14). An analysis of this table clearly teaches that the quantity of coins increased in the fourth century until 363-383, followed by a gradual decrease, and ending in a drastic collapse at the end of the century. A similar conclusion is reached after an examination of the weight of silver in the coins (Fig. 14). The economic blow in 450 constituted an additional phase in the decline of commerce in Egypt.

Few coins from Oxyrhynchus have been published, and they also indicate a decline in the fifth century (Fig. 15); in practice, the last coins are no later than the time of Arcadius.[23] The significance of this for the farmers in Palestine will be discussed below.

[19] R. S. Bagnall, "Agricultural Productivity and Taxation in the Later Roman Empire", *TAPA* 115 (1985), pp. 289-308.

[20] R. A. Haatvedt et al., *Coins from Karanis* (Michigan, 1964).

[21] West and Johnson (above, Chap. A, n. 23). The article by Milne, in contrast, mentions only a number of hoards, and as was already stated, this is insufficient to resolve the issues under discussion. See: J. A. Milne, "The Currency of Egypt in the Fifth Century", *NC* Fifth Series, 6 (1926), pp. 43-92.

[22] West and Johnson, pp. 180.

[23] J. G. Milne, "The Coins from Oxyrhynchus", *Journal of Egyptian Archaeology* 8 (1922), pp. 158-63.

The cause of the economic and demographic collapse in Egypt has not been determined. The shrinking crops brought about demographic retreat, but this leaves unanswered the question of what caused such a sharp decline in the fertility of the land. Bagnall conjectures that this was brought on by the blockage of the irrigation and drainage canals due to careless maintenance. Although no proofs have been found, this is a distinct possibility. On the other hand, the settlement processes in Egypt may very well be related to the economic-demographic situation in Palestine and in the entire East, and we must therefore search for a possible cause or system of causes whose influence reached beyond the expanse watered by the Nile.

Destruction or abandonment is also characteristic of several settlements in the Sinai Desert region, such as Bir Mazar and Qasrawet.[24]

Syria

There are no historical reports regarding the economic and settlement situation in Syria in the fifth century, and no basic and methodical study has been devoted to this subject. Even so it is clear that there was distinct settlement growth in many regions in the byzantine period, mainly to the east of Antioch.[25]

The numismatic finds from a number of sites present a slightly different picture. Thousands of coins were found in Antioch, evidencing that the peak activity of the city occurred in the fourth century. From the first half of the century, until 363, a yearly average of 54 coins were discovered. A certain decline is noticeable in the second half of this century (44-52 coins per year), while only a yearly average of 6.7 coins from the fifth century was discovered, with some recovery (19.9 coins per year) in the sixth century (Fig. 16).[26] A similar situation prevailed in Hamma in northern Syria. The city attained its maximum activity in the second half of the fourth century (363-408), while the number of coins shrinks in the fifth century to one fifth of the numbers in the preceding century (Fig. 17).[27]

Close to 100 coins were found in Dehes (northern Syria). Peak activity is reached in the first half of the fourth century, while the number of

[24] *ANEAEHL* pp. 1217-18, 1396.
[25] J. H. G. W. Liebeschuetz, *From Diocletian to the Arab Conquest, Change in the Late Roman Empire* (Variorum,
[26] D. B. Waage, *Antioch on-the-Orontes* IV,2: *Greek, Roman, Byzantine and Crusaders' Coins* (Princeton, 1952), p. 171.
[27] A. C. Christensen et al., *Hama*: III,3. The Graeco-Roman Objects of Clay, the Coins and the Necropolis (Copenhagen, 1986), pp. 59-69.

coins decreases by 50 percent in the second half of this century, and only a single coin was found from the fifth century (408-491). There is a marked rise in the sixth century, and this new level of activity continues uninterrupted until the mideighth century.[28] A similar picture, of a sharp decrease in the number of coins in the fifth century, reappears in Abu-l-Farag (Fig. 18).[29]

Another well-known commercial city is Apamea (Fig. 19), in which many coins were found. The coins are presented in an awkward fashion; we refrained from cataloging them from anew, and therefore the division is slightly different from that adopted above. A total of 544 coins were found from the period 294-395 (a yearly average of 5.5 coins), 373 coins from 395-450, and 56 coins from 450-498, for a yearly average of 4.1 coins in this century. Most of the coins attributed to the period 395-450, however, are from the end of the fourth century and until 408, and only approx. 90 are from the continuation of the fifth century. We consequently estimate that approx. 50 coins were found in 408-491, for a yearly average of approx. 1 coin.[30] The finds teach of a drastic rise in the number of coins from the middle third of the fourth century until the beginning of the fifth century, followed by a steep decrease.

This picture is repeated in other cities in Syria such as Umm el-'Amed and Tell Rifa'at, but only small numbers of coins were found at these sites.[31]

Baalbek-Heliopolis was another city which apparently suffered a decline. It was a pagan cultic center, and its weakening may be attributed to Christian pressure, and therefore the finds from Heliopolis have been excluded from our discussion.

Notwithstanding all this, there are a number of sites in which the finds are primarily from the fifth century, such as the church in Resafa (Sergiupolis), which was built in the midfourth century. The excavations uncovered many coins, the majority of which are from the fifth century. This settlement as well experienced a crisis in the middle of the fifth century, corresponding with the other coin assemblages from the East in which the fifth century is represented.[32] This century is also well-

[28] B. and S. Bavant, "Dehes: Les Monnaies", *Syria* 57 (1980), pp. 267-87.

[29] G. Hennequin, *Les Monnaies de Ballis Abu-l-Farag Al A'ush* (Damascus, 1978). The numismatic finds only partially express the international trade; see: C. Howgego, "Coin Circulation and the Integration of the Roman Empire", JRA 7 (1994), pp. 5-21.

[30] See: J. P. Callu, *Les Monnaies Romaines* (Brussels, 1979).

[31] M. Dunand and R. Duru, *Oumm el-'Amed. Une Ville de l'Epoque Hellenistique aux Echelles de Tyr* (Paris, 1962); P. A. Clayton, "The Coins from Tell Rifa'at", *Iraq* 29 (1967), pp. 143-54.

[32] Mackensen (Appendix A, n. 130), esp. pp. 193-97; cf. with all the finds from the East.

represented in Apamea.[33] There are clear signs of a crisis in the midfifth century at both sites, as in Egypt.

A number of hoards which were found in Syria[34] also are indicative of a decrease in the number of coins in the fifth century, but not a total cessation.

Tyre is another city which had close ties with Palestine and Galilee.[35] The number of coins from the excavations of the necropolis of Tyre is not large (Fig. 20), but there is clearly a decline to some extent in the second half of the fourth century, and there are no coins from the fifth century.[36] For the resemblance between the numismatic finds in Tyre and those in Galilee, see below.

The excavations of the port at Sarafand revealed that the port was active mainly in the fourth century. A total of 48 coins from this century were found, and only 2 from the following century (Fig. 21), with this site also experiencing a recovery in the sixth century (30 coins).[37]

The Hauran survey uncovered approx. 293 coins. Almost all the coins from the Byzantine period are from the first half of the fourth century, with a drastic reduction after 361.[38]

In summation: fewer coins were in circulation in fifth-century Syria than in the preceding century, therefore enabling us to assume that this province underwent a transition from a period of prosperity to one of depression and decline. The paucity of coins is indicative of a reduction in trade, and possibly also of a general settlement collapse. At any rate, the farmers of Palestine who exported their produce in the fourth century to Syria (via Tyre), could not continue this trade in the fifth century due to the impoverishment of the markets in Syria.

Transjordan

Most excavations in Jordan were conducted in the large cities, and as was noted above, the information from the urban sector is less indicative for

[33] Callu, loc. cit.

[34] See above, the end of Chap. 1.

[35] See below; also see: A. Oppenheimer, *Galilee in the Mishnaic Period* (Jerusalem, 1991), pp. 146-56 (Heb.).

[36] M. H. Chehab, *Fouilles De Tyr. La Necropole IV* (Paris, 1986), p. 91.

[37] J. B. Pritchard, "The Roman Port at Sarafand (Sarepata). Preliminary Report on the Seasons of 1969 and 1970", *Bulletin de Musee de Beyrouth* 24 (1971), pp. 52-54. We have used the definitions of the author. It is not inconceivable that the coins of the fifth century were minted before 408.

[38] C. Auge, "Les Monnaies de fouilles de Si' et la circulation monetaire antique dans le Hauran", in J. M. Dentzer, F. Villeneuve, eds. *Hauran* I (Paris, 1985), pp. 204-5.

the purposes of our discussion. An important testimony was published in 1939 by Kirkbride, who summarized the inventory of coins in the Amman Museum (5,000 coins – Fig. 22).[39] His review reveals a slight decline (15 percent) in the quantity of coins in the second half of the fourth century, beginning in the time of Julian (351/3), and the fifth century is represented in a relatively poor manner. The sixth and seventh centuries once again constitute a period of growth. Chapter 1 contains a discussion of the problems and dangers entailed in the drawing of conclusions based on the chance coin finds in the Museum. Nevertheless, the Museum's holdings comprise 5,000 coins, which is a quite large amount.

Similar Findings Were Revealed in a Majority of the Excavations in the Area:

Khirbet Siyaga (the tomb of Moses) – 18 coins were uncovered from the period 180-408, and only 2 coins from the late fourth-early fifth century (honarius coins), while, in contrast, 43 coins were found beginning from the time of Anastasius. This increase may be explained by the establishment of the churches and a pilgrimage center. These finds are confirmed by the pottery finds.[40]

Heshbon – according to the excavators, the site flourished in the period 363-527, and declined only afterwards.[41] The numismatic finds from this city are meager but interesting. There was a certain degree of growth in the fourth century, and there are almost no coins from the following century.

Pella – here, by contrast, the fifth century is represented in an impressive manner. The excavators date the establishment of the churches and the growth of the city to the fifth century, conclusions which are unsupported by the numismatic finds: the incomplete publication of the excavations lists only 19 coins from the fourth century and only two from the fifth century. Few coins were published from the 1982-1985 excavation seasons, clearly attesting to a decline in the number of coins in the fifth century.[42]

[39] A. S. Kirkbride, "Currencies in Transjordan", *PEF* 72 (1939), pp. 152-61

[40] S.J. Saller, *The Memorial of Moses on Mount Nebo.* (Jerusalem, 1941), pp. 278-89.

[41] For a summation, see: J. Bjarnai Storfjell, *The stratigraphy of Tell Hesban, Jordan, in the Byzantine Period*, Ph.D. diss., Andrews University, 1983, pp. 186-93.

[42] A. McNicoll et al., *Pella in Jordan I* (Canberra, 1982), pp. 103-23; R. H. Smith and L. P. Day, *Pella of the Decapolis*, vol. 2 (Wooster, 1989), p. 127; Idem, *Pella in Jordan II,2* (Sydney, 1992).

Dibon – only a small quantity of coins may be identified. There is a discernible decline in the fifth century, but most of the coins are small specie (minima) from the fourth-fifth centuries, and cannot be dated more precisely.[43]

Abualanda – a hoard was found with substantial representation of the fifth century.[44] As was stated above, however, hoards are of minor value as a source of information regarding chronological changes.

Gerasa – several excavations have been conducted in the city. The first numismatic report was published by Bellinger. In the 1980s, a number of excavations were conducted at different sites as part of the Jerash Archaeological Project.[45] A summation of all the finds indicates growth in the fourth century, and a severe collapse after 408 (Fig. 23). As regards the fourth century: slightly more coins from the first half of the century than from the second half of the century were discovered in the first excavations, while the second series of excavations presents the opposite picture. In general, it is doubtful if there were significant differences between the numbers of coins in the city in the two halves of the century. The differences between the excavations demonstrate, once again, the partial nature of all finds; however, the paucity of coins in the fifth century is constant in all the excavations. Most of the thousands of coins published by Arif are from the sixth and seventh centuries.[46]

Amman – a few coins were found in the fortress in Amman, mainly from the fourth century. The fifth century is not represented, while a certain amount of growth is noticeable in the sixth century.[47]

Abila Decapolis – the excavations of the city have not been published in their entirety. As is usual in Byzantine sites, the excavators are unable to date the active strata or rank the degree of activity in each stratum. The excavations yielded extremely poor numismatic finds: a

[43] F. V. Winnett, W.L. Reed, *Excavations at Dibon (Dhiban) Moab, AASOR* 36-7, New Haven 1964; Idem, *Excavations at Dibon (Dhiban) Moab 1952-3, AASOR* 40, New Haven 1972.

[44] *Coin Hoards* III (1977), p. 69, No. 224.

[45] A. R. Bellinger, "Coins", in *Gerasa: City of the Decapolis*, ed. C. H. Kraeling (New Haven, 1938), pp. 497-503; F. Zayadine, ed., *Jerash Archaeological Project, 1981-83* (Amman, 1986), pp. 82-89, 257-62; E. O. Goicoechea, *Excavationes en el Agora de Gerasaa en 1983* (Madrid, 1986), pp. 39-56.

[46] S. Arif, *A Treasury of Classical and Islamic Coins*, London 1986, pp. 49, 53-54, 65 ff.

[47] F. Zayadine, "Excavations on the Upper Citadel of Amman Area A", *ADAJ* 22 (1977-78), pp. 38-40.

total of only 17 coins. The published reports list 2 coins from 305-363, 7 from the second half of the fourth century, and only a single coin from the fifth century.[48] Such a division is suitable for most of the cities in Transjordan, but the meagerness of the finds precludes the drawing of conclusions.

The Limes line – Parker argues that the Limes line in Transjordan was abandoned in the fifth century.[49] Excavations were later conducted at a number of sites on the Limes line, and especially at the headquarters of the Legion in Lajune. The author of these reports concludes that the line was abandoned only in the late fifth century. The activity of the fortresses may be learned from a number of numismatic reports published by J. W. Batlyon, which were appended to the preliminary reports of the Limes excavations.[50] These reports still lack detail, and the division adopted by the author is not identical with ours, since he distinguishes between the "Late Roman" (284-325) and "Byzantine" (324-502) periods. These chronological distinctions, which are based on the political situation in the West, do not represent the settlement experience during the Byzantine period in the Near East.

A study of the listed coins indicates that only a few coins are from the fifth century (408-491), and the decline apparently had already begun in the midfourth century. The excavators attribute this decrease to the earthquake in 363 or to the reduction in manpower in Limes. Beginning in the sixth century, as could be expected, quite large numbers of coins are once again revealed in the various sites which were excavated.

The *Petra road* – the coins from the Petra road were published by Arif.[51] The period of peak activity, the first half of the fourth century, is represented by many coins. There are no later coins at the site (Fig. 24), as is the case in the city itself.

[48] The coins were published in *NEAS* 22 (1983), pp. 50-51; NEAS 26 (1986), pp. 25 ff.; W. H. Mare, "Coins from the 1988 Excavations at Abila Decapolis", *NEAS* 33 (1989), pp. 6-9. Activity was, however, continuous throughout the Byzantine period; see: *NEAS* 34 (1990), p. 13.

[49] S. T. Parker, *The Roman Frontier in Central Jordan: Interim Report on the Limes Arabicus Project, 1980-1985 (BAR* 340) (Oxford, 1987), pp. 818-19.

[50] Idem, "Preliminary Report, Limes Arabicus Project", *BASOR Supp*. 23 (1985), pp. 1-34; Supp. 25 (1989), pp. 131-74; Supp. 26 (1990), pp. 89-136; Supp. 27 (1991), pp. 117-54.

[51] S. Arif, loc. cit pp. 22 ff

Churches – in general, most of the churches in Transjordan date from the sixth century, and only a few were built in the fourth or fifth centuries.[52]

Obviously, settlement activity continued in most of the sites containing only a small number of coins from the fifth century. In the rural sector, there were villages which remained active, such as the village of Faris to the east of the Dead Sea.[53]

The finds lead to the conclusion that Transjordan did not generally suffer devastation in the second half of the fourth century, while there is a clear decrease in the quantity of coins in the fifth century.

The Other Provinces of the East

The economic-demographic decline of the fifth century prominently recurs in almost all the sites in the Roman East, mainly in those in which large coin assemblages were found. Thus in Sardis (Fig. 25), Ephesos (Fig. 26), Tarsus (Fig. 27), Troy (Fig. 28), and other settlements.[54]

The relatively small number of coins which were published from the excavations at Priene[55] reveal a drastic reduction of more than 50 percent in the fifth century. Only isolated structures in Istanbul have been excavated. From Sarachane, e.g., a few coins were published: 26 coins from 305-408, and only 5 from 408-491, with noticeable growth at the site in the sixth century (117 coins from 491-527). Obviously, a single site such as this cannot represent the entire large city.[56]

Foss has provided only a preliminary publication of a small number of coins from the excavations of the market in Ankara, also revealing few coins from the fifth century.[57] Many coins from Pergamon have been

[52] B. van Elderen, "Byzantine Churches and Mosaics in Transjordan", in *The Archaeology of Jordan and Other Studies*, eds. L. T. Geraty and L. G. Herr (Berrien Springs, Michigan, 1986), pp. 237-46.

[53] J. Johns and A. McQuitty, "The Faris Project: Supplementary Report on the 1986 and 1988 Seasons, the Coins and the Glass", *ADAJ* 33 (1989), pp. 250-53.

[54] See: H. Goldman, *Excavations at Goezlue Kule, Tarsus* (Princeton, 1950); A. R. Bellinger, *Troy. The Coins* (Princeton, 1961); H. W. Bell, *Sardis* XI. Coins, pt. I, 1910-1914 (Leiden, 1916); T. V. Buttrey et al., *Greek, Roman and Islamic Coins from Sardis* (Cambridge, Mass., 1981); H. Vetters, *Ephesos* (Vienna, 1976-1989); see also: J. G. Milne, "J. T. Wood's Coins from Ephesos", *NC* Fifth Series, 5 (1925), pp. 385-91.

[55] K. Regling, Die Münzen von Priene (Berlin, 1927).

[56] .M. F. Hendy, "The Coins", in *Excavations at Sarachane in Istanbul* I, ed. R. M. Harrison (Princeton, 1986), pp. 278-373.

[57] C. Foss, "Late Antique and Byzantine Ankara", in *History and Archaeology of Byzantine Asia Minor*, (Variorum, 1990), VI, p. 87 (DOP 41 [1987], p. 87).

published (Fig. 29), with the fifth century represented by only a small number of coins.[58] Similar results emerge from Alishar Hueyuek. The two excavations seasons yielded few coins: 38 from 305-408, none from the fifth century, and 14 from 491-610.[59] The few coins which have been published from the excavations at Sidi (30) present the same picture of a lack of numismatic finds from the fifth century.[60]

The cities in Greece also exhibit a decline in the fifth century, such as the major port city of Corinth. Four large assemblages from this city have been published (31-33), and additional preliminary reports have continued to appear recently. The illustration relates only to the first four assemblages;[61] there are corresponding finds from the nearby town of Kenchreai, which served as an additional port for Corinth (Fig. 34),[62] and from Athens (Fig.35),[63] Argos,[64] Arcadia,[65] Sparta,[66] and additional sites. The history of the settlement in Cyprus is worthy of a separate discussion, but the economy of this island also apparently collapsed in the fifth century, as was the case in Curium (Fig. 36), Paphos,[67] and additional cities.[68]

[58] K. Regling, "Die Stadt", in *Altertümer von Pergamon* I,2: Stadt und Landschaft (Berlin, 1912), pp. 355-63.

[59] H. H. von der Osten and E. F. Schmidt, *The Alishar Hueyek: Season of 1927 I* (Chicago, 1930) and esp.: E. T. Newell, "Coins", in H. H. von der Osten, *The Alishar Hueyek: Seasons of 1930-32 III* (Chicago, 1937), pp. 310-23.

[60] S. Atlan, *1947-1967 Yillari Side Kazilari Sirasinda Elde Edilen Sikkeler* (Ankara, 1976).

[61] A. R. Bellinger, *Catalogue of the Coins Found at Corinth, 1925* (New Haven, 1930); K. M. Edwards, *Corinth* VI: Coins, 1896-1929 (Cambridge, Mass., 1933); idem, "Report on the Coins Found in the Excavations at Corinth during the Years 1930-1935", *Hesperia* 6 (1937), pp. 241-56; J. M. Harris, "Coins Found at Corinth", *Hesperia* 10 (1941), pp. 143-62; this also may be deduced from the preliminary reports recently published in *Hesperia* 52-58.

[62] M. Hohlfelder, *Kenchreai – Eastern Port of Corinth, III: The Coins* (Leiden, 1978).

[63] M. Thompson, *The Athenian Agora II – Coins from the Roman through the Venetian Period* (Princeton, 1954).

[64] C. Waldstein, *The Argiv Heraeum II* (Cambridge, 1905), pp. 357-63; J. Bingen, "Les Monnaies Chronique des Fouilles en 1952, Argos", *BCH* 77 (1955), pp. 256-58; "... en 1953", *BCH* 78 (1954), pp. 183-89; "... en 1954", *BCH* 79 (1955), pp. 329-31.

[65] J. G. Milne, "The Currency of Arcadia", *NC* Sixth Series, 9 (1949), pp. 83-92.

[66] R. M. Dawkins, ed., *The Sanctuary of Artemis Orthia at Sparta* (London, 1929), pp. 393-98.

[67] D. H. Cox, *Coins from the Excavations at Curium, 1932-53 (Numismatic Notes and Monographs*, No. 145) (New York, 1959); I. Nicolaou, *The Coins from the House of Dionysos (Paphos II)* (Nicosia, 1990); A. H. Megaw, "Excavations at Saranda Kolonos Paphos 1966/7, 1970/1971", *Report of the Department of Antiquities, Cyprus* (1971), pp. 142 ff.

[68] For an additional survey of the finds from regions in the West and a few from the East, see: T. Lewit, *Agricultural Production in the Roman Economy 200-400* (*BAR* 568) (Oxford, 1991); see also: J. Benett and E. Scott, "The End of Roman Settlement in

Obviously Greece and Cyprus were directly influenced by the collapse of the Western Empire, and the finds from these lands should not enter into the current discussion, which is limited to the lands and provinces adjoining Palestine, and does not encompass the entire Byzantine Empire.

The data collected and presented in this work do not reflect all the excavations conducted in the eastern Mediterranean basin, nor was that the intent of the author. They are indicative, however, of a crisis, or at the very least a settlement decline, in the entire region in which the provinces of Palestina Prima and Secunda were located. This is likely to have been a demographic decrease, or at least a decline in the volume of commerce.[69] The archaeological literature dealing with these cities usually provides local explanations, such as the earthquakes in 365 and in 375 or military campaigns, which Hohlfelder argues influenced the decline of Kenchreai.[70]

Only a more nonspecific and comprehensive cause will satisfactorily explain the general lessening of commerce throughout the entire East. The simplest and most "natural" explanation would link the decline of commerce in the early fifth century with the conquests of the Western Empire by the Vandals. The subject of the influence exerted by the destruction of the Western Empire upon the East is deserving of a separate detailed examination; in order not to break the continuity of the current discussion, this topic will be reserved for the end of the chapter.

We have not discussed the Negev, since the history of this region which adjoins Palestine is distinct from that of its northern neighbor. A number of excavations have been conducted in the Negev, and a complete review of its history would exceed the scope of this work. The northern Negev flourished in the fourth century after ca. two hundred years of waning activity. This situation is graphically illustrated by the assemblage of coins from Mamphis (Fig. 37)[71] and can be deduced from

Northern England", in *Settlement in North Britain 1000 BC-AD 1000* (*BAR* 118), eds. J. C. Chapman and H. C. Mytum (Oxford, 1983), pp. 205-32; the circulation of coins in other regions north of Asia Minor has not been systematically examined, but this also clearly indicates prosperity in the fourth century and a decrease in the number of coins in the fifth century. See, e.g.: P. Kos, *The Monetary Circulation in the Southern Alpin Region* (Ljubljana, 1986).

69 For the monetary situation in the East, also see: H. Adelson, "The Monetary Deterioration in the Fifth Century", in *International Numismatic Convention, Tel-Aviv*, ed. A. Kindler (Jerusalem, 1967), pp. 262-82, and much additional literature.

70 Hohlfelder, Kenchreai, p. 3.

71 A. Negev, "The Architecture of Mamphis Final Report, II: *The Late Roman and Byzantine Periods*", *Qedem* 27 (1988), pp. 64-74.

additional excavations in the region. M. Haiman concluded on the basis of his survey of the Negev that the more southerly part of the region began to flourish only in the fifth or sixth century, somewhat later than the northern Negev.[72] This reconstruction is confirmed by the finds from Nessana, since most of the material from this village is from the sixth to the eighth centuries,[73] and the coins from the site also reflect a similar history (Fig. 38). The new excavations at the site are likely to shed additional light on its history.[74]

The Agrarian-Agricultural Process

1) *The Village Economy in the Third and Fourth Centuries*

We shall now offer an additional, and parallel, hypothesis which will resolve all the questions which have been raised and provide a possible explanation for all aspects of the entire settlement process.

The village in Palestine reached a very high level of development. Its inhabitants practiced extremely intensive agriculture, and it was settled quite densely. The village was based in large measure on an open economy, and a considerable portion of agricultural production was sold in the market, with the proceeds used to purchase imported goods which were not worthwhile for the farmer to raise himself. The Talmud speaks of villages which consumed most of their produce, while others directed most of their production to the markets. "It has been taught: where most is brought into the homes, but in a place where most is brought in to the market..."[75]

Artisans, the providers of services, and shops were common in these rural settlements. Palestine experienced slow but definite demographic growth in the second, third, and fourth centuries (see above). In order to provide for this excess population, the villagers had to fully exhaust the

[72] M. Haiman, *Shepherds and Farmers in the Kadesh Barne'a Region* (Sde Boker, 1990) (Heb.); idem, "Agricultural Settlement in Ramat Barne'a in the Seventh-Eighth Centuries CE", *'Atiqot Hebrew Series*, 10 (1990), pp. 111-24. Haiman argues that this conclusion is confirmed by additional surveys. He informed me of this orally, for which I am grateful.

[73] C. J. Kraemer, *Excavations at Nessana* I-III (Princeton, 1958).

[74] number of assemblages from way stations or fortresses in the northern Negev have been discovered, but have not been published. These assemblages stop or wane in the fifth century, but we must wait for their final publication.

[75] PT Ma'aser Sheni 2:49:c; Safrai, Economy (above, Chap. 3, n. 1), Chap. 5.

agricultural potential of their lands and to develop nonagricultural branches of production and employment. The economic balance in such an economy was dependent upon two factors: agricultural intensification, i.e., the ability to maintain maximal and optimal utilization of land resources; and a regional and national system of commerce capable of efficiently marketing the produce of the villages and providing a regular supply of commodities required by the village.[76] We do not possess the precise data required for a comparison of the level of development in various regions of Palestine, but the settlement density, agricultural intensiveness, and the centrality of commerce in Galilee were the highest in Palestine, as is shown by the following two proofs:

a) average village size. The larger Galilean villages reached a size of 90-100 dunams, while medium-sized villages covered an area of approx. 50 dunams. Evidence of this is provided by both the agricultural finds and the rabbinical literature.[77] Beth She'arim, e.g., extended over an area of 110 dunams.[78] The rural settlements in other regions were smaller.

The average settlement in the Carmel comprised an area of 20-30 dunams, such as Khirbet Summaqa (see above, Chap. 1), as did other villages which were surveyed in the Carmel. The largest known village in the Samaria hill country is Um Rihan, with an area of 36-40 dunams.[79] Early settlements in the southern Hebron hill country generally covered an area of 20-40 dunams. Horvat Susiya, e.g., which was an extremely large settlement, extended over approx. 60 dunams, and Jethira was of similar size.[80]

[76] This description of a Palestinian village is not universally accepted. For a description of the intensive agriculture in the village, see: Y. Feliks, *Agriculture in Palestine in the Period of the Mishna and Talmud* (Tel Aviv, 1963) (Heb.). For a description of the system of trade, see: Z. Safrai, *Economy*, pp. 415-30; for the demographic process and the process of economic growth, see: Z. Safrai, "The Influence of Demographic Stratification on the Agricultural and Economic Structure during the Mishnaic and Talmudic Periods", in *Man and Land in Eretz-Israel in Antiquity*, eds. A. Kasher et al. (Jerusalem, 1986), pp. 20-48 (Heb.); Idem, *The Economy*, pp. 436-458.

[77] Z. Yavin, *Survey of Settlements in Galilee and the Golan from the Period of the Mishnah in Light of the Sources*. Ph.D. diss., Hebrew University, 1971 (Heb.).

[78] B. Mazar (Maisler), *Beth She'arim* I (Jerusalem, 1975).

[79] Dar, *Um Rihan* (above, Appendix A, n. 66).

[80] These numbers are based on examinations which I conducted and on the findings of the regional surveys. See, e.g.: M. Kochavi, ed., *Judaea, Samaria and the Golan: Archaeological Survey 1967-1968* (Jerusalem, 1972), pp. 66, 71, 75, 81, 170, and many others (Heb.). In another place I will present finds from dozens of additional sites which I surveyed, but are as yet unpublished.

b) much large numbers of coins were found in the Galilean rural settlements than in other regions of Palestine. Large numbers of coins were found in almost all the excavations in Galilee. Thus in Beth She'arim, Capernaum, Chorazin, Khirbet Shema', Gischala, en-Nabratein, Meroth, Jalame, Summaqa, and other sites in this area.

Fewer coins were uncovered in excavations in southern Judea. Hundreds of coins were found only in Rimmon and in Mambre, which was the site of an international fair and a pilgrimage site. In Susiya, e.g., less than 20 coins were found, and only isolated coins were discovered in Ma'on and'Anim. Numerous coins are also characteristic of the Golan, and to a lesser degree, of the Beth Shean Valley. The Golan, however, was a relatively new area of settlement, and this datum will be of extreme importance (see below).

It may therefore be inferred that the Galilean villages were more developed, and consequently more dependent upon trade than those in the other regions of Palestine. Due to prevailing conditions and the cost of transport, reliance upon commerce was only a second choice, and the farmer probably preferred a nonmarket economy. It may therefore be assumed that the villagers applied themselves to commerce and the various trades only after exhausting the agricultural potential of the lands of the village and the surrounding area. I.e., a large volume of commerce is indicative also of extremely intensive agriculture.

This was the general agricultural situation in the third and fourth centuries. The second half of the fourth century witnessed the beginning of a "crisis" process which culminated ca. 400-430 in the decline and weakening of the village. This crisis erupted on the background of a combination of agricultural, economic, environmental, and social factors.

2) *The Agricultural Factor*

The intensive working of the land leads us to conjecture that this level of agriculture was too high, and the excessive utilization of the land was concurrent with a population explosion. Excessive working of the land exhausts the soil and leads to poorer harvests, as is known from agricultural research. For the simple peasant, decreasing crops are a strange surprise. He cannot understand the phenomenon, nor, as a general rule, is he capable of discerning that he is witnessing a progressive decline. A drop in agricultural revenues compels the farmer to make every effort to improve the level of harvests. In the first phase, the farmer will devote extra hours to working the land – extra plowing, supplementary irrigation, etc. The irrigation will improve short-term profitability, but will only acerbate the long-range depletion of land resources.

The farmer was likely to submit to the temptation to increase his harvests by switching from biannual to annual sowing. Letting the land lie fallow once every two years was the accepted practice in Palestine for restoring the earth's fertility. It was only natural, however, for the farmer to attempt to waive this limitation and "compensate" the land by increased fertilization. This course of action is characteristic of intensification processes throughout the world.[81] Such a solution is likely to yield short-term improvements, but is likely to pose a long-term threat to the food resources in the soil, and constitute a clear cause of the depletion of crops. Another solution, which had always been practiced in the East and which is known from the rabbinic literature, consisted of increasing the secondary crops in orchards.[82] The rabbis knew that such overutilization of the land was prevalent, but problematic.[83] Excessive sowing in orchards, or planting in too high a density, also may have temporarily offset a decrease in crops, but was liable to be disastrous in the long run and exhaust the farmer's lands.

Accordingly, Palestine as a whole, and especially Galilee, may have witnessed the beginning of a process of soil depletion with a consequent decrease in yields. The combination of shrinking harvests and demographic increase led to a long and protracted economic crisis.

This hypothesis cannot be proven, nor can it be easily assumed that the early sources were conscious of such slow processes. Similar explanations were offered in the past for the decline of ancient cultures in Mexico and in eastern Asia, but these are tropical regions.[84]

3) *The Environmental Factors*

The economy of Palestine, and especially that of Galilee, depended upon stable trade: the export of flax, oil, and wine, and the purchase of wheat.[85] Syria was a constant consumer of agricultural goods from

[81] Z. Safrai, *The Economy of Roman Palestine*, London 1994, pp. 427-8

[82] Feliks, Agriculture in Palestine, p. 134.

[83] Mishnah Peah 3:1; and esp. PT Peah 3:17:b-c.

[84] See, e.g.: P. Gourou, *The Tropical World* (New York, 1962), pp. 48 ff.

[85] For the import of wheat from the third century onward, see: Safrai, Economy, p. 110; Y. Dan, "Economic Life in the Byzantine Period", *in Commerce in Palestine throughout the Ages: Studies*, eds. B. Z. Kedar et al. (Jerusalem, 1990), p. 185.

Palestine. We know mainly of the ties between Galilee and Tyre, which was the main market for the produce from Galilee, as is attested by many sources.[86] Tyrean coins were in circulation in Galilee, and constituted a sizable percentage of all the coins in the region;[87] trade caravans from Galilee frequently arrived in Tyre,[88] which functioned as the nearby coast serving Galilee.[89] Consequently, there was a significant volume of trade with Syria, although both lands produced similar goods.

As was noted, there are sufficient sources attesting to the reduction of commerce in trade centers in Syria such as Tyre, the port of Sarafand, Antioch, Aphamea, and Hamma. This decrease of trade in the Syrian cities entailed the reduction or curtailment of the import of goods from Palestine, inter alia. This may have been merely "belt tightening" or a loss of "fat" for the merchants and inhabitants of Syria, while such a development severely affected the vital interests of Palestinian farmers.

Palestine was imminently suited for an economic symbiosis with Egypt. The latter exported grains which were in short supply in Palestine, and consumed oil and wine which were a rarity in Egypt. The sources speak extensively about commercial relations with Egypt,[90] and many coins from Alexandria were found in Israel.[91]

As was mentioned, the Egyptian market suffered severe damage in the fifth century. For the farmers of Palestine, this signaled the loss of an important potential market for excess production. The contraction of the Egyptian market undoubtedly led to a rise in the price of imported grain and lessened the profitability of exporting oil and wine to this neighboring land. Furthermore, Palestine lost its faith in the Egyptian market as a source of grains. This situation necessitated economic

[86] Oppenheimer, *Galilee in the Mishnaic Period*, pp. 146-53 and additional literature loc. cit.

[87] D. Barag, "Tyrian Currency in Galilee", *INJ* 6-7 (1982-83), pp. 7-13; R. Hanson, *Tyrian Influence in the Upper Galilee* (Cambridge, Mass., 1980), pp. 51-69; also see below.

[88] Z. Safrai, "On the Question of the Spacial Structure of the Settlement in Galilee in the Period of the Mishnah and Talmud", in *The Lands of Galilee*, A. Shmueli et al., eds. (1983), pp. 269-88 (Heb.).

[89] The Tyrean coins are less dominant in sites to the south of Galilee; this conclusion is based on a comprehensive study of city coins in Palestine; a detailed treatment of these data and of additional conclusions ensuing from numismatic finds in Palestine and Syria would exceed the scope of the present work; see also below, n. 76.

[90] Y. Dan, "Economic Life", loc. cit.; D. Sperber, "Objects of Trade between Palestine and Egypt in Roman Times", *JESHO* 19 (1976), pp. 113-214.

[91] Safrai, *Economy*, p. 403. This data is based on the Eretz-Israel Museum catalog; my thanks to Dr. A. Kindler, who helped me to collect the data from the catalogue.

restructuring and a different choice of crops to be raised by the Palestinian farmer.

The market in Transjordan fared no better. The settlement in Transjordan did not collapse, as is clear from, e.g., the excavations in Heshbon and in Pella, but the level of commerce in the region greatly decreased, as is attested by the numismatic finds in the Amman Museum, from Jerasa, and in other settlements (see above).

In the early fifth century, the central markets in the eastern Roman Empire were harmed. The fall of the Western Empire was responsible for the reduction of commerce in the East. It cannot be assumed that the Palestinian market was affected more severely from the fall of the Western Empire than other provinces in the East. Syria and Asia Minor probably incurred the greatest damage, but these were rich markets capable of absorbing such harm. It may be presumed that this was a more painful blow for the population of Palestine, since its farmers were dependent upon the markets of Syria, Egypt, and Transjordan. Wealthy Syria was capable of absorbing the damage and merely resort to economic "cutbacks," but such retrenchment was liable to severely harm the Palestine market. In the fifth century, then, new commercial circumstances came into existence which were likely to hamper the mercantile system of Palestine and greatly reduce the economic prospects of this region.

This leads us to believe that Galilee suffered grievously, because of its greater dependence upon trade than other regions of Palestine, and possibly also because of its relative proximity to Syria.

4) *The Socioagrarian Process*

The private agricultural sector constituted the backbone of the economy of Palestine. This small-scale and intensive agriculture made possible the demographic growth and prosperity for which it was a precondition. Jones has noted that the Roman East flourished while the West waned since the private agriculture in the East was more traditional, established, and well-rooted that its western counterpart (see above, Chap. 3). As was noted, the situation had already begun to change in the Amoraitic period, mainly from the early fourth century, but major change apparently occurred only after the completion of the Talmud.

As was demonstrated above (Chap. 3), the agrarian structure underwent change in the Byzantine period. There are sufficient proofs and allusions to support the argument that the process of the transferal of lands to the wealthy intensified in the fifth century. This process, which was aided by the economic and agricultural blows that had been inflicted on the farmers (see above), severely affected the small landowners and the poor. The farmers had difficulty in coping with the decrease in their harvests, and with the need for a complete economic reorganization and greater dependence upon their own production. Such measures obviously provided only a short-term solution.

The social and psychological influences of this agrarian process upon the growth of sharecropping were far-reaching. For the private farmer who was intimately attached to the family holdings, the transition led to a crisis of self-confidence and a sense of economic loss. The fact that the landowners belonged to a different social class, at times with differing religious affiliation as well, only compounded his distress. Such a change was directly responsible for a decrease in the farmer's earnings, and indirectly, for a drop in the population of the villages. Also to be expected was a parallel growth in the urban population and in the size of the cities, for agricultural profits streamed from the village to the city, to the residences of the landowners. Indeed, in the "Byzantine" period the number of cities increased in a methodic and constant fashion. Cities were established (or reestablished) also in the fifth century, and mainly in the sixth century (Fig. 5). In national terms, the estate economy was likely to be highly wasteful of resources, due in part to the decreased efficiency of the farmers, and mainly to the destruction of resources and waste by the wealthy classes.

Historical literature has connected many events with agrarian processes. Some scholars, e.g., claim that the Jewish revolts erupted in the wake of such processes.[92] These theories will not be discussed here, and have been mentioned only to illustrate the great potential for destruction held by agrarian processes.

The three components of the process described above: the decrease in regional trade, the exhaustion of the land's fertility, and the collapse of independent farming, can explain the economic and demographic decline in Palestine and the collapse of many Galilean villages. It is not inconceivable that a portion of the Galilee farmers moved to new regions (the Golan and southern Judea) which offered virgin, unoccupied lands. These lands could provide the experienced farmers with sufficient

[92] E.g.: S. Appelbaum, "The Agrarian Question and the Revolt of Bar Kokhba", *Eretz-Israel* 8 (1967), pp. 283-87 (Heb.); see also: idem, "Economic Life in Palestine", in *The Jewish People in the First Century*, ed. S. Safrai et al. (*CRJ*) II (Assen, 1976), pp. 692-99; idem, "The Struggle for the Soil and the Revolt of 66-73 C.E"., *Eretz-Israel* 12 (1975), pp. 125-28 (Heb.), and many additional studies.

livelihood. Many villages in eastern Galilee and the Golan which had been established in the early fourth century experienced growth in the period when the Galilean villages were on the wane, and reached their peak as the villages in Galilee were collapsing. According to the excavators of the Golan, the period of maximal activity of the villages in this region lasted for only a short period of time. According to the theory we have advanced, this resulted from the depletion of land resources due to overexploitation.

The history of the settlement in the southern Hebron hill country is not as clear. The settlements in this region may owe their growth to additional processes, those which aided in the development of the Negev in the late Byzantine period. An analysis of these processes in the Negev and in southern Judea is deserving of a separate discussion within an independent context.

5) *The Climatic Explanation*

As early as 1931 Huntigton proposed climatic changes, mainly those in the quantity of precipitation, as a possible explanation for the decline or rise of the settlement. This approach has recently been revived thanks to the learned study by Issar and Govrin.[93]

These deterministic proposals are based on the assumption that geographic conditions dictate human happenings. This approach has been thoroughly discredited, but on occasion ideas from this school are resurrected. This explanation is offered mainly as a possible background for the encroachment by the desert and the waning of the settlement it envelops, i.e., the "desertization" of the Negev. These proposals are the subject of current discussion by the scholarly community, and we will add only two comments:

a) the change in quantity of resources may be assumed to be linear in all parts of Palestine, and indeed, throughout the entire East. It is highly doubtful if this was the case. As has been demonstrated, not all parts of Palestine were damaged in equal measure or at the same time. The potential for damage due to lack of rain should be greatest in the Negev and in the desert fringe, but these regions suffered the least in the late fourth century.
b) some of the proofs regarding changes in the flora and ground cover of Palestine are possibly due to settlement changes. The absence of a

[93] A. Issar and Y. Govrin, "Climatic Change and the Desertification of the Negev at the End of the Byzantine Period", *Cathedra* 61 (1991), pp. 67-83 (Heb.).

settlement and deficient care of agricultural areas are likely to cause a deterioration in cultivated plants and their replacement by wild growths or weedlike flora. Thus the mere observation of such changes does not explain their cause.

The concept of climatic change was also proposed and discussed within the wider context of the entire Middle East. According to Vita-Finzi, there is a noticeable phenomenon of "younger fill" throughout the Middle East. This fill began to accumulate in all regions ca. the fifth century, as a result of the decline of the settlement, which in turn may possibly be attributed to climatic change.[94] Later studies, however, have raised serious doubts regarding the simultaneous start of this process in all regions, consequently lowering the value of climatic change as the chief cause of this process.[95] Needless to say, the archaeological dating of the beginning of the fill is extremely problematic.

At this stage of research, therefore, climatic change is insufficient as an explanation of the causes and scope of the crisis. The detection and mapping of the crisis is a precondition for understanding its causes, which is the contribution of the current discussion.

One method of discerning the quantities of rain in previous ages consists of analyzing the changing thickness of trees. The sole finds from this period consists of the beams in the el-Aqsa mosque.[96] All the wood which was examined is indicative of a short period of ca. 50 years in the midfifth century of narrow bands, which leads the authors to conclude that a local climatic change, i.e., a short period of drought, may have occurred in this time span. The finds correspond to our conclusions regarding a settlement decline in the fifth century, and may be a possible explanation of this trend. The origin of these trees, however, has not been determined; moreover, the short bands may have had other causes, such as lack of care of the trees, if these were in fact cultivated trees. The subject of climatic change awaits further study. At this stage of the research, proofs which would confirm these conjectures have not been collected.

[94] C. Vita-Finzi, *The Mediterranean Valleys: Geological Changes in Historical Times* (Cambridge, 1969).

[95] J. M. Wagstaff, "Buried Assumptions: Some Problems in the Interpretation of the 'Younger Fill' Raised by Recent Data from Greece", *Journal of Archaeological Science* 8 (1981), pp. 247-64.

[96] S. Lev-Yadun et al., "Ring Analysis of *Cedrus libani* Beams from the Roof of El-Aqsa Mosque", *Eretz-Israel* 17 (1984), pp. 92-96 (Heb.).

Appendix

The Influence of the Barbarian Conquests on the Byzantine Empire

The explanation that economic and\or demographic decline in Palestine was caused by general weakening throughout the Empire suffices for the limited scope of this work, which deals with the history of Palestine. Nevertheless, we are duty bound to offer an explanation for the general regression in the entire Empire, a process which was deduced through the use of the experimental tool of quantitative numismatic research. The decrease in the number of coins began after the time of Arcadius in 408. The raids and conquests by the barbarian tribes began in this period, thereby leading to the obvious deduction that the barbarian conquests and the fall of the West influenced the Eastern Empire.

This explanation would seem to be simple and self-evident, but this is not so, since this theory must confront and corroborate with other theories regarding the influence of the barbarian conquests on the East and on the West. If the severance of the ties with the Western Empire was responsible for the decline of commerce in the East, it must then be assumed that similar or even more severe damage was caused in the western provinces, or, stated more simply: if Egypt and Syria were harmed by the conquest of Gaul and Carthage, then these latter two centers must have suffered damage at least as great. The degree of influence exerted by the conquest of the Western Empire by the barbarians is, however, controversial, and constitutes one of the most central and important issues regarding the history of the ancient world.

The central question is: what caused the end of the ancient world, and what was responsible for the destruction of Roman culture and the beginning of the Dark Ages? A great deal of literature has been written on this topic, and this is undoubtedly one of the most important and intriguing questions in the history of human development.

The End of the Roman Age in Europe and the Conquests of the Barbarians – a Survey of the Research.

The theory of Pirenne: The survey of the research should begin with Pirenne. It has been said that great historians and central historical theories become part of history itself and are studied accordingly. This general statement undoubtedly applies to the theory of Pirenne, and this concise survey will therefore begin with this theory and the discussions of it.[97]

Pirenne's theory postulates two phases:

1) the Arab conquests isolated the commercial and cultural system in the Eastern Empire, with a consequent deterioration of cultural and commercial values in the West, which then descended into the long night of the Dark Ages. One of the proofs on which Pirenne bases his theory consists of the "four deficiencies," i.e., the lack of essential items which were produced in the East: papyrus, spices, fabrics, and luxury items.
2) the smashing of the Mediterranean trading cycle caused Gaul to redirect its traditional orientation toward the south and the east to the north, thus bringing into existence the (Christian) Gallic-Germanic-Celtic economic and cultural sphere which slowly led to the development of European culture.[98]

Pirenne's theory has aroused great interest, is the subject of dozens of books and articles, and quite naturally has prompted many respondents, both supporters and opponents. Most recent discussions begin with a survey of the research, which obviously grows longer and more complicated as time passes.[99] In place of a comprehensive survey, we will merely mention several ideas which have ben raised in the context of this international inquiry.

a) Lopez argues that the "four deficiencies" were to be found in the markets of the West during the medieval period as well, but there is not a great deal of information concerning this point.[100] Quite unintentionally, Lopez may have directed attention to the main touchstone

[97] H. Pirenne, *Mohammed and Charlemagne*, trans. B. Miall (London, 1939).

[98] This part of Pirenne's theory conflicts with the hypothesis of Dopsch, who argues that European civilization had already developed among the Germanic tribes in the Roman period; see: A. Dopsch, *The Economic and the Social Foundation of European Civilization* (London, 1937). The different cultural-political realities separating the two authors cannot be ignored.

[99] See, e.g.: P. Grierson, "Commerce in the Dark Ages: a Critique of the Evidence", *Transactions of the Royal Historical Society* Fifth Series, 9 (1959), pp. 123-40; P. Van Dam, "The Pirenne Thesis and Fifth-Century Gaul", *in Fifth Century Gaul: A Crisis of Identity*, ed. J. Drinkwater and H. Elton, eds. (Cambridge, 1992), pp. 321-33; for a comprehensive survey, see: Z. Rubin, "The Mediterranean and the Dilemma of the Roman Empire in Late Antiquity", *Mediterranean Historical Review* 1 (1986), pp. 13-62; P. Lambrechts, "Les theses de Henri Pirenne sur la fin du monde antique et les debuts du moyen age", *Byzantion* 14 (1939), pp. 513-36.

[100] R. S. Lopez, "Mohammed and Charlemagne: A Revision", *Speculum* 18 (1943), pp. 14-38.

of change: prosperity or decline. In the final analysis the question is not whether the fabrics of the East reached the markets of France or Spain, but rather how frequently they did so. This question is quantitative in nature, and the absence of quantitative data hinders the drawing of conclusions.

b) According to Baynes, the decline of the West had already begun in the wake of the conquests of the barbarians. This hypothesis has not been presented in a methodical fashion, and has appeared only concisely, in the form of a critique of a number of other works dealing with the economic history of the Byzantine empire.[101]

c) In the past decade, this effort has been joined by archaeologists attempting to examine Pirenne's theory in the light of archaeological finds. Hodges and Whitehouse collected a small amount of material from North Africa and Italy.[102] They argue that North Africa maintained normal commercial ties with the East, while a decrease ca. the midfifth century is noticeable in the rural sector in Italy, but this reduction is not reflected in Rome itself.[103] Despite this convoluted formulation, the authors conclude that the barbarian conquests cannot be held responsible for the decline of the West. As for the East, they argue that the collected material evidences that it remained "economically active" until the Arab conquest.[104] In our opinion, the material collected in the Eastern Empire is not sufficiently significant to draw such a conclusion.

A collection edited by Drinkwater and Elton contains a number of essays about fifth-century Gaul.[105] Hitchner asserts that imported ware noticeably decreased in Gaul,[106] although there are testimonies of the import of wine from the East,[107] and Van Dam correctly concludes that in the fifth century Gaul was no longer a province Mediterranean in nature,[108] and consequently Baynes rightly attributed the "end of the Roman era" to the barbarian incursions and conquests.

[101] N.H. Baynes, "Reviews and Discussions", *JRS* 19 (1929), pp. 229-33.

[102] R. Hodges and D. Whitehouse, *Mohammed, Charlemagne and the Origins of Europe: Archaeology and the Pirenne Thesis* (Ithaca, N.Y., 1983).

[103] Ibid., pp. 20-53.

[104] Ibid., pp. 54-76, esp. p. 75.

[105] Drinkwater and Elton, above note 99.

[106] R. B. Hitchner, "Meridional Gaul, Trade and the Mediterranean Economy in Late Antiquity", in Drinkwater and Elton, pp. 122-31.

[107] Ibid., p. 128.

[108] R. Van Dam, "The Pirenne Thesis and Fifth-Century Gaul", in Drinkwater and Elton, pp. 321-33.

The End of the Roman World in the Western Empire

Totally divorced from Pirenne and his theory, researchers have sought the reasons for the disintegration of Byzantine rule in the West. This question has greatly troubled scholars investigating the Empire, who have proposed a number of solutions. The researchers generally emphasize the internal decay and the cultural regression.[109] Jones stressed the economic and agrarian decline brought on by the collapse of the private farmer class and the agrarian processes; the strengthening of the estates and the colonate law.[110] Lot claims that the process began as early as the third century.[111] Lewit has recently shown that there is no evidence of the collapse or weakening of the rural sector in the West in the fourth century. It is possible that societal and governmental order was undermined, but the agricultural economy continued to be active and productive. This sector undoubtedly constituted the economic backbone of the Byzantine empire as a whole, and consequently, any description of the collapse of the Empire must include proofs and explanations of the collapse of the productive rural sector. Lewit does not relate directly to Pirenne's theory,[112] but the large body of material accumulated in hundreds of excavations throughout the West clearly shows that the number of rural and urban sites containing remains dated to the fifth century is extremely low (excluding Carthage – see below).[113] The decrease encompasses all the western provinces, and occurred in all sectors of society. Hodges and Whitehouse based their conclusions on fewer than ten field surveys, and therefore Lewit, who summarized information from hundreds of excavations, is to be preferred to these earlier attempts.

Lewit did not confine herself to the mere collection of data, but provided a detailed and scholarly analysis in order to explain why the absence of fifth-century sites did not ensue from a lack of settlements, nor is it indicative of a demographic or settlement decline. Her main arguments follow:

a) in the fifth century, use was no longer made of the fine imported pottery vessels, mainly those from Africa (ARS), and in their stead extensive use was made of simple local ware.

[109] A. H. M. Jones, *The Later Roman Empire 284-602: a Social, Economic and Administrative Survey* (Oxford, 1964), pp. 1025-68; W. E. Kaegi, *Byzantium and the Decline of Rome* (Princeton, 1968).

[110] Jones, loc. cit.

[111] F. Lot, *The End of the Ancient World and the Beginnings of the Middle Ages* (New York, 1961); also see Baynes (above, n. 101).

[112] Lewit (above, n. 68).

[113] Ibid, pp. 37 ff.

b) the local pottery vessels of the fifth century have not been identified or dated, since they are still not well-known. Furthermore, in the past certain types of vessels were erroneously dated to the fourth century, instead of the fifth century to which they belong.
c) little use was made of new pottery vessels in the fifth century, while extensive use was made of old wares from the preceding century.
Regarding the other archaeological finds:
d) the lack of coins does not indicate the absence of a settlement, since the use of coins in commerce was limited. The residents used coins from the fourth century, and barter trade was common.
e) many village structures were abandoned, and a large number of "villa" structures were turned into churches and burial sites, since the estate was connected to a specific social structure which was typical of the Roman period but had collapsed, and the estate system disintegrated.
f) the farmers of the fifth and succeeding centuries who abandoned the estate houses built new buildings for themselves of wood, and only few remains of these structures have been preserved.
g) extensive use was made of wooden construction in the cities as well.
h) the population did not construct public buildings, wrote few inscriptions, did not build new roads, etc.

It would seem, however, that these data lead to a different conclusion. The society of the fifth century, based on Lewit's data, was one which experienced a decisive change in the structure of the village, and in which the system of estates prevalent in the Roman-Byzantine Empire collapsed. The villagers constructed simple wood and thatch structures, and the few pottery vessels they used lacked unique features and character. The extensive import of clay vessels and products from Africa came to a virtual halt. Jewelry and buildings were simpler and poorer, the method of construction was of lesser quality (wood construction is inferior to stone), public buildings were not erected, and the norm of public buildings and dedicatory inscriptions came to an end. The nature of burials also changed, and the practice of emorial inscriptions was reduced. The difference between the Roman period and the early medieval period in the sphere of construction and the use of public buildings, on the one hand, along with the continued usage of such structures, on the other hand, has been treated extensively in the research literature.[114]

[114] J. B. Ward-Perkins, *From Classical Antiquity to the Middle Ages: Urban Public Building in Northern and Central Italy, A.D. 300-850* (Oxford, 1984). Greenhalgh presents a different approach: M. Greenhalgh, *The Survival of Roman Antiquities in*

We would be hard-pressed to find a sharper and clearer formulation for the term "the end of the Roman era" than this. If such a series of changes occurred, then it attests to a radical change in the governmental, societal, economic, and cultural realms. It is this change which is labeled "the end of the Roman era", and according to the extant material, it did in fact take place in the fifth century.

The question must now be asked: does "the end of the Roman era" refer only to the social, cultural, and economic change, or was it also accompanied by an economic and demographic decline? The archaeology of the fifth and sixth centuries is patently less well developed than that of the Roman period. Consequently, the level of information regarding this period is inferior to what we are accustomed in the research of the first to fourth centuries, although it is difficult to accept that the excavators have not fully uncovered the complete remains of the extensive fifth-century settlement. Modern archaeology has even discovered the remains of bands of nomads, and it is inconceivable that the presumed hundreds and thousands of villages from the fifth century have not yet been found. Consequently, the settlement did not completely disappear, and it is obvious that the full extent of the settlement has not been delineated, but is it improbable that the settlement in Gaul or in Spain in the fifth century had not diminished in relation to the settlement of the preceding century.

Furthermore, the economic law of supply and demand states that supply will always overtake demand. Developed economic life of the fifth century implies that whenever there was a demand for coins there would be a corresponding further supply. The kingdoms of the barbarians also were familiar with the techniques of minting coins, which in fact they issued. If the demand proved to be extensive, additional coins would be minted. It should be emphasized that the minting of coins is technically

the Middle Ages (London, 1989). The difference between their approaches does not ensue from different historical material, but rather from differences in their understanding of the sources. In our opinion, Ward-Perkins is correct: the social, cultural, political, and economic structure of the classical world changed in great measure, but the entire ancient way of life patently did not disappear, nor was the degree of change uniform in all lands. Thus, e.g., the laws pertaining to the preservation of ancient monuments which are cited by Greenhalgh (pp. 11-15) prove that these structures no longer functioned in an ongoing fashion; in the final analysis, there is no need to afford legal protection to an active structure that is defended by those using it. On the other hand, these structures, or a portion of them, still stood and were impressive, even though they were in only partial use. In this realm as well the distinctions must be made more acute, and greater use must be made of the quantitative data; the fundamental question is not one of "change" or "continuity", but rather to *what extent the change was significant, and whether the change was solely quantitative, or whether the quantitative change thereby became qualitative.*

quite simple, and it is improbable that this was beyond the abilities of the Vandal kingdoms.

If the population had maintained its standard of living, new pottery vessels would have been produced, and new types of fine ware would have developed. Their absence teaches of an economic change, and a clear process of degeneration. In effect, there are three processes, in theory separate, but which were most likely linked in a causal relationship:

1. the end of the Roman era in the west;
2. the severance of the connection between the eastern and western Mediterranean;
3. the economic decline in the West and in the East.

The evidence leads to the conclusion that the "end of the Roman era" in the West was influenced in great degree by the barbarian invasions, which constituted the main factor beginning the process; this was obviously a protracted process, and not a sharp turning point.

The following discussion will examine the cessation, or more precisely, the limitation of the economic link between the East and the West; the economic decline in the East, which lies at the center of our investigation, will be discussed separately. The economic decrease in the West, in contrast, is of lesser interest for us, for if the Eastern Empire and the western provinces ceased to be a single integrated economic system, then we are freed from the need to examine the events in the western Mediterranean.

The End of the Roman Era in the Eastern Empire

It is generally assumed that the Arabs were responsible for the destruction of the Eastern Empire. The conquests by the desert tribes turned the East into a wilderness. The Arabs are therefore not only the sons of the desert, but its creators and fathers. This general agreement has recently come under attack, and two likely explanations have been proposed.

I. Foss argues that the East suffered severe damage in the Persian conquest of 614-617.[115] He bases his thesis on a number of data:

(1) the large number of hoards indicates a great deal of tension and destruction.[116]

[115] C. Foss, "The Persians in Asia Minor and the End of Antiquity", *EHR* 90 (1975), pp. 721-47.

[116] Foss wrote his article in 1975. A number of hoards from Israel could be added to his data, but this is not the place for such a discussion.

(2) the absence or small number of coins of Heraclius, the emperor who ruled in this period, in several coin assemblages. This datum is problematic, because the small numbers of coins of an emperor who ruled ca. only thirty years are of doubtful significance, as was already noted in the methodological discussions.[117]

(3) the meager results from a number of sites in major cities in Syria and Asia Minor, in which streets and structures were damaged or abandoned in the early seventh century. The dating of the damage is problematical, and the determination of the early seventh century is generally not proven. The main problem encountered by researchers is the inability to distinguish between pottery from the beginning of the seventh century and pieces from the second or third quarters of this century, thus depriving the scholar of a reliable research tool which would aid in distinguishing between and dating the different events.

In general, Foss's grounds do not succeed in bearing the burden of proof for his thesis. Sites were damaged in the course of the Persian conquest, and the settlement fabric was harmed to some degree in the wake of the conquest, but there is insufficient proof to charge the Persian king Shapur with the destruction of the ancient world. Foss retreats somewhat from this position in a later article, by concluding that the destruction of the twenty central cities in Asia Minor came in the wake of the Persian conquest or of the Muslim conquest.[118] The information from Palestine itself is not very helpful. Based on the data which he succeeded in obtaining, Schick concluded that the damage directly caused by the Persians was significant, but was not of a long-term nature. The Jewish forces, in contrast, were directly responsible for the damage in Jerusalem and the destruction of churches in "the Tyre region," i.e., in western Upper Galilee.[119] Schick's conclusions also appear to be insufficiently based and only partial in nature, because the dating in most of the sites he mentions is not sufficiently founded. Notwithstanding all these reservations, Schick's conclusions undoubtedly indicate a well-known phenomenon: the end of the Byzantine era in Palestine was characterized by

[117] See Above Chap. 1.

[118] C. F. Foss, Archaeology and the 'Twenty Cities' of Byzantine Asia", in History and Archaeology of Byzantine Asia Minor (above, n. 57) II (*AJA* 81 [1977]), pp. 305 ff.

[119] R. Schick, "*The Fate of the Christians in Palestine in the Byzantine-Ummayyad Transition, AD 600-750*". Ph.D. diss., University of Chicago, 1987; idem, in *Bilad al-Sham during the Byzantine Period*, eds. M. A. Bakhit and R. Schick (Amman, 1989), pp. 37-48.

the abandonment of settlements, and not by a wave of destruction and burning. (The question of the division of "blame" between the Persian army and the Jewish population is not relevant to the current discussion.)

Only a meager amount of quantitative numismatic data was available to Foss. Based on new data from additional excavations (see above, Chaps. 1 and 5), the following conclusions may be drawn:

1. Egypt did not recover from the economic collapse in the fifth century. This conclusion is based on the finds from two assemblages, and obviously is only an interim finding, because two excavations are insufficient to be representative. At any rate, in Oxyrhynchus there is a rise in the number of coins after 610.
2. There is a clear and significant decrease in the number of coins after 610 in many cities. This is true of all the large assemblages from Palestine and Transjordan, such as: Jerusalem, Sebaste, Caesarea, Jerasa, and the Amman Museum, as well as Shiloh (with a small number of coins). This also the case in two of the three rich assemblages from Greece: Athens and Corinth. This phenomenon is known in Syria and in Asia Minor only in some cities, e.g.: Antioch, Ephesos.[120]
3. In a number of cities, the decrease in the number of coins had already begun in the time of Heraclius. Thus, e.g., in Troy the crisis began after 518; in Kenchreai (Greece), the crisis occurred before 602, i.e., before the reign of Focas. In Palestine, the assemblages from the Golan, Gush Halav, Membre, and other sites end in the late fifth or early sixth centuries. As in Kenchreai, there is an extremely drastic decline in Capernaum in the early seventh century.
4. In another portion of the cities of Syria and Asia Minor, the reign of Heraclius appears to be a period of continuity, and even as one of improvement and a certain amount of growth, at least according to the quantitative numismatic data. This is the case in Dehes, Ankara, Pergamon, Priene, Sardis, Constantinople, Sidi, and Curium in Cyprus.[121]

This list enables us to summarize the major processes of the sixth and seventh centuries as follows:

[120] Below Appendix A 1 and above this Chap.; for a number of examples, see: D. M. Metcalf, "The Currency of Byzantine Coins in Syrmia and Slavonia", *HBN* (Hamburg Beiträge zur Numismatik) 14 (1960), pp. 442-44.

[121] For the bibliographical data for this list, see above the current chap..

1. after the crisis of the fifth century, most portions of the Byzantine Empire recovered and rehabilitated their economy and both local and international trade.
2. Ca. the second quarter of the sixth century, a nonuniform process of decline set in. In some cities this process had already begun in 518, in other cities in 603, and in a large group of cities only in 610. In a number of cities, the economic decline began only later.
3. Although the Persian invasion certainly did not aid in the recovery of the Empire and the strengthening of its economy, there is insufficient evidence to conclude that King Shapur of Persia was chiefly responsible for the decline of the Byzantine Empire and for the undermining of its economy. The Persian invasion was included in a more general process of decline and degeneration; and the success of the invasion was more a consequence of the latter than its cause. The Persian conquest wreaked much havoc among the population at large, and was especially disastrous for the churches and the Christian leadership, but it cannot be proved that the events of these years brought about the end of the Byzantine era.

II. According to Kennedy, the Byzantine decline began in the midsixth century. No damage was caused by the Arab invasion, and the settlement system began to collapse only in the midseventh century, in the wake of the earthquake in 747/8.[122] Kennedy was quick to adopt Foss's initial conclusions and to base his theory on a number of literary testimonies regarding the agrarian nature of Byzantine cities in the early phases of Muslim rule. He blames a series of earthquakes and a widespread plague in the midsixth century for the damage suffered by the rural and urban settlement.[123] The current study will not concern itself with the possible consequences of the Arab conquest, and the discussion will be limited to the sixth century.

The literary testimonies cited by Kennedy are not convincing. Thus, e.g., Laodicea is depicted in the midseventh century as a quiet rural settlement (with Kennedy seeking to demonstrate that the city had ceased

[122] For the dating of the earthquake, see: Y. Tsafrir and G. Förster, "On the Date of the 'Sabbatical Year Earthquake'", *Tarbiz* 58 (1989), pp. 357-62, with a survey of the literature on this earthquake (Heb.).

[123] Kennedy, "The Last Century of Byzantine Syria" (above, chap. 1, n. 11), pp. 141-183; idem, "The Towns of Bilad al-Sham" (above, chap. A, n. 11), pp. 88-99. For the great famine, see: L. L. Conrad, "The Plague in Bilad al-Sham in pre-Islamic Times", in *Bilad al-Sham*, eds. Bakhit and Schick (above, n. 119), pp. 143-63.

to function as an economic center). Jones, however, has already shown that even at the apex of their growth, agriculture constituted the main branch of employment and livelihood in the Byzantine cities.[124] It is not surprising, therefore, that Laodicea is depicted as a city of farmers, and this portrayal contains no new elements. Regarding the earthquakes, we have already stated our opinion (above) that an earthquake, as an isolated factor, can cause only temporary damage, and if the settlement is sufficiently robust, it will renew and restore its buildings. An earthquake is likely to expose the weakness of a settlement which is incapable of rebuilding its dwellings, but it cannot constitute the sole source of this weakness or of the degeneration and decline suffered by the settlement.[125]

The influence of epidemics on settlement development over a span of decades is similarly unclear. Europe, e.g., required only two decades to recover from the effects of the Black Plague. Accordingly, it still remains to be shown that one or more epidemics in the seventh century exerted a significant and longlasting effect upon the settlement.[126]

Noteworthy in this context is Conrad's comment that the weakening of the settlement is likely to cause a strengthening of the nomads, who would become more powerful in the settled areas. There is no proof that such a scenario did in fact occur.[127]

Nevertheless, the quantitative numismatic data supports Kennedy's theory to a certain extent. The gradual decline did not occur in all the cities of the East, and in some the number of coins decreases only later (these processes lie beyond the scope of the present work).

Most of the surveys conducted in Israel and Jordan do not distinguish between the intermediate phases of the Byzantine period. Until recently, the distinctions between different phases of pottery were not sufficiently clear. In the Apollonia region[128] and a number of surveys in Transjordan,[129] a distinction is drawn between the "Early Byzantine" and the

[124] A. H. M. Jones, *The Roman Economy* (Oxford, 1974), pp. 35-60.

[125] See above.

[126] In Tell Kison, the authors emphasize the vast difference in the nature of the pottery vessels in the middle of the sixth century. The use of imported ware ceased in the second half of this century, with a clear shift to the use of simple, local vessels. The excavators are of the opinion that this change was due to a settlement decline caused by a major epidemic in 540. See Conrad (above, n. 92).

[127] See Conrad, loc. cit.

[128] Roll and Ayalon, *Apollonia* (below, appendix A, n. 73), p. 176.

[129] K. Yassine et al., "The East Jordan Valley Survey 1975", in *Archaeology of Jordan: Essays and Reports*, ed. K. Yassine (Amman, 1988), pp. 157-86; idem, II (Amman, 1989), pp. 187-207; G. King et al., "Survey of Byzantine and Islamic Sites in Jordan.

"Late Byzantine" periods. In two instances, there is a clear decrease in the number of settlements in the late Byzantine period. This decline may be dated between the late fifth century and the late sixth century, and it obviously may be interpreted as evidence of a protracted process of depletion and damage in the rural sector. Consequently, the testimony of the surveys is likely to serve as proof for the theory advanced in this work, of a decline in the early fifth century, for the hypothesis of Kennedy, or even as support for Foss's theory.

Was the Fifth Century Marked by Economic and/or Demographic Deterioration and the End of the Byzantine Period?

We have systematically collected proofs of impoverishment in the East in the fifth century. This process, however, is not directly connected to the end of the Byzantine era. The numismatic evidence teaches that the settlement was restored in the sixth century and recovered to a certain degree, although the extent to which this recovery was complete, comprehensive, profound, and all-inclusive cannot be unequivocally determined. In other words: if the conquest of the Western Empire influenced the East and was the cause of economic and demographic damage there, its effects were only temporary. In the sixth century almost all the markets regained their former vigor, and there is a clear increase in the number of coins. New cities were established in Palestine (Fig. 5) and in Syria. The evidence of this recovery is inconsistent with the information from rural surveys, because the rural settlement in the fifth century (to be precise, the "Late Byzantine period") experienced a permanent (and not merely temporary) decline. (Such temporary fluctuations are not expressed in surveys.) This inconsistency cannot be resolved at present. The decrease in the rural settlement may possibly have been a consequence of the growth of the cities or of the migration from small villages to larger townships;[130] it is also possible that there are merely partial, and marginal phenomena. Additional information is needed to clarify this picture.

The term "the influence of the barbarian conquests" recurs in our discussion and should be clarified. Pirenne devotes a lengthy discussion to the economic significance of the Mediterranean basin. In his estimation,

Second Preliminary Season Report", *ADAJ* 27 (1983), pp. 385-436; idem, "... Third Season Preliminary Report (1982): The Southern Ghor", *ADAJ* 31 (1987), pp. 439-59; "... Third Preliminary Report (1982), The Wadi Arabah (Part 2)", *ADAJ* 33 (1989), pp. 199-215, and several additional surveys.

130 In the Apollonia region, the decrease in a number of sites may possibly be due to the movement of villagers to the city of Apollonia, which grew considerably in the Byzantine period; see: Roll and Ayalon, loc. cit.

maritime trade made possible, and was a necessary condition for, the growth of all the lands bordering the Mediterranean. This hypothesis should be clarified. The severance of the commercial systems of the Mediterranean basin is not in itself sufficient to explain the economic decline in the East as in the West, because the markets of the former recovered in less than a century. Accordingly, an additional element in this system should be stressed. The agrarian economy of the Mediterranean lands was an integrated economy which incorporated different components from the various provinces. Each "national" economy was capable of flourishing as an independent entity, but the nature of this "national" economy had already changed in the third and fourth centuries, with a great degree of interdependence between the provinces. The sudden cessation of international commerce was responsible for the degeneration of urban trade. The influence of this severance on the rural sector is less clear (see above). This economic blow was greater in the West than in the East. At any rate, the economy of the eastern provinces succeeded in recovering, in restoring their trade systems, and in adapting the latter to the new reality of a split between East and West.

The Break between East and West

We may learn about the separation of the Byzantine Empire from the lands conquered by the barbarians from two additional sources of information which have not been fully utilized for the subject of our study. At this stage of the research, however, these two types of examination arouse methodological problems.

1. The Pottery Vessels Imported from the West to the East, or Vice Versa

Presumably, the quantity of imported pottery vessels in East-West trade should be indicative of the degree to which the two parts of the Empire were connected, as did Hodges and Whitehouse with the information regarding the ware imported from the East to North Africa.[131]

The presence or absence in the East of imported vessels from the West does not suffice for this purpose; comparative quantitative data is required. I.e., what was the percentage of amphorae or bowls from the Western Empire in the fifth century, *as compared with the third or fourth centuries*?

[131] Hodges and Whitehouse (above, n. 102).

Current research does not possess sufficient quantitative data regarding the import of vessels from the West to the East. It may be stated with certainty that throughout this entire period, the quantity of such vessels was not great.

Thanks to Hayes, it is possible to determine which types arrived in the East from the West and to date the production times of these types.[132] The data collected by Hayes from a number of sites in the eastern Mediterranean in which ARS sherds (of North African manufacture) were found reveal a clear decrease in the fifth century.[133] The number of sites in which this imported ware is represented increases once again the sixth century.[134] In the Supplement, Hayes includes an additional site, the church in Shavei Zion (in the fringe of Palestine), which contains ARS material from the fifth or sixth century.[135]

Fulford and Riley enable us to advance somewhat in this area as well. Fulford showed that the decline in pottery vessels had already begun in the early fifth century, slightly preceding the barbarian conquests.[136] This latter comment is of interest, but the degree to which accuracy of 8-10 years is obtainable in such spheres is questionable. Riley, who reexamined Hayes's data, concurs with the opinion that the import of pottery to the Eastern Empire from North Africa and from the West was greatly reduced in the fifth century.[137]

The import of pottery vessels from the East to the Western Empire as well ceased or was extremely reduced in the fifth century.[138] The city of Carthage is an exception to this general phenomenon. It experienced a dramatic upsurge in the import of amphorae from Syria, Egypt, and Palestine.[139] Fulford is most likely correct in explaining that Carthage owed its prosperity to the barbarian victories. Until the conquest,

[132] J. W. Hayes, *Late Roman Pottery* (London, 1972); idem, Supp. (London, 1980).

[133] See Hayes, maps 7-8, and cf. maps 9-16 and 27.

[134] Ibid., maps 10-11.

[135] M. W. Prausnitz, *Excavations at Shavei Zion* (Rome, 1967).

[136] M. G. Fulford, "The Red-Slipped Wares", in *Excavations at Carthage: The British Mission* I, 2 (above, chap., n. 52), pp. 113 ff.

[137] J. A. Riley, "The Coarse Pottery from Berenice", in *Excavations at Sidi Khrebish Benghasi* (above, chap. 1, n. 52), pp. 417-18. It should be noted that the pottery from a number of excavations in Israel is unpublished, or was published in languages or forums unknown to Hayes and Riley, thus leaving their conclusions open to a reexamination. Furthermore, we do not possess quantitative data regarding the pottery vessels from the East. One of the sole datum is from Caesarea: J. A. Riley, "The First Season of Excavation in the Caesarea Hippodrome", *BASOR* 218 (1975), pp. 25-63.

[138] Lewit, loc. cit.

[139] Fulford, "Carthage: Overseas Trade" (above, chap., 1, n. 52), pp. 68-80; idem, "Long Distance Trade" (above, chap., 1, n. 51), pp. 255-61.

Carthage had supplied Rome with a large quantity of grain, and it now was freed of this obligation. In purely economic terms, the export of grain as payment of taxes constitutes a flight of capital, which ceased after the barbarian conquests. The individual farmer may not have enjoyed any alleviation of tax payments, since they were merely transferred to the new rulers; the national economy, however, benefited greatly from the new conditions.

Furthermore, Carthage became the capital of a new empire, and its ensuing prosperity was easily predictable. This growth was also expressed in the quantities of coins. Carthage was exceptional in that the quantity of fifth-century coins found in the city was relatively greater than those from earlier periods (Figs. 39-42)[140]

Carthage was unique in experiencing such prosperity, which was not found in other cities in North Africa which were excavated. Quantitative finds were collected only in the excavations in Bengazi. The fifth century was a depressed period in the history of the latter city, which is expressed in a very small quantity of imported amphorae.[141] The fourth century also was a depressed period in Bengazi, the reasons for which are not pertinent to the current discussion. The numismatic finds from the African cities demonstrate that the prosperity of Carthage in the fifth century was not a general phenomenon in North Africa. A decline in the number of coins in the fifth century was perceived in Ptolemais, Apollonia, Setiff, Banasa, Sabrata (Fig. 43) and Bengazi.[142] As was noted in

[140] Humphrey, *Excavations at Carthage* I (above, chap., n. 51), pp. 151-98; idem, *Excavations at Carthage* IV (above, chap., n. 51), pp. 99-163; idem, Excavations at Carthage V (above, chap.,1, n. 51), pp. 185-269; idem, *Excavations at Carthage* VII (above, chap., 1, n. 51), pp. 63-168. For a partial summation, see: W. E. Metcalf, "Michigan Finds at Carthage 1975-1979", *AMNM* 32 (1987), pp. 61-84; idem, "The Coins – 1982" (above, Introduction, n. 50), pp. 337-82; Visona, "The Coins – 1983" (above, chap., 1, n. 51), pp. 382-422. For a summation of the coin finds from the sixth and seventh centuries, see: C. Morrison, "Coin Finds in Vandal and Byzantine Carthage", in *The Circus and a Byzantine Cemetery at Carthage* I (above, chap., 1, n. 51), pp. 423-36; R. Reece, "The Coins", in *Excavations at Carthage: The British Mission* I,1 (above, chap., 1, n. 51), pp. 171-81.

[141] J. A. Riley, "The Coarse Pottery from Berenice", in *Excavations at Sidi Khrebish Benghasi* (above, chap., 1, n. 52), pp. 253 ff.

[142] C. H. Kraeling, *Ptolemais, City of the Libyan Pentapolis* (Chicago, 1962), pp. 263-69; R. G. Goodchild et al., *Apollonia, the Port of Cyrene* (Tripoli, 1980), pp. 335 ff.; A. Mohamedi et al., *Fouilles de S'etiff 1977-1984* (unknown place 1991), pp. 230-46; R. Thouvenot, *Une colonie Romaine de Mauretanie Tingitane Valentia Banasa* (Paris, 1941), pp. 69-70; J. A. Lloyd, ed., *Excavations at Sidi Khrebish Benghazi (Berenice)* II (Tripoli, 1982), pp. 229-33; D. M. Kenrick, *Excavations at Sabratha, 1948-1951* I (London, 1986), pp. 246-74; E. Joly and F. Tomasello, *Il Tempio a Divinita' Ignota di Sabratha* (Rome, 1984), pp. 167-88; J. N. Dore and N. Keay, *Excavations at Sabratha*, 1948-1951 II (London, 1989).

chap., 1, the correlation between the quantitative pottery finds and the quantitative numismatic finds in Carthage and in Bengazi is most impressive and demonstrates their suitability as research tools.

Thus, excluding the exceptional Carthage and its environs, we may surmise that trade between the western and eastern Mediterranean was extremely limited in the fifth century. This conclusion is definite for the goods which were marketed in amphorae. We do not possess data regarding other goods, nor has research discovered the geographical bounds of the "Carthage phenomenon." Furthermore, the decrease cannot be quantified, and this conclusion is based on the collection of types and not on quantities of pottery vessels.

A large concentration of Vandal coins was found in Carthage, in contrast to the other North African cities, in which only more limited numbers of such coins were unearthed.

2. The Numismatic Evidence

The extant numismatic assemblages enable the researcher to determine the circulation in the markets of the East of the coins minted by the Vandal rulers.[143] In the absence of full comparative data, the information we possess is inconclusive. A comparison may be conducted of the quantities of Vandal coins in the various cities in the same period, thus enabling the researcher to determine that such coins were common in Greece but rare in Syria (see below), but chronological comparative data are lacking. I.e., it cannot be determined if more coins reached the markets of the West in the fifth century than in the third century. Fulford has advanced our understanding of this point,[144] and enables the researcher to propose a possible methodology. Fulford demonstrated that the supply of bronze coins was planned and not incidental, with elements of a clearly systematic policy, although the goals of such a policy are unclear. It is evident from the material that has been collected that each mint supplied coins to a specific geographic area, and adjoining mints also bore this responsibility. Fulford's data would seem to imply that the coins produced in distant mints were brought by mer-

[143] At the same time, it is possible to examine the circulation of the coins of the Byzantine emperors in the marketplaces of the West (see below).

[144] M.G. Fulford, "Coin Circulation and Mint Activity in the Late Roman Empire: Some Economic Implications", *The Archaeological Journal* 135 (1978), pp. 67-114; R. Duncan-Jones, *Money and Government in the Roman Empire* (Cambridge, 1994), pp. 172.

chants, tourists, or administrative and military officials who traveled from one region to another.[145] This assumption, although logical, is as yet unproved.[146]

The basic factual material was collected by Kienast, Carson and Kent, King and Spaer, and especially by Kent, Ryan, and Depeyrot (Gaul).[147] It may be concluded in a most general manner that approx. 10-20 percent of the coins did not originate in local mints, which may possibly attest to the volume of international trade in these specific markets.[148]

Also to be examined are the numbers of coins issued by the Vandal rulers that reached the markets of the East, and the quantities of Byzantine coins from the fifth and sixth centuries that appeared in the West. The quantities of Vandal coins in the markets of the East were undoubtedly very limited. In Sidi, Pergamon, Troy, Apamea, Priene, Tarsus, and Karanis, there are no Vandal coins; a single coin of this type was found in Sardis; and only 25 coins (less than 3 percent) in Antioch. In Palestine and Syria: there are no traces of such coins in Jerasa, Sebaste, and Jerusalem; a concentration of Vandal coins was found in Caesarea, but this may be attributed to the movement of pilgrims to the holy places in Palestine.[149] One of the many hoards from Egypt contains numerous

[145] The calculation of the coins must take into account the possibility, e.g., that a merchant coming from Antioch to Gaul would bring with him copper coins from his city. This assemblage, however, already included coins from the West, corresponding to the representation of such coins in the marketplaces of Antioch.

[146] If coins from distant mints are indeed reflective of trade, then it may be assumed that faraway mints would have a greater representation in cities which were trade centers. It also follows that distant mints would be underrepresented in villages and centers in which trade did not play a major role. Consequently, material must be gathered from throughout the Empire, in order to determine whether the proposed modes of behavior are present.

[147] J. P. C. Kent, *The Roman Imperial Coinage VIII: The Family of Constantine* I (London, 1981), pp. 91-115; C. E. King and A. Spaer, "A Hoard of Folles from Northern Sinai", *NC* 137 (1977), pp. 64-112; R. A. G. Carson and J. P. C. Kent, "Constantinian Hoards and Other Studies in the Later Roman Bronze Coinage", *NC* Sixth Series, 16 (1956), pp. 83-161; D. Kienast, "Der Münzfund von Ankara", *Jahrbuch für Numismatic und Geldgeschichte* 12 (1962), pp. 65-112; N. S. Ryan, *Fourth Century Coin Finds from Roman Britain, a Computer Analysis* (*BAR* 183) (Oxford, 1988), pp. 94-109; G. Depeyrot, *Le Numeraire gaulois de iv siecle* (*BAR* 127) (Oxford, 1982).

[148] Kent collected data from excavations and from hoards, and distinguished between the two. In our opinion, the hoard represents the currency of an individual person which he buried. Consequently, this evidence is incidental and episodic. Thus, e.g., the coins in the hoard of an innkeeper whose establishment was located at the exit from the harbor would be more "international" in composition than that of a large-scale real estate dealer or of a wealthy slave trader. Accordingly, data based on excavations are to be preferred.

[149] Hamburger (below Appendix a, n. 81).

Vandal coins, but this is insufficient to determine that these coins were common in Egypt.[150]

In Curium and in Athens, on the other hand, these coins are represented in large numbers, thus attesting to trade between these regions and Carthage. All in all, only a very small quantity of coins from the conquered part of the Empire reached the East in the fifth century. This finding corresponds precisely with the extremely small quantity of ARS ware in excavations of sites in the East from this period (see above).

Similarly, few fifth-century Byzantine coins appeared in the markets of Italy, Gaul, Germany, Spain, or Britain.[151]

Nevertheless, all the above data still do not constitute decisive proof of a small volume of trade between East and West. Coins from the fourth century were used in the fifth century in the markets of the western Mediterranean.[152] Accordingly, when, e.g., merchants from Gaul came to Syria in the fifth century, they brought with them their local coins, i.e., those that had been minted in the previous century. Consequently, the absence of coins that had been struck in the barbarian states in the fifth century from the markets of the East does not indicate a paucity of trade with these lands, but rather represents the coins in circulation in the latter. One would expect, however, that the merchants of Syria, who came to Treves, Carnuntum, Leon, or London in the fifth century would have brought with them Byzantine coins minted in the fifth century, for such coins were in use in the East (see above, chapter 1). The fact that there are few extant Byzantine coins from the sixth and seventh centuries in the Western Empire, and even fewer from the fifth century, teaches of the tenuous ties between the East and the West. A clear change occurred in the fifth century, due to the barbarian conquests, as is indicated by an analysis of all the numismatic assemblages in the West.[153]

Consequently, the two methods of investigation which we have proposed teach of the low level of East-West trade after 408. These two examinations are not methodically perfect, but they undoubtedly provide

[150] W. R. O. Hahn, "A Sixth-Century Hoard of Byzantine Small Change from Egypt, and Its Contribution to the Classification of African Minimi", *NC* 140 (1980), pp. 64-70.

[151] The situation was different in Cyrenaica, and esp. in Carthage.

[152] See above, Chap. 1.

[153] Theree is no need to collect data regarding the relative scarcity of Byzantine coins in excavations in the Western Empire after the time of Arcadius-Honorius, since this well-known fact is taught in every introduction to the subject, and is represented in every chronological registration of coin assemblages from the West. In this instance, the claimed later usage of fourth-century coins is more probable.

data which enable us to identify the developing trends and indicate reduced commercial ties between the Byzantine East and the barbarian West. This does not relate to the question, if the lands of the western Mediterranean suffered economic damage and if they experienced a demographic and economic decline. This work is concerned with the Eastern Empire, and all that has been proven regarding the West is that the barbarian invasions disrupted the ties between the two parts of the Empire. This severance would critically affect the East; its influence upon the Western Empire is deserving of a separate discussion.

Conclusion

All the data we possess tend to support the opinion of Baynes, that the barbarian conquests severely damaged the economy of the western Mediterranean and led to the end of the Roman era in the region. The fall of most of the western provinces and the reduction of East-West trade proved to be a crushing economic blow to the previously flourishing major markets in the Eastern Empire. It would take the East 85 years to recover and adapt itself to the new political reality.

This discussion would not be complete without a chronological note: the decrease in the number of coins began in 408. The decline may possibly have begun a few years earlier, during the reign of Arcadius; or even somewhat later, since coins remain in circulation for several decades.

If the decline was indeed brought on by a political event, we should not expect to find an acute and well-defined turning point. No change took place the day after the fall of Rome, Carthage, or Londinium, neither in agricultural production nor in commercial transactions, beyond the limited damage directly caused by the conquest and the victorious armies. Instead, we should anticipate a prolonged process the influences of which would be felt only decades later.

CHAPTER SIX

Conclusions

In the course of our discussion, we have examined a number of processes which occurred in Palestine in the fourth and fifth centuries, after devoting an entire chapter to methodological discussions concerning the methods of examining the data.

I. The Settlement-Economic Data

a) The process of growth and development, which had already begun in the third century, intensified throughout Palestine in the first half of the fourth century.
b) Two contradictory processes evolved in the second half of the fourth century:
   i) a process of degeneration began in western Galilee, the Carmel, Samaria, and Judea, and to some extent in the coastal plain as well;
   ii) in contrast, growth continued in the Golan, eastern Upper Galilee, the Tiberias Valley, and possibly also in the southern Hebron hill country and in Transjordan, with a strengthening of the settlement.
c) The settlement regressed greatly in the fifth century. In the settlements belonging to group b(i), the decrease became a general collapse, with a slower decline in group b(ii).
d) The sixth century was marked by some degree of recovery throughout Palestine. This phenomenon lies beyond the extent of the current work, and we have been content to cite a number of archaeological proofs of its existence.
e) the settlement decline was expressed, inter alia, in severe damage to trade. The devastation in the economic sphere was naturally more acute than the demographic loss.

II. The Ethno-Religious Data

a) The Jewish community was weakened in the second half of the fourth century, and suffered severe damage in the fifth century. This situation was intimately connected to the settlement fluctuations in Galilee, which was the heart of the Jewish settlement. The Jewish community in the Golan and southern Judea maintained stability, but this population was incapable of renewing religious and cultural life and the batei midrash, or of reconstructing the unique nature of the Talmudic literary output of the Talmudic period.

b) Christianity became the religion of the masses only in the second half of the fifth century.
c) The movement of conversion to Christianity apparently began to assume significant dimensions only in the sixth century, mainly among the pagan population.
d) The nature and quality of the Talmudic literary product changed after the fourth century. This change corresponds chronologically to the changes in the fate of the Jewish community in Galilee, and apparently was a consequence of them.

III. The Economic-Agrarian Data

a) Processes of economic degeneration and decreased trade were discerned throughout the entire East in the fifth century (see below, [d]).
b) A change or upheaval occurred in the agrarian structure of Palestine. The agrarian society based on small-scale agriculture became one based on sharecropping and on large estate owners. This process led to the transfer of resources from the village to the city and to intensified urbanization in Palestine.

IV. Settlement History in the Eastern Mediterranean

a) In the first half of the fifth century, beginning after 408, the number of coins decreased throughout the Byzantine Mediterranean basin (Syria, Asia Minor, Cyprus, Transjordan, and Judea).
b) It may be assumed that this decrease reflects economic ruin, and probably a demographic collapse as well.
c) The incursions by the barbarians and the conquest of the West and its ensuing economic disengagement apparently were the main causes of the process of economic decline.
d) A process of decline in the number of coins began in the early seventh century, or possibly somewhat earlier. This pattern of economic decay was neither uniform nor constant.

V. The Background of the Economic and Demographic Processes

We have attempted to assemble all the known data and propose one or more explanations for all these processes.

a) We suggested that the main process in Palestine was one of a rapidly expanding population and over-utilization of land. This situation intensified in the fourth century and was responsible for a crisis in the following century. This crisis would naturally have been more severe in the areas of longer settlement, in which the depletion of land resources had occurred over a longer period.
b) In addition, the entire East suffered an economic crisis. There was a clear demographic and economic decline in Egypt, and a reduction in commerce in Syria, Phoenicia, and Transjordan. Consequently, the excess income of the wealthy provinces in the East diminished, and their ability to purchase consumer goods dwindled. The agricultural economy in Palestine, which had been based in great measure on this trade, accordingly suffered and was forced to undergo structural change.
c) A parallel, or consequential, agrarian change occurred which also led to many difficulties in the economy of Palestine. We have not offered an explanation for this change; it may possibly have been a general and "natural" pattern affecting the entire Byzantine Empire.

VI. Events of Local Importance

These central processes were accompanied by local processes and events which merged with the general pattern and imparted to it a critical nature.

a) The revolt of Gallus: we have demonstrated that the revolt in 351/2 caused serious harm to only a limited number of Jewish communities and settlements; the population as a whole did not incur significant damage.
b) The earthquake in 363 destroyed many settlements. We regard this as a localized phenomenon which by itself was incapable of effecting settlement processes. It did, however, serve as a sort of coup de grace, and exposed a profound, but previously obscure, process.

c) The Christian pressure constituted an additional factor:
   1) Until the fifth century, there were few Christian attacks against non-Christian ritual sites.
   2) The anti-Jewish legislation only marginally affected the life of the Jews, but did, however, contribute to the sensation of suffocation and pressure felt by the Jewish community at the time.
3) The daily and tangible social pressure exerted against the Jewish communities was marginal in extent, although its emotional effect cannot be evaluated.

Appendix A

The Archaeological Finds and Numismatic Material in Palestine

Many hundreds of excavations have been conducted throughout Israel, of tels, entire neighborhoods, structures (especially public structures), and installations. Surveys have also been conducted of extensive areas in the country. As was stated above, the dating of the Byzantine material in many excavations is problematic, because of the difficulty entailed in distinguishing between pottery from the fourth century, the fifth century, and the succeeding centuries. This appendix summarizes data from many of the major excavations, mainly those whose final reports have been published. Major emphasis was placed on excavations and surveys in which significant numismatic assemblages were uncovered. At this stage of the research, the numismatic finds constitute the best basis for settlement dating, and also serve the researcher as an important tool for quantifying the processes of growth, decline, and regression in the various sites.

The sites are presented by a regional division indicated by the quantitative numismatic examination. This categorization approximates, but is not identical with, the administrative division of the province.

Western Galilee

Jalame – An estate house or village and the surrounding area were excavated.[1] The site was most active in the fourth century, until 363, although a decline in the numismatic finds is not noticeable in this year, but only ca. 383, in which the site collapsed. The fifth century is represented by extremely sparse finds (Fig. 44).

'Ammudim – the finds consist solely of pottery in the synagogue (Fig. 45). The quantity of sherds indicate that the settlement reached its apex in the second half of the third century, followed by a gradual decline, with no pottery finds from the fifth century. It may be assumed that the settlement ceased to be active or, at the very least, deteriorated drastically.[2]

[1] G. D. Weinberg, ed., *Excavations at Jalame and Their Chronological Implications* (Columbia, Miss., 1988), p. 104.

[2] D. Adan-Bayewitz, "The Ceramics from the Synagogue of Horvat 'Ammudim", *IEJ* 32 (1982), pp. 28-29. An inspection tour I conducted seemed to indicate later activity at

Kefar Hananyah – There is a noticeable decline in the second half of the fourth century, and the near cessation of activity in the fifth century.[3]

Meron – there is a drastic decrease in the number of coins in the second half of the fourth century. The fifth and sixth centuries are barely represented (Fig. 46).[4]

Khirbet Shema'– according to the results of Meyers et al., the height of activity at the site was in the first half of the fourth century. There is a noticeable decline in the second half of the century, and an almost total cessation of activity in the fifth century. The quantitative numismatic analysis yields slightly different results (Fig. 47). The numismatic finds do not attest to a sharp decline in the second half of the fourth century; there is only a minor difference between the two periods, and it is not expressed in the graph.[5] In the fifth century there is a drastic decrease.

Sepphoris – Only the assemblage of coins discovered in the excavations conducted in the 1930s has been published in its entirety.[6] The extensive excavations conducted in the 1980s are as yet unpublished (Fig. 48), but the publications and summation of the numismatic finds seem to indicate a severe decline in the degree of activity in the city in the midfourth century.[7] The excavations conducted in 1931 provide only a small amount of information of greater accuracy. Based on the hundreds of coins which were discovered, the city apparently underwent a crisis in 364, and the quantity of coins from this and following years is smaller (104 coins from 305-364, compared with only 22 coins from 364-408). This collection contains no coins from the fifth century, and the following two centuries are represented by poor finds consisting of only 12 coins.

the site. A structure located approx. 50 m. to the south of the synagogue contained evidence possibly attesting to later and secondary usage of architectural elements which were taken from the synagogue or from another magnificent structure. It was not possible to date this activity.

3 My thanks to D. Adan-Bayewitz for this information.

4 J. Raynor and Y. Meshorer, *The Coins of Ancient Meiron* (Winona Lake, 1988), pp. 83 ff.

5 A number of coins are attributed in this catalog to the late fourth and early fifth centuries. In order to conduct the analysis, these coins were listed as belonging to the second half of the fourth century; in their analysis, the authors listed only a portion of them as fourth century coins. See: E. M. Meyers et al., *Ancient Synagogue Excavations at Khirbet Shema', Upper Galilee, Israel 1970-1972* (Durham, 1976), pp. 155-63, 281-89.

6 L. Watterman, *Preliminary Report of the University of Michigan Excavations at Sepphoris*, Palestine, in 1931 (Ann Arbor, 1937), pp. 35-77.

7 E. Meyers et al., "Sepphoris – 'Ornament of all Galilee'", *BA* 49 (1986), p. 9.

It is obvious that the city continued to exist, as is evident from literary sources. This is corroborated by the new excavations (as yet unpublished).

Qedesh – the temple in this Phoenician town ceased its activity in 363. The town itself was not excavated.[8]

Tel Dan – The activity of the altar also finally ceased its activity in this period.[9] The subject of the total suspension of activity of the temples entails an examination of the Christianization of Palestine.[10]

Nahf – the kiln in the settlement ceased its activity in the fourth century.[11] A tomb in the settlement also was abandoned in the midfourth century, after the time of Constantine I.[12]

Yehi'am – a well-dated tomb which fell into disuse in the midfourth century.[13]

Peki'in and *'Arabah* – tombs in which activity ceased in the late fourth century.[14]

Rama – A bathhouse was discovered which had been active until the middle or end of the fourth century. In the fifth century a house or villa was established on its ruins.[15]

Hanita-Nahariyah region – a number of tombs were excavated, in all of which burial ceased in the midfourth century, probably after 363.[16] In contrast, in the tombs, excavated by D. Barag in the same region, burials ceased only in the late fourth century.[17] These finds are less significant, because a tomb may have fallen into disuse because of personal reasons.

8 A. Ovadiah et al, "the Roman Temple at Qedesh in Upper Galilee", *Qadmoniot* 60 (*1983*), pp. 121-25 (Heb.).

9 See: A. Biran, "An Incense Altar and Other Discoveries at Dan", *Qadmoniot* 73-74 (1986), p. 28 (Heb.); A. Biran and V. Tsaferis, "A Bilingual Dedicatory Inscription from Tel Dan", Qadmoniot 40 (1978), pp. 114-16 (Heb.).

10 Also see below, Chap. 4.

11 P. Vito, "The Potter's Workshop in Kfar Nahf", in *The Western Galilee Antiquities*, ed. M. Yedaya (Tel Aviv, 1986), pp. 451-56 (Heb.).

12 V. Sussman, "A Tomb at Nahf", *'Atiqot Hebrew Series* 8, pp. 31-32.

13 V. Tsaferis, "Tombs in Western Galilee", *'Atiqot Hebrew Series* 5 (1969), pp. 72-75 (Heb.).

14 Tsaferis (above, n. 13), pp. 75-77.

15 V. Tsaferis, "A Roman Bath at Rama", *'Atiqot English Series* 14 (1980), pp. 66-75.

16 For the literature, see: Barag (below, n. 17), p. 400; M. Peleg, "Persian, Hellenistic and Roman Burials at Lohamei HaGeta'ot", 'Atiqot 20 (1991), pp. 131-52; M. Sharabani, "Coins from Lohamei HaGeta'ot", ibid., pp. 156-58.

17 D. Barag, "Cemeteries from the Roman Period in Nahariya", in The *Western Galilee Antiquities*, pp. 397-405 (Heb.).

This instance, however, consists of a series of tombs, and should be considered together with the above-mentioned testimony. The tombs apparently served a non-Jewish population. Tombs in the vicinity of Kibbutz Lohamei ha-Geta'ot present a similar picture of the abandonment of tombs in the midfourth century, which is also confirmed by the small number of coins found at the site.[18]

Many other tombs throughout Israel which are dated to this period of the fourth century fell into disuse at the end of the century, or, at the very least, the numismatic finds cease at the end of this century. Each individual tomb may be interpreted as a random find, but their very numbers constitute testimony of some importance.[19]

Nahariyah – The coins are unpublished. The initial report indicates that many of the 100 coins are from the fourth century and a few from the sixth century, while the fifth century is not represented at all.[20]

The *Galilee panhandle* is marked by a settlement decline in the late fourth century. We don't know much about Paneas, although this city is known from literary sources.[21] A fine Jewish cave tomb which fell into disuse in the midfourth century was excavated in Tel Hai.[22] In Metulla, in contrast, a cave tomb was uncovered which remained in constant use throughout the entire Byzantine period.[23] In the absence of coins or other clear evidence, this find is doubtful, and it cannot negate the possibility of a decline in the use of the tomb, or total cessation of its activity, in the fifth century.

Beth She'arim – the activity at this central site stopped in the midfourth century. The rich hoard from the synagogue area (1200 coins) dates from the period 307-352, when the settlement apparently suffered severe damage

[18] Sharabani, loc. cit.

[19] E.g., J. H. Iliffe, "Rock-Cut Tomb at Tarshisha", *QDAP* 3 (1934), pp. 9-16; idem, "A Tomb at el Bassa of c. A.D. 396", *QDAP* 3 (1934), pp. 81-91.

[20] "Numismatic News: Coins from Excavations in Nahariya", *INJ* II:1-2 (1964), p. 45. The delay in publication is regrettable, as is the fact that the material in the museum in Nahariya is neither cataloged nor registered.

[21] U. Z. Maoz, "Banias, Temple of Pan – 1989", *Hadashot Arkheologiyot* 95 (1990), pp. 1-2 (Heb.). The excavator has recently proposed that the temple precinct was destroyed only in the sixth century, see: Z. U. Ma'oz, "The Sacred Precinct of Pan – Banias", in *The Eighteenth Archaeological Congress in Israel*: *Booklet of Abstracts* (Tel Aviv, 1992), p. 26 (Heb.).

[22] N. Feig, "A Burial Cave at Tel Hai", *'Atiqot Hebrew Series* 10 (1990), pp. 165-67 (Heb.).

[23] V. Tsaferis, "A Tomb Near Metulla", *'Atiqot Hebrew Series* 8 (1982), pp. 26-30 (Heb.).

during the rebellion of Gallus.[24] Activity at the site resumed in the sixth century. The pottery finds attest to a Christian presence.[25] In addition, an estate house was excavated in the upper part of the settlement.[26]

Summaqa – Approx. 80 coins were discovered during the four excavation seasons, all from the fourth century (Fig. 49). No coins from the fifth century were discovered at the site, while there is a clear renewal of activity in the sixth and seventh centuries.[27]

This list is complemented by a series of unpublished sites, all of which experienced a severe reduction in the number of coins in the second half of the fourth century, and the complete or almost complete absence of coins in the fifth century, after the year 408, including: Kh. Tiriya, Even Menahem, Mazuba, Horvat Mamziyah, the "Abdon road" site, Tirat ha-Carmel, and Tel Wawiyat; only a small number of coins was discovered in each of these sites.[28]

Beth Shean Valley

Scythopolis – The numismatic finds from the excavations of Fitzgerald attest to continued activity in the fifth century,[29] as is also indicated by the preliminary reports of the current excavators. According to this initial report, the current excavations uncovered 974 coins from the fourth century, and 2,666 bronze coins and many gold coins from the fifth century.[30] These finds and the pottery evidence attest to unprecedented growth in Scythopolis in the fifth century. Recent excavations have begun to uncover settlement phases from the fourth century; these finds are as yet unpublished.

[24] See below, Chap. 4. The coins are presently in the collection of the Israel Antiquities Authority. See *NEAEHL* (1993), p. 239. I examined the collection in the IAA archives.

[25] B. Mazar, "Those Who Buried Their Dead in Beth-Shearim", *Eretz-Israel* 18 (1985), p. 293 (Heb.).

[26] P. Vitto, Byzantine Mosaics at Bet She'arim. New Evidence for the History of the Site, *Atiqot* 28 (1996), pp. 115-146.

[27] My thanks to S. Dar, the excavator of the site, who showed me the material and permitted me to publish this information in his name.

[28] According to the IAA archives. My thanks to V. Tsaferis for allowing me to publish this datum.

[29] G. M. Fitzgerald, *Beth-Shan Excavations 1921-23: The Arab and Byzantine Levels*, vol. III (Philadelphia, 1931), pp. 51-60; idem, A *Sixth Century Monastery at Beth-Shan (Scythopolis)* (Philadelphia, 1939), pp. 11-12.

[30] Y. M. Yannai, "The Numismatic Finds from the 1988-1989 Seasons", *Hadashot Arkheologiyot* 95 (1990), p. 37 (Heb.).

[31] The hoard discovered in the settlement contains coins from these centuries See A. Paltiel, "A Hoard of Byzantine Gold Coins from the City of Rehob", *Alon – Internal Quarterly of the Israel Numismatic Society* 3 (1969), pp. 101-6 (Heb.).

The synagogue in *Rehob* was established in the fifth century and was active until the late Byzantine period, and perhaps afterwards as well.

Beth Alpha – the synagogue was established in the sixth century.[32]

Ma'oz Hayyim – the first synagogue was constructed in the late third-early fourth century and restored in the fifth century, when it reached its peak, while a third synagogue from the sixth century is of very inferior construction.[33] Coins from the fourth and sixth centuries were uncovered at the site, and the fifth century is not represented at all.[34]

A few coins were found in *Tel Bazul* and in Kibbutz Gesher. In both instances, the second half of the fourth century is most heavily represented, and only a few fifth-century coins were found.[35]

Golan – Eastern Upper Galilee

'En Nashut – (Fig. 50)[36], *Horvat Kanaf*[37] (Fig. 51) and *Dabiyye* (Fig. 52)[38] – this sites characterized by few coins from the first half of the fourth century, while the finds from the second half of the century are predominant The fifth century is not represented, because the sites consists of the foundations of a synagogue which apparently was established in the fifth century and which was active only briefly.

Qasrin – the finds have not been published in their entirety; in this case as well, the synagogue apparently was established only in the fifth century, the period in which the settlement was active and flourished.[39]

There is a brief description of a hoard from the Golan from the time of Diocletian to Constantinus I.[40] This private hoard is of importance only in conjunction with additional early fourth century testimonies of the growth of the Golan.

32 E. L. Sukenik, *The Ancient Synagogue of Beth Alpha* (Jerusalem and London, 1932), p. 48.

33 V. Tsaferis, "The Ancient Synagogue at Ma'oz Hayyim", *IEJ* 32 (1982), pp. 215-44.

34 According to the IAA archives.

35 According to the IAA archives.

36 D. T. Ariel, "Coins from the Synagogue at 'En Nashut", *IEJ* 37 (1987), pp. 147-57.

37 Ibid., "Coins from the Synagogue at Horvat Kanef, Preliminary Report", *INJ* 4 (1980), pp. 59-62. I used the draft of the final report, which Ariel graciously showed me, for which I am grateful.

38 Ibid., "Coins from the Synagogue at Dabiyye", *'Atiqot* 20 (1991), pp. 74-80.

39 Z. U. Ma'oz and A. Killebrew, "Ancient Qasrin: Synagogue and Village", *BA* 51 (1988), pp. 5-19.

40 Coin Hoards III (1977), p. 64, No. 190.

Givat'Orha – the settlement was destroyed in the midfourth century.[41]

Meroth – the synagogue in Meroth (Upper Galilee), like its counterparts in the Golan, was established in the late fourth-early fifth century. Coins dating until the end of the fourth century were found in the foundations of the structure, some of which were from the hoard of the synagogue fund. The excavator reports briefly of additional coins discovered in the settlement from the fifth and sixth centuries.[42] Partial information regarding another group of these coins indicates that most of the coins in the assemblage are from the second half of the fourth century. There is a 50 percent decline in the number of coins from the fifth century. It should be emphasized that these finds are partial in nature.[43]

Capernaum – (Figs. 53-4). Scholarly opinion differs concerning the dating of the synagogue. The date of the establishment of the synagogue is not relevant for the purposes of the current discussion. All scholars agree, however, that significant activity was conducted at the site in the fifth century.[44] The numismatic and pottery finds indicate the growth and prosperity of the settlement in the early fourth century and of additional growth (an increase in the second half of the century, and decline in the following century.[45] Some of the coins were found under the pavement of the synagogue, and it presumably could be argued that their meager numbers are a consequence of the establishment of the structure and the "sealing" of the hoard. The numismatic finds in the other parts of the settlement, however, are similar (Fig. 54). Consequently, the activity in the settlement continued, as it did in the Golan settlements and in Meroth, but with a smaller number of coins, ensuing either from a reduction of general activity in the settlement or from a decline in cash transactions.

The additional excavations conducted throughout the settlement have yielded only small quantities of coins, but they clearly attest to settlement continuity into the Arab period.[46]

[41] *NEAEHL* (1993), pp. 522-23.

[42] Z. Ilan and E. Damati, *Meroth: The Ancient Jewish Village* (Tel Aviv, 1987), pp. 118, 126-27 (Heb.).

[43] The material is as yet unpublished; A. Kindler was kind enough to show me the material and his summations.

[44] For this discussion, see: Y. Tsafrir, "The Synagogue at Meroth, the Synagogue at Capernaum, and the Dating of the Galilean Synagogues: A Reconsideration", *Eretz-Israel* 20 (1989), pp. 337-44 (Heb.).

[45] A. Spijkerman, *Cafarnao III Catalogo Della Monete della Citta* (Jerusalem, 1975).

[46] V. Tsaferis, *Excavations at Capernaum, I 1978-1982* (Winona Lake, 1989), pp. 131-38, 213-21; V. Tsaferis and M. Peleg, "Excavations at Capernaum", *Qadmoniot* 16 (1983), pp. 72-76 (Heb.).

En-Nabratein – the complete results are as yet unpublished. This synagogue is located in the geographical corridor between Gischala and Meron, on the one hand, and Meroth, on the other hand. The synagogue was damaged in the midfourth century and was abandoned in the fifth century, as were Meron and Gischala, but flourished anew in the sixth century, as did Meroth.[47]

Kursi – only a few coins were found at the site, mainly from the first half of the fourth century. The second half of the fourth century and the sixth century are not represented.[48] The holy site continued to attract pilgrims in the eighth century.[49]

Tiberias – intensive excavations are currently being conducted in the city, and the history of the finds in the area cannot be summarized before the publication of the excavations. A large synagogue from the fourth century which was destroyed in the early fifth century was uncovered in nearby Hammath Tiberias (stratum IIB). The excavator proposes the earthquake in 419 as the cause of the destruction.[50] The structure was later rebuilt in the sixth century.

Chorazin – the final report has not been published, but the numismatic data are clear (Fig. 55) Most of the coins are from the fourth century, with a distinct increase in the second half of the century, and a major decrease in the number of coins after 408.[51]

Part of the decline in the number of coins may be explained by the normal activity of the synagogue in the fifth century, which precluded the placement of coins from this century in its foundations. The coins were also collected, however, from other loci, and they therefore are indicative of the settlement as a whole, as is clearly attested by a comparison of the finds in different loci at the site.[52]

[47] E. M. Meyers et al., "Preliminary Report of the 1980 Excavations at en-Nabratein, Israel", *BASOR* 244 (1981), p. 23.

[48] M. Sharabani, "Coins", in V. Tsaferis, "The Excavations of Kursi-Gergesa", *'Atiqot* 16 (1983), pp. 39-40.

[49] See: Eutyches of Alexandria, para. 321.

[50] M. Dothan, *Hammath Tiberias: Early Synagogues and the Hellenistic and Roman Remains* (Jerusalem, 1983), pp. 64-66, 71-74.

[51] For the first publication, see: Z. Yeivin, "Excavations at Khorazin", *Eretz-Israel* 11 (1973), pp. 144-57 (Heb.). A few coins were published by Meshorer: Y. Meshorer, "Coins from the Excavations at Khorazin", *idem*, pp. 158-62 (Heb.). Our summary was prepared with the aid of the final report prepared by D. Ariel. The report is unpublished, and my thanks to the author for showing me the material and confirming the data. These finds were combined with the coins published by Kloetzli (below, n. 52).

[52] See, e.g., G. Kloetzli, "Coins from Khorazin", *LA* 20 (1970), pp. 359-69.

Hammath-by-Gadera – the bathhouse was constructed or restored in the fifth century, while the finds in the rest of the site are of interest. Coins dating until the midfourth century were found in the theater, but only from the sixth century in the synagogue.[53] Coins from the fifth century were found in the bathhouse and the surrounding area. The excavations of the bathhouse have not been published in their entirety, and therefore our conclusions are only partial.

Arbel – the settlement was surveyed quite carefully, and more than 170 coins were collected as random finds. The publication provided only a schematic division, 74 coins from the fourth century were found and 19 from the fifth century, all of them "from before 450".[54] It may be presumed that at least some of the coins from the "fifth century" were minted before 408, and it is clear that the settlement continued to exist in the fifth century, but with a sharp decrease in its activity.

Khirbet al-Karak – the monastery at the site was established in the sixth century. Few coins were found at the site, and there is a clear settlement gap between 337 and 565.[55]

Gush Halav (Gischala) – the pottery finds indicate that activity reached a peak in the first half of the fourth century. There is a drastic decline beginning in the second half of the century, encompassing the years 360-460. The excavators attribute sparse continued activity to a later period.[56] The numismatic finds indicate a significant decline in the second half of the fourth century [57] and an additional sharp drop in the fifth century, but the site was not abandoned in this century as well (Fig. 56 Furthermore a hoard from the fifth century was found in the synagogue (Fig. 57 consequently, the activity at the site and in the synagogue continued in this century, as it did in the other "eastern" sites. The settlement continued to exist in the sixth century, but the small number of coins (only 4) attests to its decline and poverty.

[53] E. L. Sukenik, *The Ancient Synagogue of el-Hammeh (Hammath-by-Gadara)* (Jerusalem, 1935).

[54] M. Dolev, "Coins from Horvat Arbel", in *Arbel*, eds. Z. Ilan and A. Izdarecht (Tel Aviv, 1988), p. 30 (Heb.). The material in this article is different from that in the IAA archives.

[55] P. Delougaz and K. C. Haines, *A Byzantine Church at Khirbat al-Karak* (Chicago, 1960), pp. 50-52. These excavations, which were concentrated in the church, unearthed two coins from the third and fourth centuries, and 12 from 565-641.

[56] E. M. and C. L. Meyers, eds., *Meiron Excavations Project 5. Excavations at the Ancient Synagogue of Gush Halav* (Winona Lake, 1990), pp. 7-13.

[57] Ibid., pp. 230-45.

Not far from the synagogue, within the bounds of the present-day Gush Halav, previous excavations revealed a Christian tomb with Jewish-Christian amulets.[58]

Samaria

Qedumim – the village was active in the third-fifth centuries, and was destroyed only in the late fifth century, apparently in the Samaritan revolts, and was not rebuilt.[59]

Shiloh – (fig. 58) coins were found only in the Danish excavations, in which a church from the Roman-Byzantine period was uncovered. The site began to expand in the fourth and fifth centuries. 26 coins from the fourth century (to 408) and 37 coins from the fifth century were discovered. This was followed by a certain decline in the quantity of coins; the church was established at the site in the fifth century.[60] Shiloh was a pilgrimage site, and the growth of the settlement is not necessarily indicative of the regional history. Only meager remains from the Roman-Byzantine period were found within the village itself.[61] Similar finds were discovered in additional churches in Bahan and in Ramat Rahel.

Samaria-Sebaste – (Fig. 59) Samaria was excavated twice. Reisner et al., provided only partial report of the numismatic finds, and the later coins are described in a concise and general manner, since they were not of sufficient interest from the limited viewpoint of these pioneering scholars.[62] The second excavations, which were conducted by Crowfoot et al., yielded many coins which were properly documented.[63] About a generation later, additional finds of coins from Sebaste were published.[64] For our purposes, the researcher has at his disposal three assemblages of coins from antiquity: the Second Temple period (Reisner

[58] N. Makhouly, "Rock-Cut Tombs at El Jish", *QDAP* 8 (1939), pp. 45-50.

[59] Y. Magen, "Qedumim – A Samaritan Site of the Roman-Byzantine Period", *Qadmoniot* 62-63 (1983), pp. 76-83 (Heb.).

[60] *F. G. Andersen, Shiloh II: The Remains from the Hellenistic to the Mamluk Periods* (Copenhagen, 1985), pp. 102-7.

[61] I. Finkelstein informed me of this orally. See: I. Finkelstein, *Shiloh, The Archaeology of a Biblical Site* (Tel Aviv, 1993).

[62] G. A. Reisner et al., *Harvard Excavations at Samaria, 1908-1910* (Cambridge, 1924), pp. 252 ff.

[63] J. W. Crowfoot, *The Objects from Samaria* (London, 1957), pp. 43-70.

[64] W. J. Fulco and F. Zayadine, "Coins from Samaria-Sebaste", *ADAJ* 25 (1981), pp. 197-225.

et al.; Crowfoot et al.; Fulco and Zayadine), but only the latter two assemblages, from the Roman and Byzantine periods, are relevant to our discussion.

There was significant economic growth in Sebaste in the first half of the fourth century (the quantity of coins is five times as large!). The second half of the century is marked by a drastic decline, with an acute collapse in the fifth century. The sixth and seventh centuries witnessed a minor recovery, which continued until ca. 750 (until the earthquake in 747).

Northern Samaria – a private hoard of coins from the time of Constans I to Julian (363). Since this is a private and random hoard, it is not highly indicative of the settlement in the entire region.[65]

Umm Rihan – a large rural settlement which was thoroughly surveyed. According to the surveyors, the settlement ceased in the late third century.[66] Approx. 40 coins are from the first half of the fourth century, and only 9 from the second half of the century (Fig. 60). The last coin is from the time of Arcadius (late fourth century). It accordingly would seem that the abandonment of the settlement is to be dated to the end of the fourth century. In this instance, the absence of coins is connected with the total abandonment of the settlement.

Many settlements in Samaria and its environs suffered damage in the late fifth century. The dating of the crisis is based on the pottery finds, and may be attributed to the Samaritan revolts.[67]

Shechem – a number of (as yet unpublished) important excavations have been conducted at the city and at Mount Gerizim. Three coin assemblages were discovered in the city: in the theater; in the hippodrome, which became the amphitheater; and in the sacred precinct on Mount Gerizim. The amphitheater remained in constant use until the end of the fifth century, and many coins were found which were generally attributed to the "fifth century" with no additional detail. This general formulation, which is a consequence of the poor state of preservation of the coins, raises

[65] J. Baramki, "Coin Hoards from Palestine", *QDAP* 11 (1945), pp. 30-36.

[66] S. Dar et al., *Um Rihan: A Village of the Mishnah* (Tel Aviv, 1986) (Heb.). After the publication of this work, Dar and I conducted an additional survey, which is as yet unpublished. A total of 63 coins were found in the settlement, of which 55 were dated. The coins were examined by A. Kindler, to whom we are grateful for his assistance.

[67] S. Dar, "Archaeological Evidence on the Samaritan Revolts of the Byzantine Period", in *Jews, Samaritans and Christians in Byzantine Palestine*, eds. D. Jacoby and Y. Tsafrir (Jerusalem, 1988), pp. 228-37 (Heb.).

difficulties for the proper utilization of the data.[68] Dozens of coins were found in the theater, including approx. 50 coins from the fourth century, and only 3 from the fifth century.[69] The same picture of a drastic decline in the number of coins in the fifth century recurs in the sacred precinct.[70]

The Samaritan synagogues – a number of synagogues have been excavated. A large assemblage of coins was discovered in *Deir Serur*, containing approx. 80 coins, almost all from the fourth century, and only 8 in the fifth century.[71] The synagogue in *Deir Sharaf* contained only 8 coins from the fourth century. This picture is repeated in the holy Samariran precinct on Mount Gerizim.[72]

Accordingly, all these Samaritan sites, which have not been published in their entirety, contain an ash and destruction stratum from the late fifth century, apparently in the wake of the Samaritan rebellions. In most a significant decline has been identified at the beginning of this century.

The Coastal Plain

Apollonia – there was continuous activity in the city until the fourth century, and it especially flourished in the sixth century. The excavators could not indicate a settlement stratum from the fifth century, although they argue that it was not totally abandoned.[73]

Apollonia apparently already was a polis in the fifth century, for the bishop of this city already participated in the Council of Ephesus in 449; however, the city was small and poor, and flourished only in the sixth century.[74] A certain decline was noticed in the rural sector of the coastal plain in the early fifth century or the midfourth century,[75] but this is only a tentative conclusion.

[68] I. am extremely grateful to Y. Magen, the excavator of the Samaria sites, who provided me with this information. Also see: Y. Magen, "*The History and Archaeology of Shechem (Neapolis) in the First-Fourth Centuries C.E.*", Ph.D. diss., Hebrew University, 1989, pp. 180-84 (Heb.).

[69] Ibid., p. 141.

[70] Y. Magen informed me of this orally. I am grateful to him for the information, for his willingness to explain the finds, and for permitting their publication.

[71] Y. Magen provided me with this information orally, for which I am grateful.

[72] See above, n. 71.

[73] I. Roll and E. Ayalon, *Apollonia and Southern Sharon: Model of a Coastal City and Its Hinterland* (Tel Aviv, 1989), p. 65 (Heb.).

[74] Z. Safrai, *Boundaries and Government in Palestine in the Period of the Mishnah and Talmud* (Tel Aviv, 1980), p. 161 (Heb.).

[75] Roll and Ayalon, p. 176.

Antipatris – the city was destroyed in the earthquake of 363.[76] Only a meager settlement was later established at the site. Nevertheless, the bishop of the city participated in the Councils of Ephesus (449) and Chalcedon (451).

Tel Hefer – the tel was not damaged in the late fourth century, and apparently was destroyed only at the end of the fifth century, in the Samaritan revolts.[77] This conclusion is based solely on preliminary reports, without the coins, and differs from the other sites in this list, possibly because all the numismatic finds from the site are as yet unpublished.

Caesarea – many excavations have been conducted in the city. Based on the rich numismatic finds at the site, the synagogue apparently was destroyed in 352.[78] The excavations conducted by Levine and Netzer revealed a decline in the city itself in the fifth century, according to the numismatic finds.[79]

A few coins from Caesarea Maritima have been published.[80] Hamburger has published coins from the dunes of Caesarea, but his collection does not deal with the relevant period. Since he was selective in his choice of material, his finds do not reflect the chronological quantitative distribution of the material.[81] The excavations conducted by the American expedition yielded many coins, the results of the first two seasons were published in their entirety,[82] but most of the coins from the six seasons have not been published in their entirety, since Hohelfelder published only a short schematic summary of the numismatic material.[83] Hohelfelder relates to the century between 395 and 491 as a single period. His analysis clearly reveals that there was an impressive rise in

[76] M. Kochavi, *Aphek-Antipatris: Five Thousand Years of History* (Tel Aviv, 1989), p. 121 (Heb.). The coin finds have not been published.

[77] Y. Porath et al., *The History and Archaeology of Emek-Hefer* (Tel Aviv, 1985), pp. 168-70 (Heb.).

[78] See *NEAEHL* (1993), q.v. "Caesarea".

[79] D. T. Ariel, "The Coins", in L. I. Levine and E. Netzer, "Excavations at Caesarea Maritima 1975, 1976, 1979 – Final Report", *Qedem* 21 (1986), pp. 137-48; A. Frova, ed., *Scavi di Caesarea Maritima* (Milano, 1965), pp. 229-34.

[80] R. L. Hohlfelder, "Byzantine Coin Finds from the Sea: A Glimpse of Caesarea Maritima's Later History", in *Harbour Archaeology: Proceedings of the First International Workshop on Ancient Mediterranean Harbours*. Caesarea Maritima (BAR 257), ed. A. Raban (Oxford, 1958), pp. 179-84.

[81] H. Hamburger, "Minute Coins from Caesarea", *'Atiqot* 1 (1955), pp. 115-38.

[82] C. J. Lenzen, *The Byzantine-Islamic Occupation at Caesarea Maritima as Evidenced through the Pottery* (Ann Arbor, 1983), Part II, pp. 466-88; and other studies.

[83] R. L. Hohlfelder, "Caesarea Maritima in Late Antiquity", in *Ancient Coins of the Greco-Roman World*, eds. W. Heckel and R. Sullivan (Ontario, 1984), pp. 186-261.

the number of coins in the fourth century, while their numbers declined by more than 50% in the fifth century (after 395). It may be assumed that there was an even sharper decline after 408, but we lack the information necessary to prove this hypothesis. Clear support for this argument is provided by Table 2[84], in which Hohelfelder provides a detailed listing of the 128 coins whose mint has been identified (approx. 30 percent of all the coins from the Byzantine period). A similar picture is indicated by the three assemblages which have been published: in the fourth century the number of coins rose, there was a major increase in the number of coins in the second half of the fourth century, although many coins from this period are identified only generally as "late fourth-early fifth century."[85] In the fifth century, the number of coins drops, before rising once again in an impressive manner in the sixth century. Since the finds are partial, they have not been presented in graphic form, as have the other data in this work.

Tel Mevorakh – these tombs remained in continual use to the end of the sixth century. All the 10 coins found at the site, however, are until 361, indicating that the small numismatic finds do not represent all the activity at the site.[86]

The Nahsholim-Dora road – the use of this cemetery ceased by the end of the fifth century, and possibly as early as the beginning of this century.[87]

Dora – the early city declined in the third century. The Byzantine city has not been excavated. The church which had been established in the fourth century was destroyed by the end of that century.[88]

Emeq-Hefer – Appelbaum concentrated all the private collections of coins from Emeq-Hefer (fig. 61). [89] The period of greatest activity was the first half of the fourth century, there was a reduction of 50-80 percent in the second half of the century (there is a general decline of 50-85 percent in the entire region, while the numbers of coins decreased by 85 percent in *Khirbet Jalame*, in which the largest number of coins was

[84] Ibid., p. 267.

[85] Ariel, "The Coins" (above, n. 79).

[86] E. Stern, "Excavations at Tel Mevorakh", Qedem 9 (1978), pp. 10-21.

[87] A. Ovadiah, "Soundings on the Hadera-Haifa Road between Nahsholim and Habonim, *'Atiqot* 17 (1985), pp. 161-67.

[88] C. Dauphin and S. Gibson, The Byzantine city at Dor/Dora, *Bulletin of the Anglo-Israel Archaeological Society*, 14 (1944-5), pp. 9-38.

[89] S. Appelbaum, "The Ancient Coin Finds in Emek-Hefer", in *The History and Archaeology of Emek-Hefer*, eds. Y. Porath et al., pp. 271-77 (Heb.).

collected), and with an even steeper decrease in the fifth century. To these numbers we must add the "Byzantine" coins which have not been identified in detail, but which are described only in general formulations such as "and many Byzantine coins," which are difficult to express in graphic form.

Jamnitarum Portus – the rich numismatic finds (400 coins) have not been published. According to our count, the greatest number of coins is from the fourth century (Fig. 62). There is a clear drop of 50 percent in the second half of this century, and a severe collapse in the fifth century, although some coins from this century obviously were found as well.[90]

Joppa (Fig. 63) – the finds are as yet unpublished. Based on partial information, the situation in the fourth and fifth centuries is identical with that in Jamnitarum Portus.[91]

Tel Keisan – in contrast with the other settlements in Galilee, this apparently Phoenician settlement flourished only in the sixth century.[92]

Judea

Jerusalem – the thousands of coins which were found in Jerusalem in a series of excavations (Fig. 64) were collected and analyzed by D. Ariel.[93] There was a yearly average of approx. 3.2 coins during the first half of the fourth century (305-363), and only 2.2 in the second half of the century. Many fourth-century coins which could not be identified with precision also were found, for a total yearly average of 3.2 coins in this century. In marked contrast, only a total of 17 coins (average of 0.2 per year) were found from the entire fifth century (408-491). The sixth and seventh centuries constituted a period of relative growth, even exceeding that of the fourth century. This is despite the fact that the literary sources portray the fifth century as the high point in the history of the city; the building projects of Eudocia are well-known from the sources.[94]

[90] The coins were identified by A. Kindler, and I am grateful to him and to D. Zahavi, the director of the museum, for permission to publish these finds in their name. The coins were collected above ground, mainly by the late A. Sadeh. These totals do not include the few coins found in the excavations in the area.

[91] The finds were examined by D. T. Ariel, to whom I am grateful for his permission to study the material and cite it.

[92] J. Briend et al., *Tell Keisan (1971-1976)* (Paris, 1980).

[93] D. T. Ariel, "A Survey of Coin Finds in Jerusalem", *LA* 32 (1982), pp. 273-326.

[94] See above, chap., 4. n. 45

Gibeon – only a few coins were found. The fifth century is not represented, but the finds are too meagere.[95]

Mambre (Fig. 65) – the numismatic finds indicate that the site was most active in the first half of the fourth century (until Constantius II in 363). Few coins from the fifth century were found, and this century is poorly represented.[96] The site is not representative of the region as a whole, because it hosted an international fair and a Jewish, pagan, and Christian holy site until the midfourth century. Constantius II decided to build a church on the site, thereby drastically reducing the use of the site and its attraction for pilgrims.

Horvat Hazzan – a large villa was apparently established in the fourth century (phase B of the settlement) and was active until the end of the Byzantine period.[97] This conclusion is based only on the pottery finds.

Lachish – most of the material in Lachish is from the early periods preceding the purview of the current work, but the excavations of the tombs also uncovered coins: 14 from the second and third centuries, 20 from the first half of the fourth century (305-363), 30 from the second half of the century (364-408), 2 from the fifth century, and 7 from the sixth and seventh centuries.[98] Once again, there are very few coins from the fifth century.

Thala – the cemetery which was excavated was in use until the end of the fourth century, and possibly into the beginning of the fifth century.[99] This information is based solely on the pottery finds.

Herodion – Herodion was destroyed in the Bar Kokhba revolt and was rebuilt as a church and monastic center in the sixth century.[100] The history of this settlement is not characteristic of the region, and reflects the unique experience of the site.

Eleutheropolis (Beit Guvrin) – a total of 355 coins were found in a tomb adjoining Beit Guvrin and were published at the beginning of this cen-

[95] J. B. Pritchard, *Winery, Defenses and Soundings at Gibeon* (Philadelphia, 1964), pp. 52-62.

[96] E. Mader, *Mambre* (Freiburg im Breisgau, 1957), pp. 177-79.

[97] G. Avni et al., "Ahuzat Hazzan", *The Hiding Complexes in the Judean Shephelah*, eds. A. Kloner and Y. Tepper (Tel Aviv, 1987), p. 127 (Heb.).

[98] O. Tufnell et al., *Lachish III: The Iron Age* (London, 1953), pp. 164-68, 412-15.

[99] A. Kloner, "The Cemetery at Horvat Thala", *Eretz-Israel* 17 (1984), pp. 325-32 (Heb.).

[100] A. Spijkerman, *Herodion III: Catalogo delle Monete* (Jerusalem, 1972).

tury.[101] The major body of the numismatic finds represents the period between the two revolts, from the time of Nero to that of Hadrian, followed by a prolonged gap until the time of Anastasius; the sixth century is represented by 8 coins. This lone tomb most probably does not reflect the history of Eleutheropolis, which became a flourishing polis in the third century.[102]

Jericho – Arif reports of an interesting concentration of coins, in which, here as well, the number of coins greatly increases in the early fourth century (25 coins from 138 to 235, a gap until 305, and 65 coins between 305-363).[103] There is no mention of later coins at the site.

Susiya – a number of excavations were conducted in the settlement, but the final results of only one has been published (Fig. 66). The synagogue is dated to the post byzantine period on the basis of the language of the inscription. But, for the purposes of our discussion, this dating method should not be relied upon.[104] The meager numismatic finds [105] indicate a decline in the second half of the fourth century, and an additional decrease in the sixth century. The pottery finds clearly attest to settlement continuity until the medieval period. In another summation of the excavations, A. Negev reports of the abandonment of the settlement from the fifth century to the Middle Ages.[106] The term "abandonment" does not correspond to the results of the synagogue excavations, leading to the conclusion that the settlement suffered a drastic decline, or that a certain quarter which was excavated had been abandoned.

The structure containing the shops of the settlement was constructed in the sixth century.[107] The new excavations in the settlement have not been published in their entirety, and do not provide a firm basis for the dating of the settlement.[108]

101 J. N. Svoronos, "Prosktema to Nomismatikou Mouseiou", *JIAN* (1907), pp. 230-52 (Greek).

102 In addition, there are also a number of hoards from Eleutheropolis which end in the Great Revolt or in the Bar Kokhba revolt; see, inter alia, Arif (below, n. 103), p. 23.

103 A. S. Arif, *A Treasury of Classical and Islamic Coins: The Collection of Amman Museum* (London, 1986). The material is presented in a misleading and confusing manner, and the registration and reporting do not follow accepted methods.

104 S. Gutman et al., "Excavations in the Synagogue at Khirbet Susiya", *Qadmoniot* 5 (1972), pp. 47-52 (Heb.).

105 My thanks to D. T. Ariel, who showed me the manuscript of his article before publication.

106 *NEAEHL* (1993), pp. 1416-17.

107 Y. Hirschfeld, "Excavation of a Jewish Dwelling at Khirbet Susiya", *Eretz-Israel* 17 (1984), pp. 168-80 (Heb.).

108 A. Negev, "Excavations at Carmel (Kh. Susiya) in 1984: Preliminary Report", *IEJ* 35 (1985), pp. 231-52.

Hebron – the *el-Khalil* excavations used quantitative methods to examine the pottery finds with extreme care. The quantities of sherds led the excavator to conclude that there was a large decrease in the population (i.e., in the quantity of sherds) in the fifth century (stratum 13). The settlement recovered in the late fifth century and flourished in the following century.[109]

Horvat Rimmon – the synagogue was established in the fifth century. Two hoards found in the synagogue contained 3 coins from the fourth century, while the remaining coins (44 in number) are all from the fifth century.[110] An examination of the coins in the settlement presents a different picture (Fig. 67). The settlement began to flourish in the time of Diocletian, and this growth increased in the first half of the fourth century. The second half of the fourth century marked the period of greatest settlement activity (68 coins). The quantity of coins decreases by approx. 80 percent after 408. The decrease in the number of coins continued in the sixth century, but the small quantity of coins does not enable us to determine if the situation in the settlement had improved or further deteriorated.[111]

Ma'on and *Anim* – although only a few coins were found, the excavators are of the opinion that these settlements, including their synagogues, were established in the fourth century and experienced growth in the fifth and following centuries.[112] In the absence of a significant number of coins, it is difficult to rely solely upon the ceramic.

Magen – one of the earliest churches in Palestine, was built at the end of the fourth century.[113] A larger church was built in the late fifth century, in the process destroying the earlier structure. According to the excavators, there is a gap, or at the very least diminished use of the structure, in the fifth century.[114] A synagogue was built in Ma'on

[109] M. A. Bennet, *Byzantine and Islamic Ceramics from Hebron (El Khalil): The Common Wares* (Ann Arbor, 1972), p. 286.

[110] A. Kloner and T. Mindel, "Two Byzantine Hoards from the Ancient Synagogue of Horvat Rimmon", *INJ* 5 (1981), pp. 60-68.

[111] My thanks to A. Kloner for giving me the material to study. The coins were identified by R. Barkai.

[112] Z. Ilan, *Ancient Synagogues in Israel* (Tel Aviv, 1991), pp. 302-4, 308-10 (Heb.).

[113] V. Tsaferis, "An Early Christian Church Complex at Magen", *BASOR* 258 (1985), pp. 1-15; N. Feig, "Pottery, Glass, and Coins from Magen", *idem*, pp. 33-40.

[114] N. Feig (above, n. 113), pp. 34-38.

(Nirim) in the coastal plain only in the sixth century.[115] The hoard of coins found in Deir Dassawi (near Meflasim) also begins in the sixth century.[116]

Coin Hoards from Syria and Palestine

Coin hoards are problematic, and their use for the purposes of this book raises methodical problems. The hoard was concealed by its owner, who died, fled, or abandoned his money for personal reasons. Such an event could have been connected with general circumstances, such as war, plague, or earthquake, but may also have been a wholly personal occasion. The "lifetime" of a hoard, i.e., the length of the period whose coins it represents, may be influenced by various factors. Nevertheless, it may reasonably be expected that a hoard from the early sixth century would contain coins from the fifth century. The absence of such coins in a number of hoards is likely to indicate the paucity of coins in this century, or at least to provide support for such an argument. Hoards from the fifth century would indicate that economic activity did not cease in this period as well, but the unearthing of such a hoard constitutes a random discovery, and is of no greater significance than the discovery of a single pottery vessel or structure from this period. The existence of hundreds of hoards from the entire period would enable the researcher to draw conclusions based on their relative frequency within given time spans, and studies of this type have been conducted for the Western Empire. Unfortunately, the number of hoards from Syria and Palestine is not sufficiently large for examinations of this sort.

The major value of the hoards lies in an analysis of the material they contain, and they are indicative to a certain degree of the circulation of coins in the period represented by the hoard. They teach nothing of the period after the sealing of the hoard, and very little of the period preceding its beginning.

Most of the hoards from the Byzantine period in Syria and Palestine are from the fourth and sixth centuries. Especially prominent are hoards from the sixth and seventh centuries which begin in the late fifth century (from the time of Anastasius – 491) or even later. There are many exam-

[115] J. Magness, "The Pottery from the 1980 Excavations at Ma'on (Nirim)", *Eretz-Israel* 19 (1987), pp. 216-24 (Heb.).

[116] L. Y. Rachmani, "Two Hoards of Byzantine Coins and a Roman Charm from Khirbet Deir Dassawi", *INJ* 2 (1964), pp. 21-23.

ples of such hoards, such as the hoard from Tell Kalak published by Metcalf,[117] that published by Bates,[118] and others.[119]

Excavations in Palestine also have uncovered a number of similar hoards which begin in the late fifth or early sixth century.[120] This group includes the hoard in Fandaqumia in Samaria, that from Khirbet Dubel in the Carmel,[121] that near Kibbutz Miflasim,[122] the Jericho hoard,[123], the hoard from Raphia,[124] and that from Tel Rehob.[125]

The fund from the synagogue in Rimmon is contemporaneous, but different. It is exceptional in that the earliest coins it contains are from the fifth century.[126] Additional hoards from the fifth century were found in Gush Halav [127] and in Abualanda in Transjordan.[128]

A few hoards from the fifth century were also discovered in Syria. Adelson and Kustas published such a hoard found in Syria, and also discuss two additional hoards from this period: the Volo hoard and the Yale hoard.[129] A similar hoard from Beirut or northern Syria is also reported,[130] as are additional discoveries.[131] These hoards, along with those from Rimmon and Gush Halav, attest that not only did commercial activity not cease, coins from the fifth century were in circulation

[117] W. E. Metcalf, "The Tell Kalak Hoard and Trajan's Arabian Mint", *ANMN* 20 (1975), pp. 39-108.

[118] G. E. Bates, "A Byzantine Hoard from Coelesyria", *ANMN* 14 (1968), p. 81.

[119] E.g., the Sarafand hoard from southern Lebanon, *Coin Hoards* III (1977), p. 82, No. 229; W. E. Metcalf, "Three Seventh-Century Byzantine Gold Hoards", *ANMN* 25 (1980), pp. 87-108.

[120] Not included were hoards from the seventh century, such as the Bat Galim hoard, ca. 610: *Coin Hoards* I (1975), p. 60, No. 235; or a hoard from Awarta, Nablus: *ADAJ* 1 (1951), pp. 41-43; and similarly, the Carmiel hoard, which has not been published.

[121] C. Lambert, "A Hoard of Byzantine Coins", *QDAP* 1 (1932), pp. 55-68; J. Baramki, "A Hoard of Byzantine Coins", *QDAP* 8 (1939), pp. 81-85.

[122] L. Y. Rachmani, "Two Hoards" (above, n. 116), loc. cit. 139.*Coin Hoards* III (1977), p. 82, No. 228.

[123] *Coin Hoards* III (1997), No. 225.

[124] A. Spaer, "The Rafah Hoard: Byzantine Sixth-Century Folles", *NC* 138 (1978), pp. 66-70.

[125] A. Paltiel, "A Hoard of Byzantine Gold Coins" (above, n. 31), loc. cit.

[126] Kloner and Mindel, loc. cit.

[127] Meyers and Meyers, loc. cit.

[128] *Coin Hoards* III (1977), p. 69, No. 224.

[129] Adelson and Kustas 1962 (above, chapter 1 n. 36).

[130] *Coin Hoards* II (1976), pp. 55-60, No. 187.

[131] E.g.: J. W. E. Pearce, "A Late Roman Hoard from South-west Asia Minor", *NC* 15 (1935), pp. 21-24. Additional information on the hoards of the fifth century was collected by Mackensen: M. Mackensen, "Die spätantiken Fundmünzen", in T. Ulbert, *Resafa III: Die Basilika des Heiligen Kreuzes in Resafa-Sergiupolis* (Mainz am Rhein, 1986), pp. 181-225; H. L. Adelsen, *Roman Monetary Policy from Diocletian to Heraclius*, Ph.D. diss., Princeton University, 1952 (Ann Arbor, 1979).

in this period, and use was not made of "old" coins from the fourth century.

A similar picture is portrayed by hoards from Asia Minor, such as the Taburabat hoard and additional hoards.[132]

The information we possess regarding hoards may be summarized as follows:

1. Almost all the hoards in Palestine begin in the late fifth century, leading to the conclusion that coins from this century were rare, thereby indicating the limited extent of commerce in this century.
2. The fifth century is not represented in most of the hoards from Syria. Nonetheless, a small number of hoards from this century were uncovered, clearly indicating that the continuation of commerce in this century, albeit with limited volume.
3. The hoards from the fifth century contain coins from this century, demonstrating that such coins were in regular circulation. The hoards from the sixth century contain coins from that century, and only rarely begin with coins from the fifth century.
4. No hoards were found composed exclusively of coins from the fourth and sixth centuries and totally lacking coins from the fifth century. For the importance and methodical significance of the last two points, see above, the end of chapter a.

[132] M. Arslan, "The Taburabat Hoard", in *Recent Turkish Coin Hoards and Numismatic Studies*, ed. C. S. Lighfoot (Oxbow, 1991), pp. 43-58.

Appendix B

Military Influence upon the Monetary Situation

In another essay, we presented a theory regarding the cardinal influence of the Roman army upon the economy of Palestine and the level of trade in the province.[1] Two legions (the Xth in Judea, and the VIth in Galilee) and auxiliary units, were stationed in Palestine from ca. 130 CE to the early fourth century. This force is estimated to have comprised 25,000 men. The Xth Legion was then transferred to the Limes line in the Negev, and the VIth Legion to Limes Arabicus.

At this time the garrison force in Judea was the largest in the Empire, relative to the size of the province. Other large garrison forces exerted far-reaching economic influence in the provinces in which they were stationed, as many studies have shown. It may therefore be reasonably assumed that the army exerted formidable economic influence in Judea as well, possessing at it did great purchasing power, as a consumer of quality goods, as a producer and supplier of products, and as a living example of Roman life.[2]

According to this theory, the presence of the army should have influenced the general level of commerce, and especially that in Galilee, mainly in the period 130-300. As was noted above, the numismatic finds are indicative of the level of trade in Palestine. To the extent that this can be verified, there is no significant chronological correlation between the military presence and the quantity of coins in the settlements of Palestine. The quantity of coins is the greatest in the fourth century, after the Roman legions moved to the south, where only few coins were found; while in the second and third centuries there was a major military presence in this province. It had been proven, however, that the Negev and southern Judea began to flourish in the period in which the army moved to the south. There are a number of reasons for this phenomenon, and the improvement in security and the economic influence of the army only partially explain this growth. Consequently, there is no correlation

[1] Z. Safrai, "The Roman Army in the Galilee", in *The Galilee in Late Antiquity*, ed. L. I. Levine (Cambridge, Mass., 1992), pp. 103-14.
[2] *Ibid.*

between the chronology of trade in Palestine and that of the Roman army in the land.

The lack of such a correlation does not prove that the army did not exert any economic influence, nor does it attest that such influence was not central to the life of the land. The transfer of the army to the south did not greatly change the economic system of the province, since, throughout this entire period, all parts of Palestine shared equally in both the burdens imposed by the military presence and the benefits ensuing from such a presence. The encampment of the VIth Legion, e.g., did not rely solely on Galilee for its supplies, but drew upon the resources of the entire province; consequently, the transfer to the south did not necessarily entail damage to the Galilean economy. Moreover, if the settlements of Galilee did in fact suffer from the transfer, its effects are noticeable only several decades later. This takes us close to the midfourth century, and the transfer of the Roman army may therefore be regarded as an additional cause of the turning point in the life of the settlement and the beginning of the deterioration of the settlement in Galilee.

Consequently, the method of research we have adopted neither proves the centrality of the army in the economic life of Palestine, nor rules out such a possibility.

Glossary

Amoraitic period – 220-400 CE. The sages of the period are known as "Amoraim". The Talmud and midrashei aggadah were composed in this period.

Anastasius – Byzantine emperor (491-518).

Arcadius – Byzantine emperor (395-408).

Colonatus law – a Byzantine law enacted in the fourth century, which prohibited sharecroppers from leaving the land and established that the farmer and his land compromise a single entity for tax purposes.

Epiphanius – fourth-century Church Father born in the Eleutheropolis region.

Episcopus (bishop)- Christian administrative term for the head of the church in a polis. The Greek word originally had various meanings.

Eusebius – Church leader in Palestine (late third-early fourth centuries).

Euthymius – leader of Judean Desert monasticism (ca. 377-473).

Gallus revolt – a midfourth century revolt in Palestine.

Genizah – Jewish law dictates that wornout religious books must be preserved. A repository containing a large collection of religious books and letters was found in the upper chamber of a Cairo synagogue (the Cairo Genizah). This collection is our main source of textual variants and books which were lost.

Geonic period – ca. the ninth-twelfth centuries. "Gaon" is an abreviation of the title "Rosh Yeshivat Gaon Yaakov", the title of the head of the Gaon Yaakov yeshivah.

Hadashot Arkheologiyot (Archaeological News) – current Israeli periodical containing concise initial archaeological reports. Until ca. 1991 the reports appeared without author attribution.

Halakhot Kezuvot – a Geonic collection of halakhot.

Harba de-Moshe – a popular mystical work composed sometime in the early medieval period.

helev – fatty part of meat; its consumption is forbidden by Jewish law.

Hilarion – the first monk in Palestine; born in the midfourth century in the Gaza region, and died in Cyprus.

Hilkhot Arayot – a collection of laws pertaining to sexual relations; written in Palestine in the late Byzantine or early Islamic period.

Honorius – Roman emperor (393-423).

Ibbur ha-shanah – Intercalation of the lunar year. In the Jewish calendar, an additional year must be added approx. every third year, in order to adjust the lunar year to the solar one. The additional month is called hodesh ha-ibbur (the intercalated month), and the year, shanah me'uberet (leap year).

Iggeret Rav Sherira Gaon – a letter written by Rav Sherira, one of the last sages of the Geonic period in Babylonia. The Iggeret summarizes the history of the scholarship in the preceding period. There are two extant versions of the Iggeret, the Spanish and the French.

Justin – Byzantine emperor (518-527).

Kashrut – the dietary prohibitions and restrictions in Jewish law.

Kiddush ha-hodesh – each month in the Hebrew calendar is, alternately, 29 or 30 days in length. The decision to add a day, which is dependent upon the "molad", the appearance of the new moon, is called kiddush ha-hodesh.

Madaba map – a mosaic pavement from the late Byzantine period found in a church in Madaba (Transjordan) containing a map of Palestine.

Manicheans – heretical sect, followers of Manes.

Mark the Deacon – see Porphyrius of Gaza.

Ma'asim literature – the general name for a series of collections on halakhic matters composed in Palestine in the late Byzantine or early Islamic period.

Megillat Aviatar – an eleventh-century biography of the Italian sage R. Shephatiah.

Midrash – an ancient system of study used by the Rabbis for Scriptural exegesis. A large number of works were written employing this method.

Midrashei aggadah – a series of works, each comprising a commentary on a book of the Bible. Most of the material they contain is aggadic in nature. The midrashei ha-aggadah were written in the Amoraitic period or slightly later.

Midrashei ge'ulah – general name for a group of eschatological and apocalyptic midrashim, some of early composition (fourth-sixth centuries), and others from a later period (eighth-twelfth centuries).

Midrashei halakhah – a series of works comprising a commentary, each of a different book of the Pentateuch. Most of the material they contain derives legal conclusions from Scriptural verses. All the Midrashei ha-halakhah are Tannaitic in origin.

Nevelah – an animal not slaughtered in accordance with Jewish law; its flesh may not be eaten.

Onomasticon – book of names written by Eusebius and containing a list of Biblical names and their identifications.

Peter the Iberian – Church Father born in Spain; active in Palestine late fifth-early sixth centuries.

Pirkei de-Rabbi Eliezer – a midrash aggadah composed in the fourth century in Palestine*

Pirkei Heikhalot – a mystical book written sometime in the early medieval period.

Porphyrius of Gaza – a Church Father and the head of the church in Gaza in the fifth century. His disciple Mark the Deacon wrote a book about his proselytizing efforts in Gaza and its environs.

Samaritan revolts – a series of revolts between 484 and 536 C.E. Savoraitic period – the interim period between the Amoraitic period and the period of the Geonim in Babylonia. The sages of the period were known as "Savoraim". Little is known of the period. The corresponding period in Palestine is unnamed.

Sozomenus – fifth-century Church Father born in Gaza.

Talmud – the most important work composed in the Amoraitic period. The Jerusalem or palestinian Talmud, composed in Palestine, and the Babylonian Talmud, redacted in Babylonia.

Tannaitic period – 70-220 CE. The sages of the period are known as "Tannaim".

Illustrations

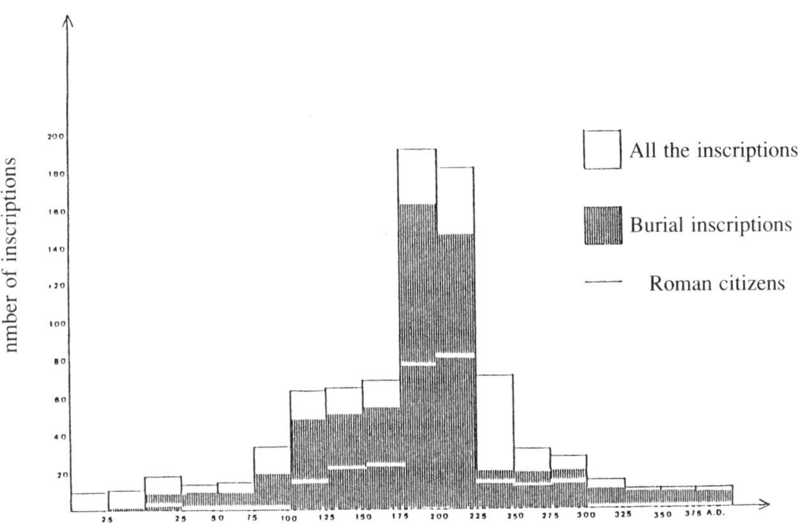

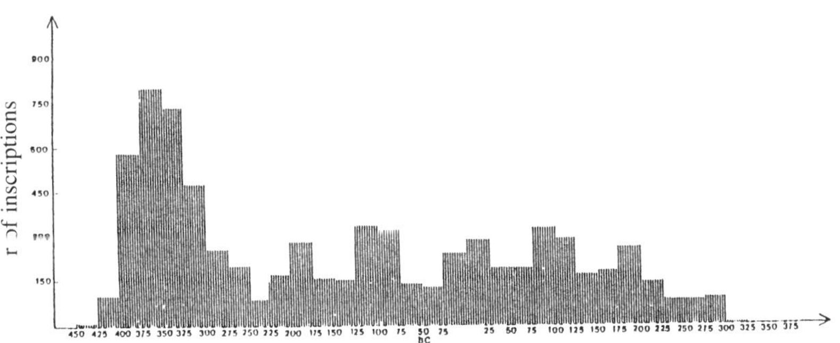

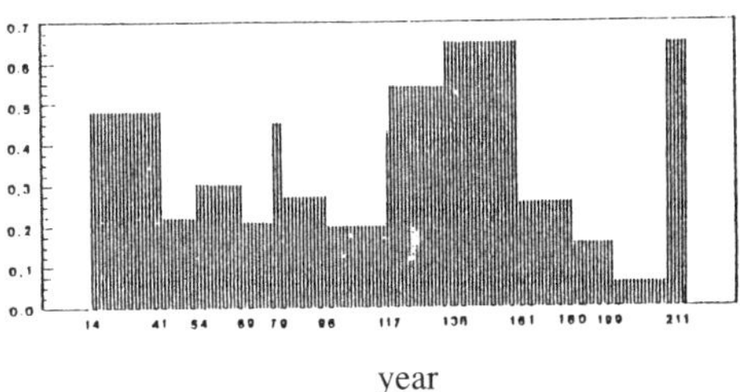

year

Fig. 1. Quantities of dedicatory inscriptions by chronological division (MacMullen 1988, p. 13).

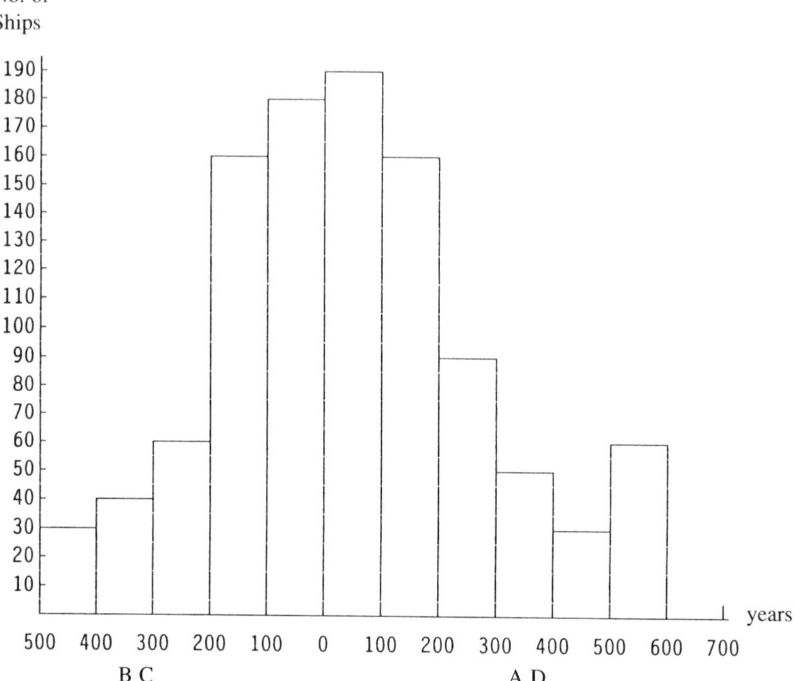

A.J. Parker, *Ancient Shipwrecks of the Mediterranean & the Roman Epire*, *BAR* 580 (Oxford 1992).

Fig. 2. Sunken ships in the western Mediterranean Sea

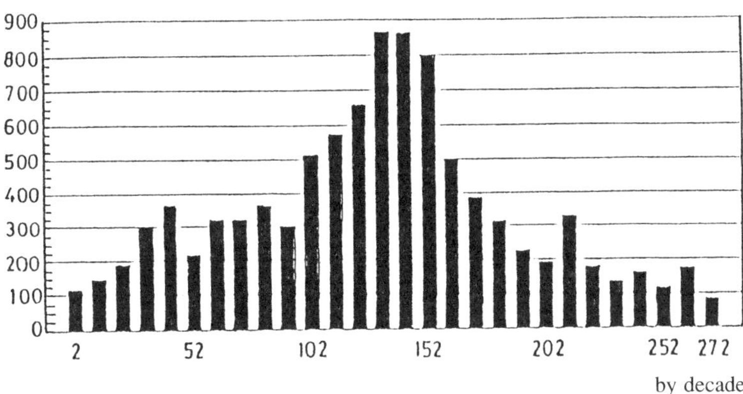

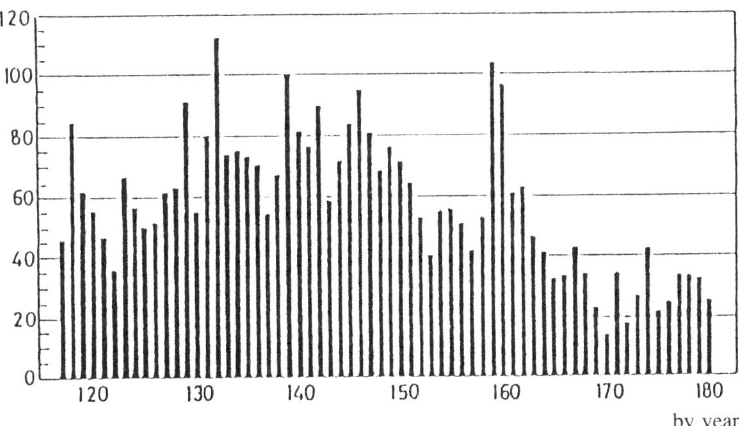

Quantities of papyruses in Egypt, by chronological division
(Duncan-Jones 1990, pp. 68-69)

Fig. 3. Quantities of papyruses in Egypt, by chronological division

DEMOGRAPHIC MULTIPLICATION AND ECONOMIC GROWTH

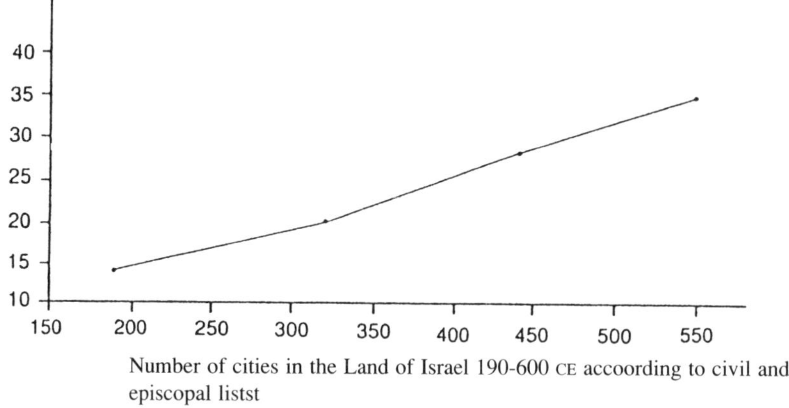

Number of cities in the Land of Israel 190-600 CE accoording to civil and episcopal listst

Urbanization in Palestine.

Fig. 4. Urbanization in Palestine in the Byzantine period

average quantity of
coins per year or
population size

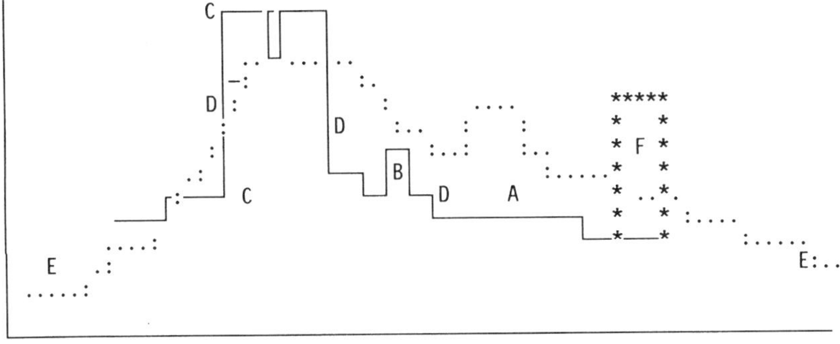

period

. . . . . Population size and economic situation in a settlement
- - - - - - Average quantity of coins per year
****** Quantity of coins in hoard

Explanation:

1. The quantity of coins is influenced by the economic situation (volume of commerce) and population size; consequently, the quantity of coins generally reflecths the demographic and economic fluctuations in the city. However:

A. the numismatic finds do not reflect short-term fluctuations.

B. a randon factor may account for over- or underrepresentation of coins of a specific emperor within a short period of time.

C. the settlement process is slow and fradual. The numismatic finds are naturally revealed to the researcher in an artificial manner, as a set of acute changes, since the dating of coins is almost exclusively based on the name of the issuing emperor.

D. the chronological correlation between changes in the quantity of coins and demographic change is neither complete nor precise.

E. the lack of coins is not necessarily indicative of the destruction or absence of a settlement, but rather attests to a decline in the settlement and a reduction of its population and/or commerce in it. The numismatic activity therefore is mainly reflective of periods of growth marked by a great deal of economic activity.

F. an incidental hoard from a period of decline in the settlement, in which case the large number of coins does not testify to economic strength in the settlement. The composition of the hoard is not indicative of the settlement. The composition of the hoard is not indicative of the economic history of the settlement, but rather of the circulation of coins at the site and its markets during this specific period.

Fig. 5. Quantities of coins and economic and demographic fluctuations in a settlement: a theoretical model

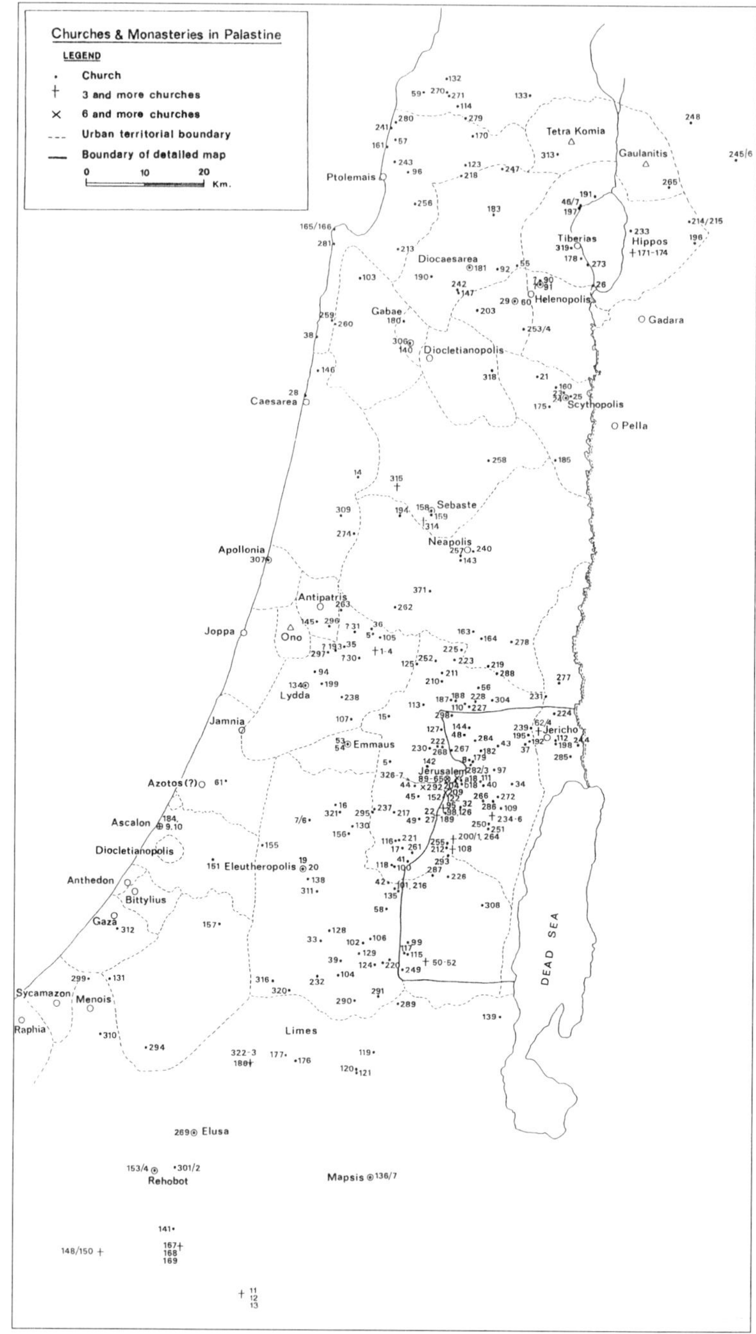

Fig. 6. Churches in Palestine

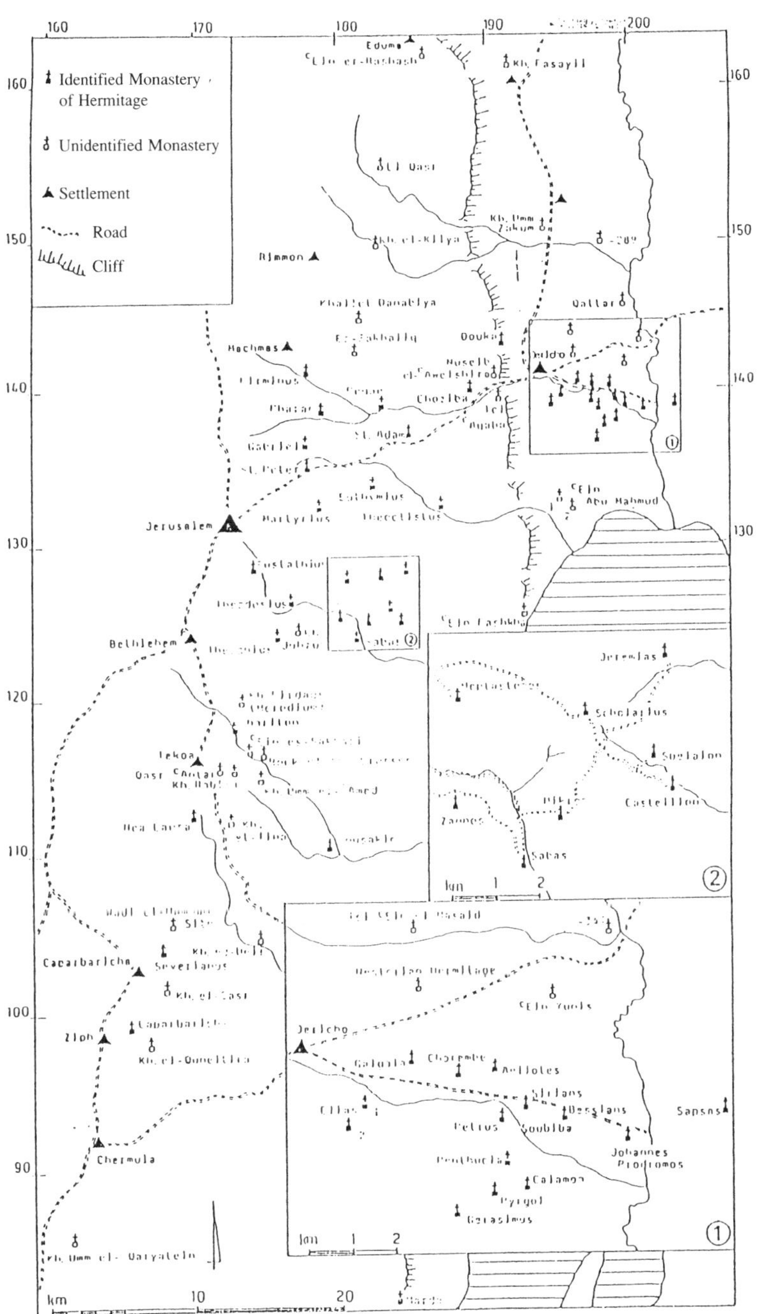

Fig. 7. Monasteries in the wilderness of Judea.
A detailed map of no. 6

Diocese in Palestine in the fourth century

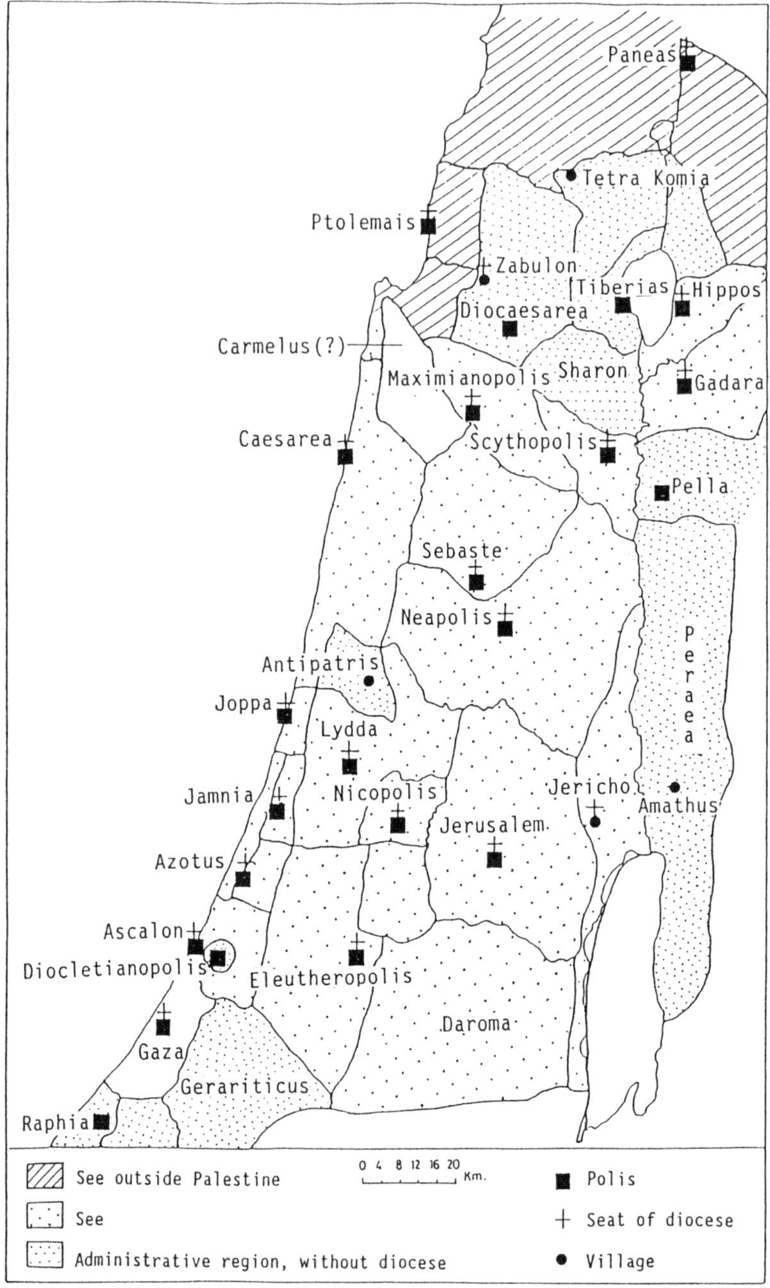

Fig. 8. Dioceses in Palestine in the fourth century

Dioceses in Palestine in the second half of the fifth century

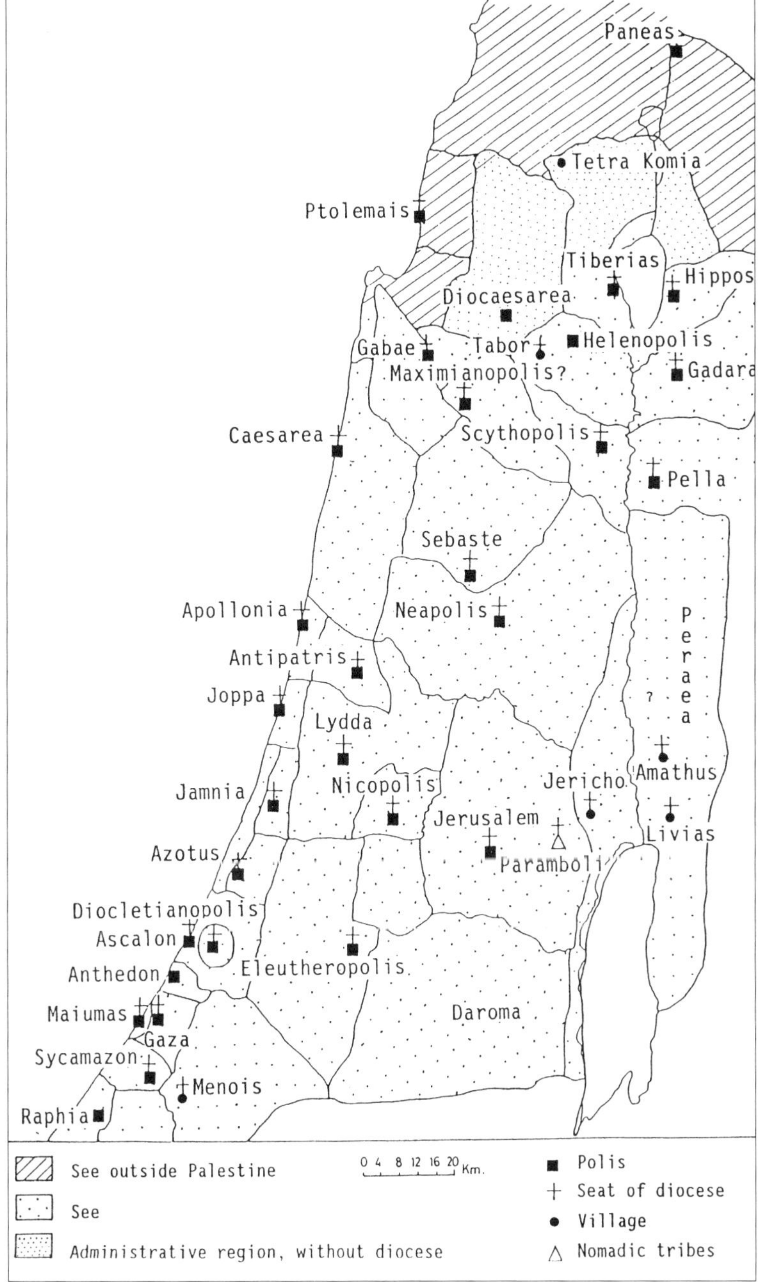

Fig. 9. Dioceses in Palestine* in the second half of the fifth century

Dioceses in Palestine in the sixth century

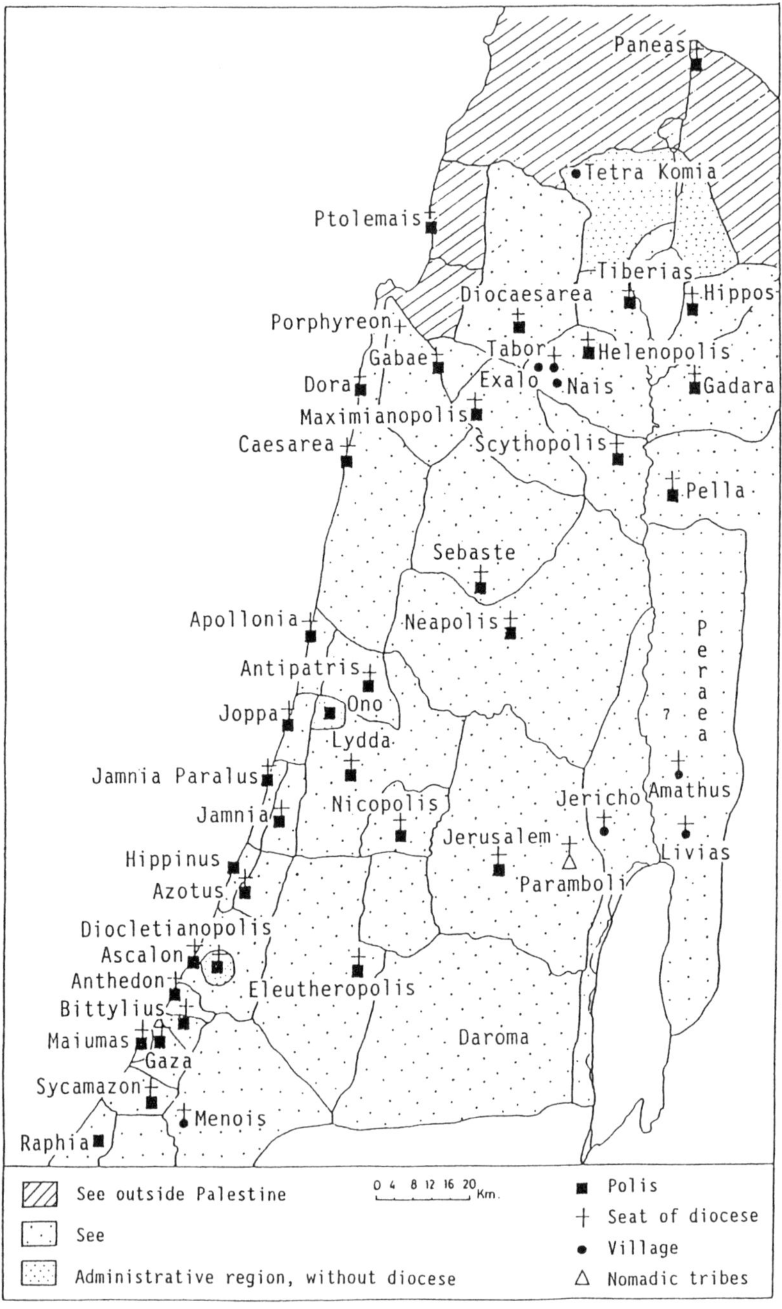

Fig. 10. Dioceses in Palestine in the sixth century

The Earthquake in 363

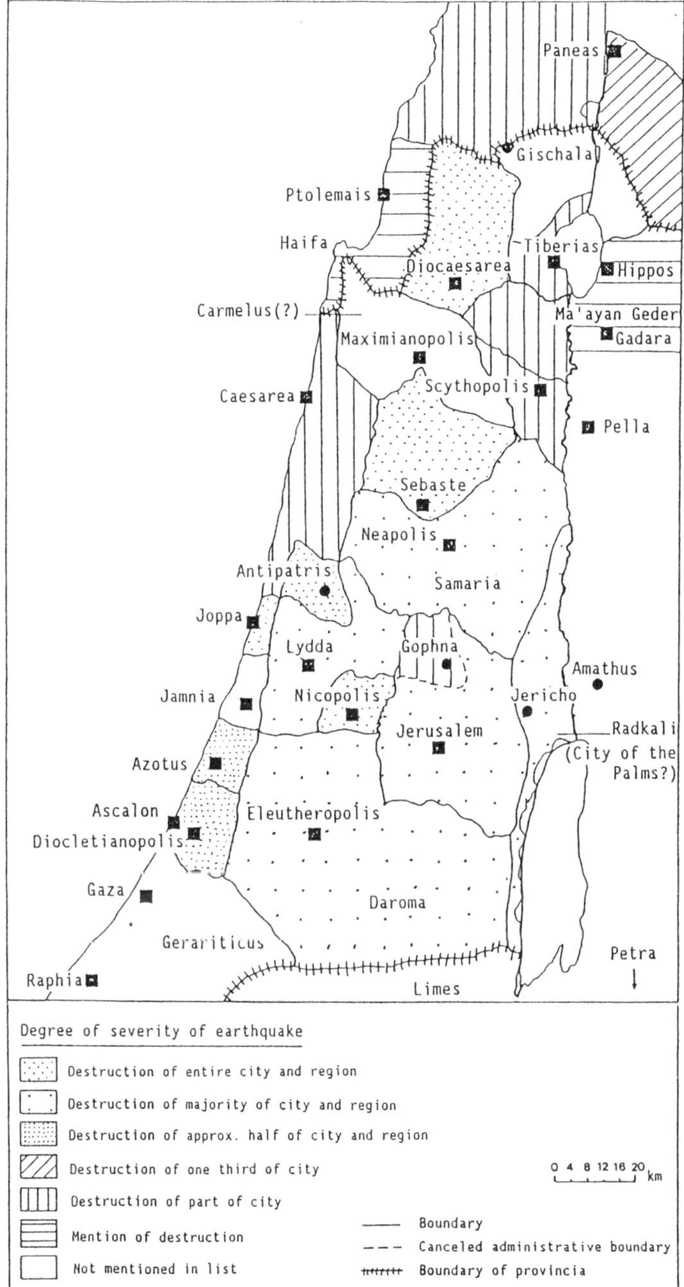

Fig. 11. The earthquake in 363

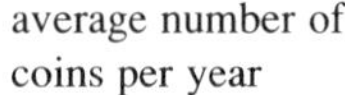

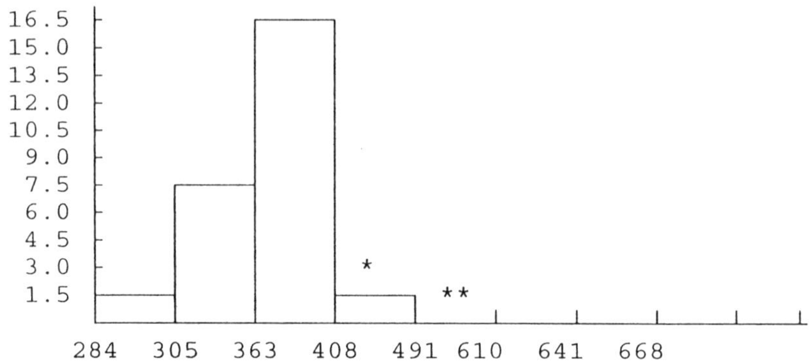

* 82% – coins of Emperor Honorius
** coins from this period

Fig. 12. Quantities of coins in Karanis, Egypt (yearly average)

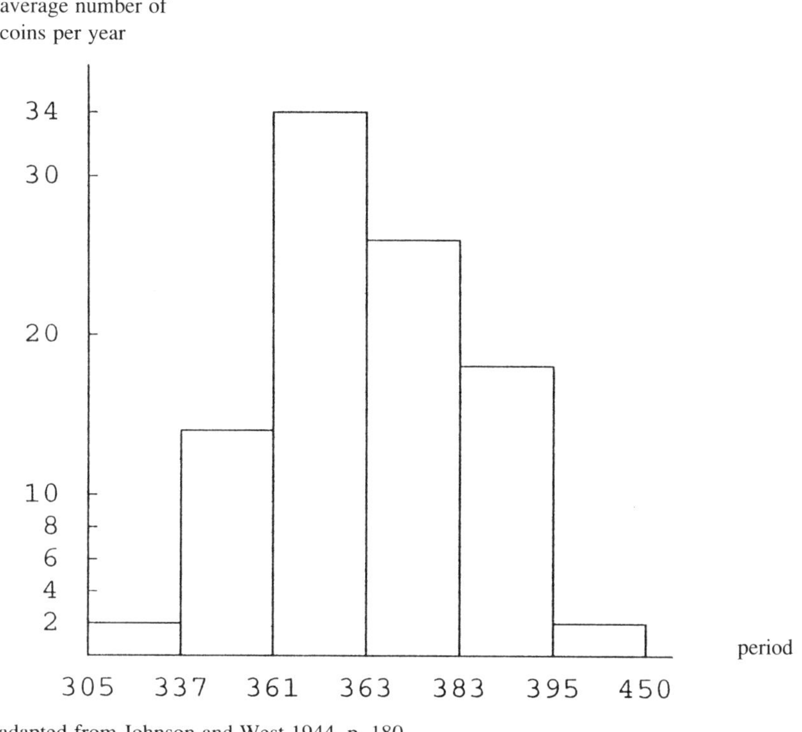

adapted from Johnson and West 1944, p. 180.

Fig. 13. Quantities of coins in Egypt (yearly average)

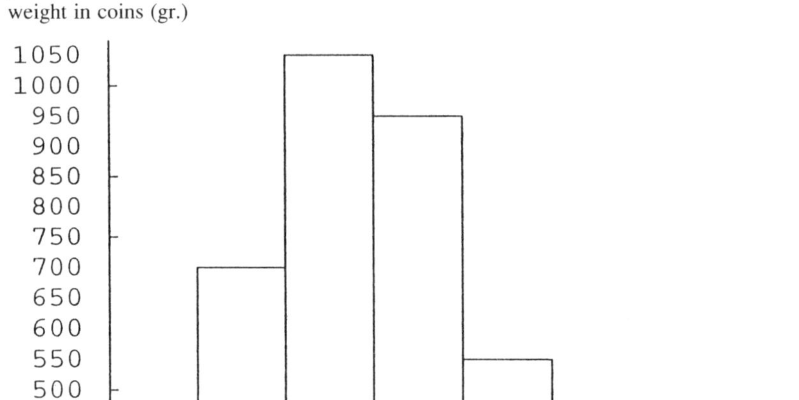

adapted from Johnson and West, p. 180.

Fig. 14. Silver weight in coins in Egypt (yearly average)

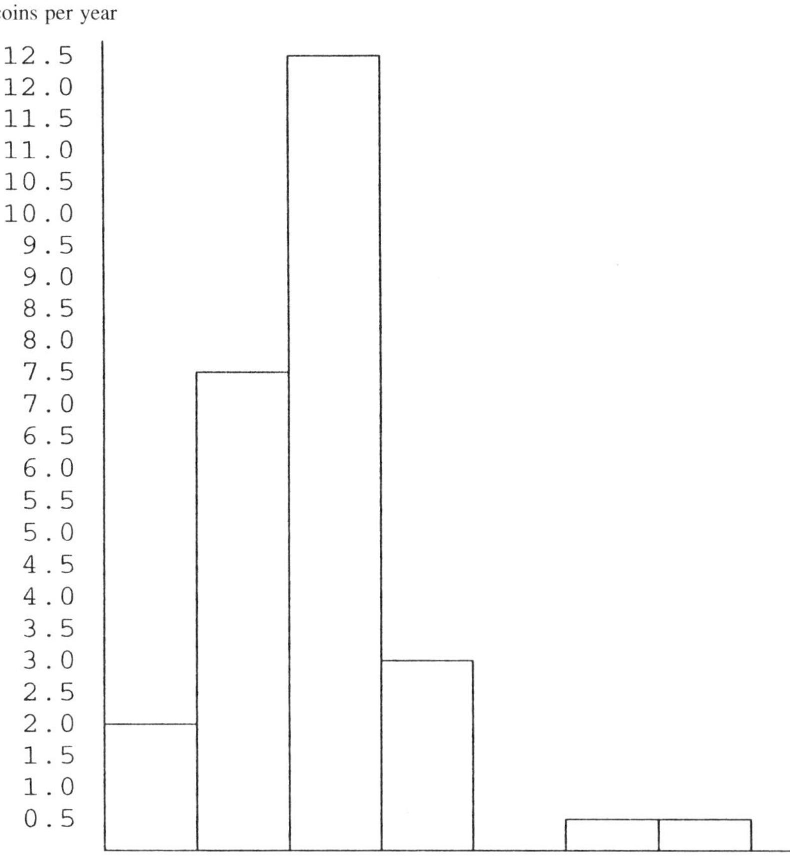

Fig. 15 Quantities of coins in Oxyrhynchus (yearly average)

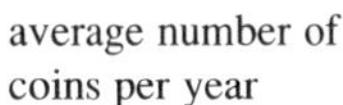

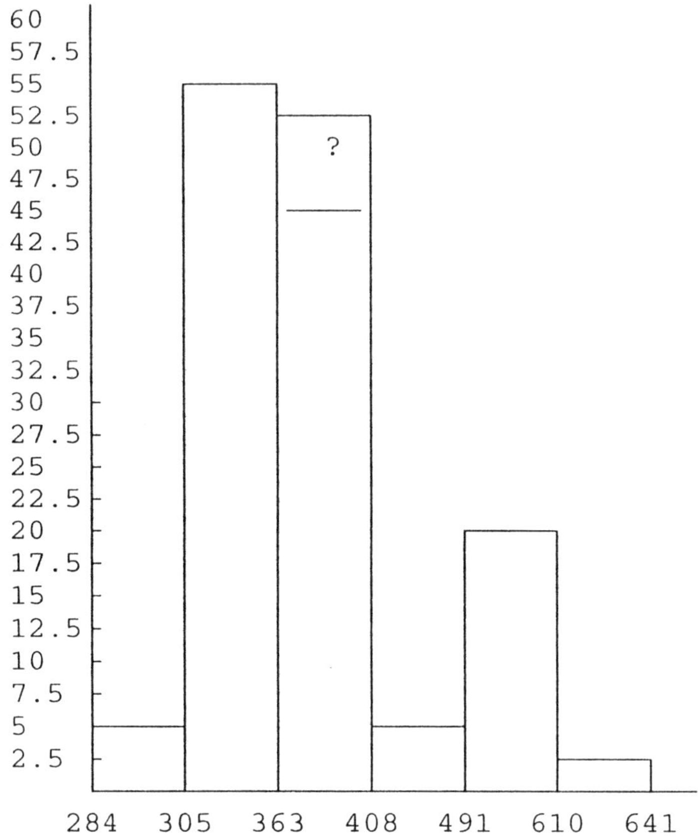

Fig. 16. Quantities of coins in Antioch (yearly average)

average number of
coins per year

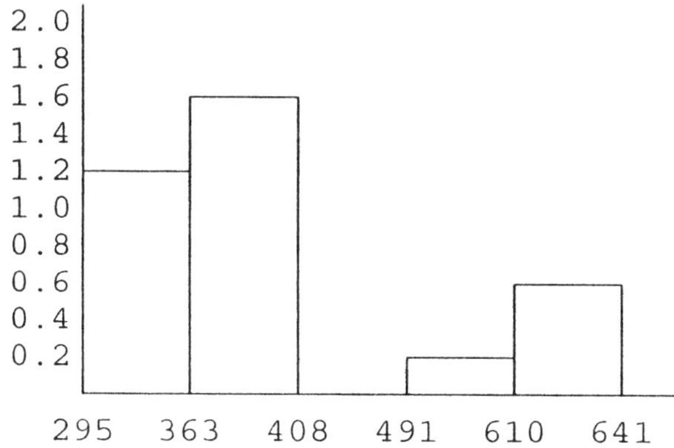

Fig. 17. Quantities of coins in Hammah, Syria (yearly average)

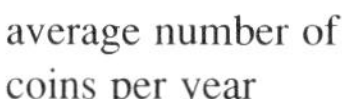

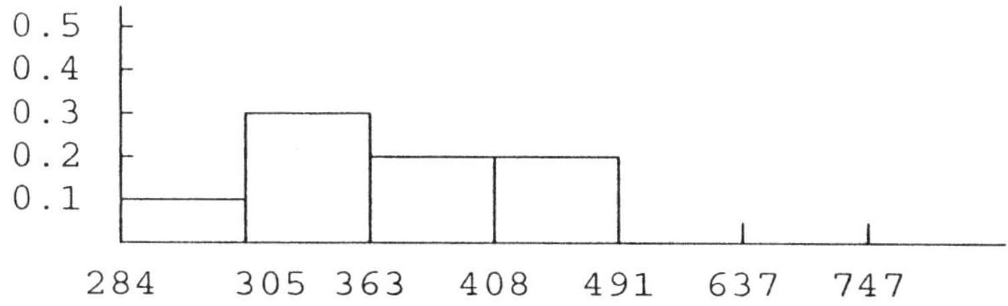

Fig. 18. Quantities of coins in Abu-l-Faraj (yearly average)

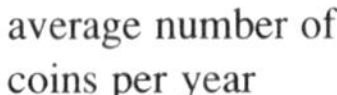

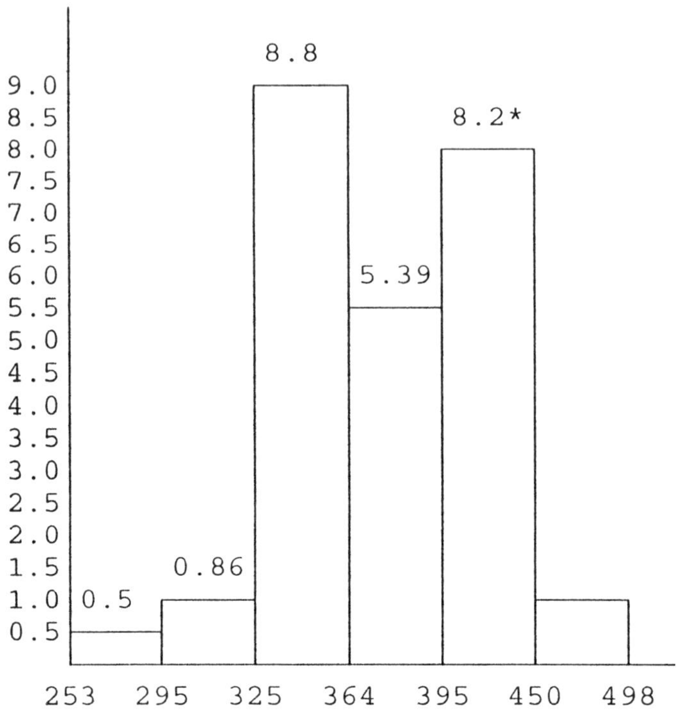

Due to the nature of the publication, the method of division of the author has been used, despite its unsuitability for our purposes. Our excamination indicated that most of the coins in this group are from 395-408.

Fig. 19. Quantities of coins in Apamea (yearly average)

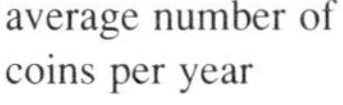

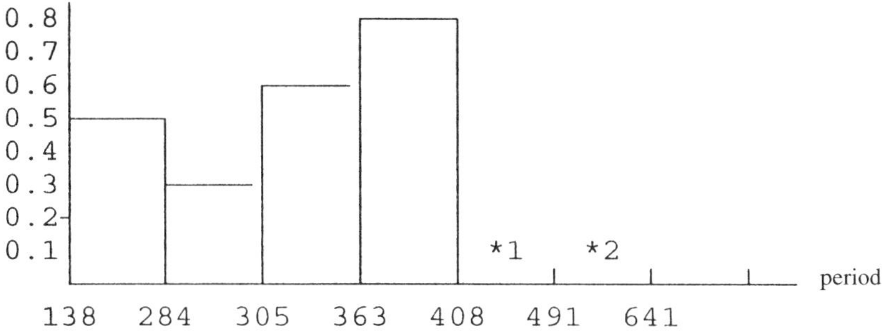

* Nominal number of coins from this period

Fig. 20. Quantities of coins in Tyre (yearly average)

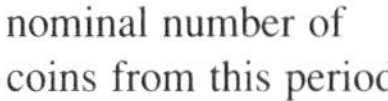

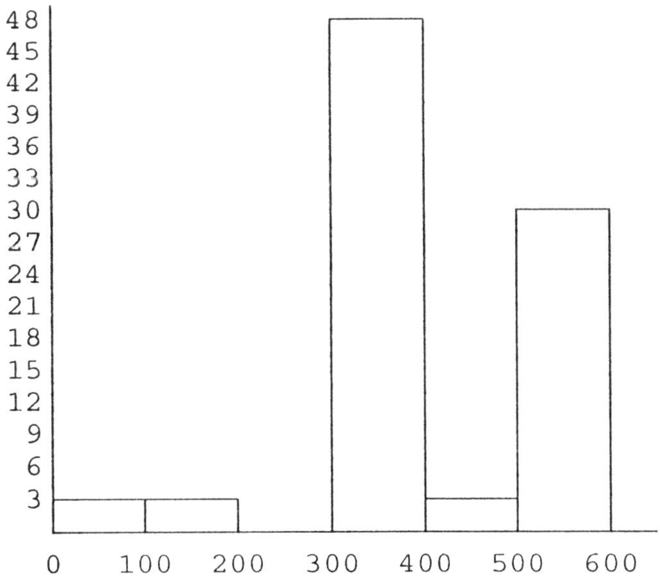

Fig. 21. Quantities of coins in Sidon

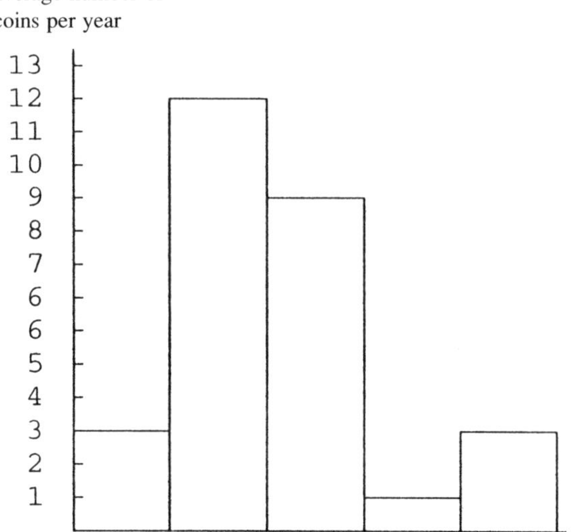

Fig. 22. Quantities of coins in the Amman Museum (yearly average)

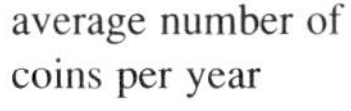

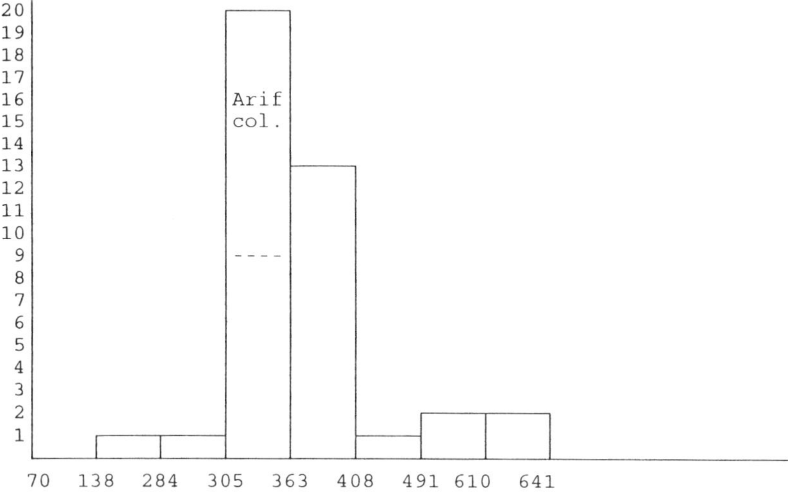

The data comprises all the excavations, including the Arif collection. For the first half of the fourth century, this collection is marked separately; it contains no coins from the second half of this century.

Fig. 23. Quantities of coins in Gerasa in the second-seventh centuries (yearly average)

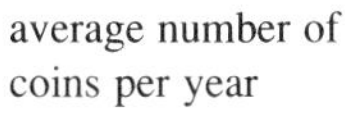

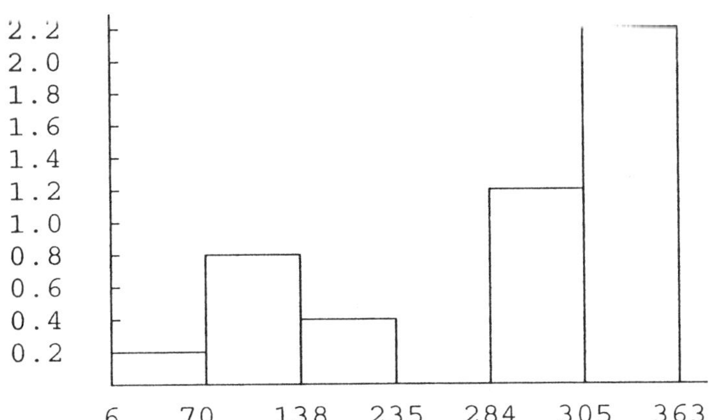

Fig. 24. Quantities of coins in Petra road (yearly average)

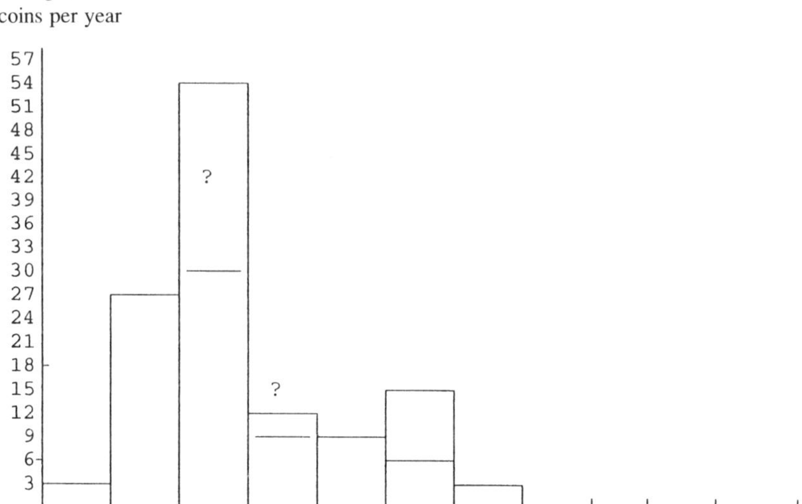

Fig. 25. Quantities of coins in Sardis (yearly average)

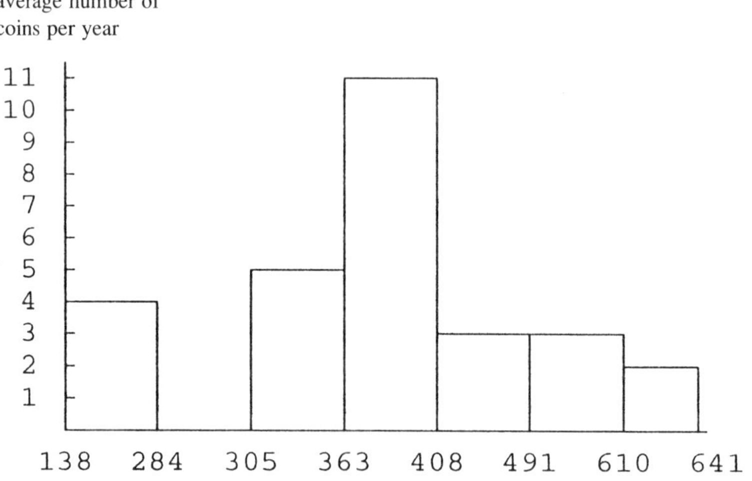

Fig. 26. Quantities of coins in Ephesos (yearly average)

average number of
coins per year

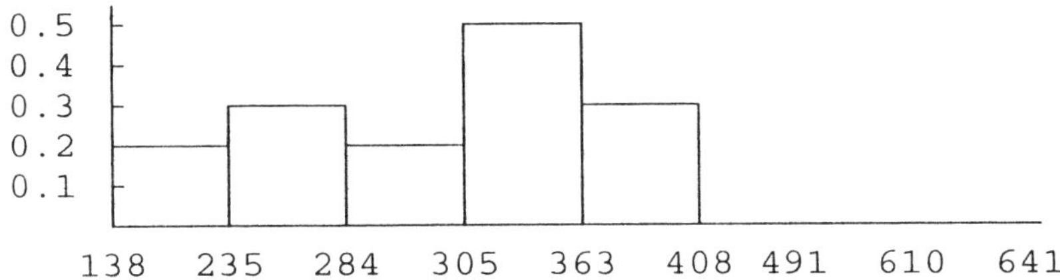

Fig. 27. Quantities of coins in Tarsos (yearly average)

average number of
coins per year

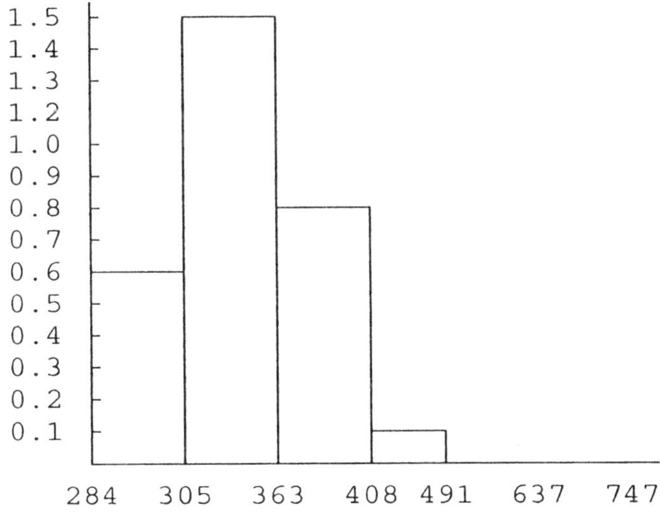

Fig. 28. Quantities of coins in Troy (yearly average)

average number of
coins per year

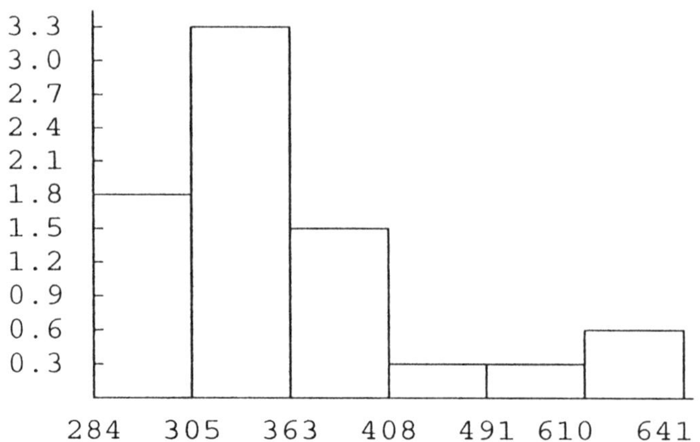

Fig. 29. Quantities of coins in Pergamon (yearly average)

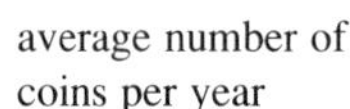

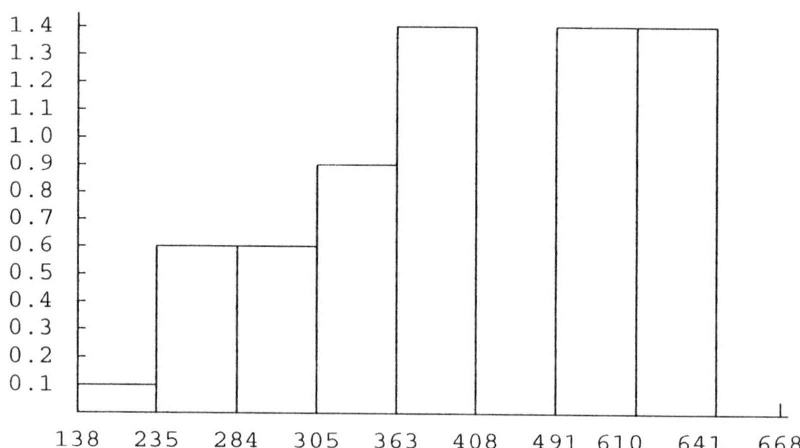

Fig. 30. Quantities of coins in Sidi (yearly average)

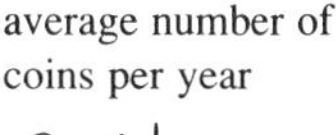

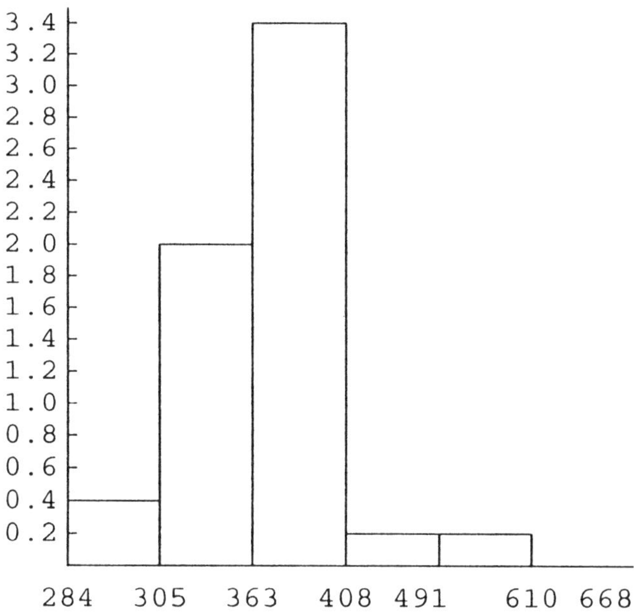

Fig. 31. Quantities of coins in Corinth (1925) (yearly average)

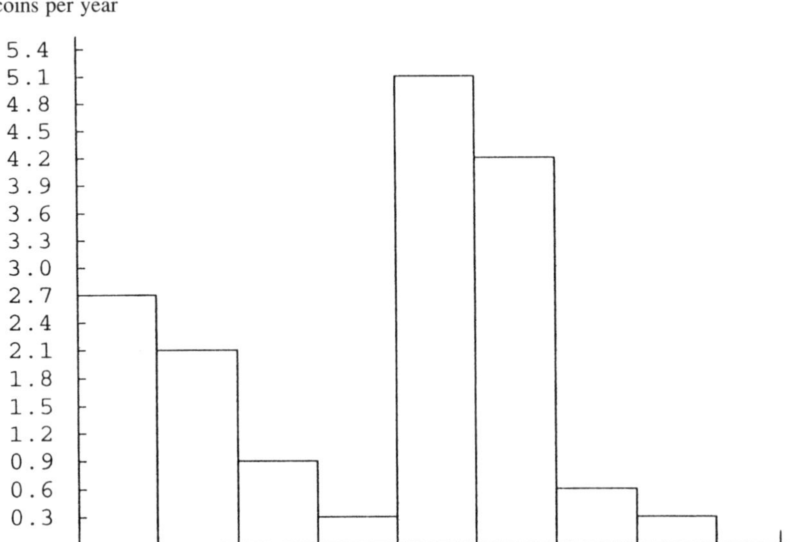

Fig. 32. Quantities of coins in Corinth (1933) (yearly average)

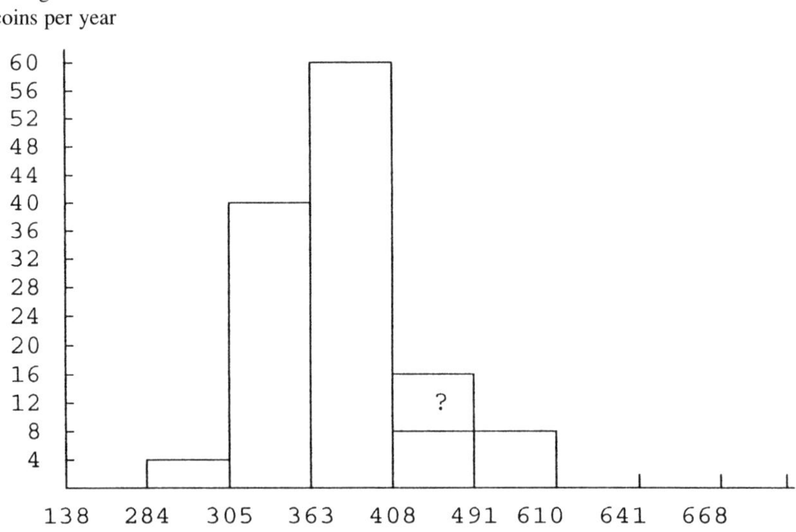

Fig. 33. Quantities of coins in Corinth (overall total) (yearly average)

average number of
coins per year

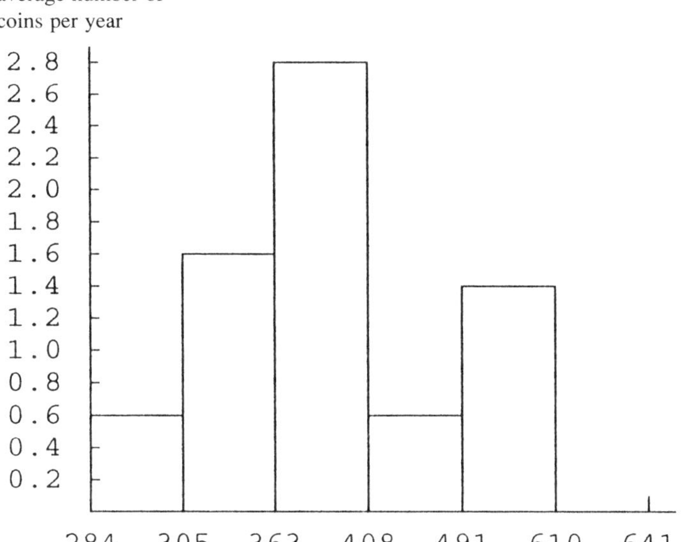

Fig. 34. Quantities of coins in Kenchreai, Greece (yearly average)

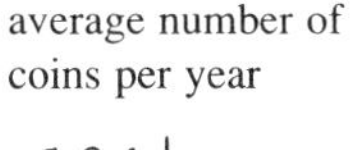

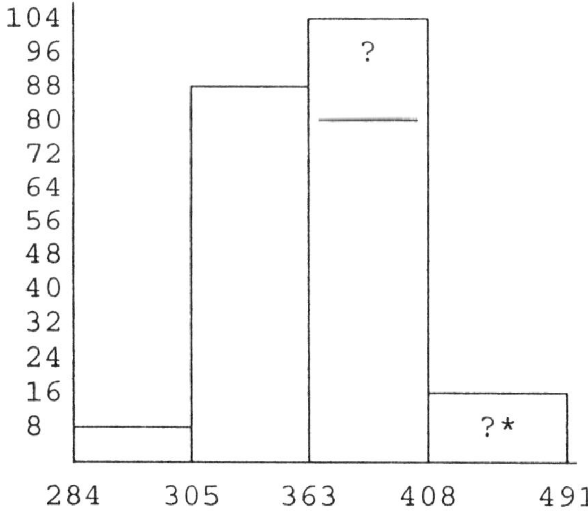

* maximal number of coins in this period; only 3.3 coins per year are certain

Fig. 35. Quantities of coins in Athens (yearly average)

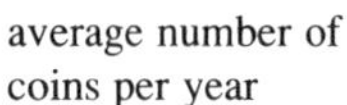

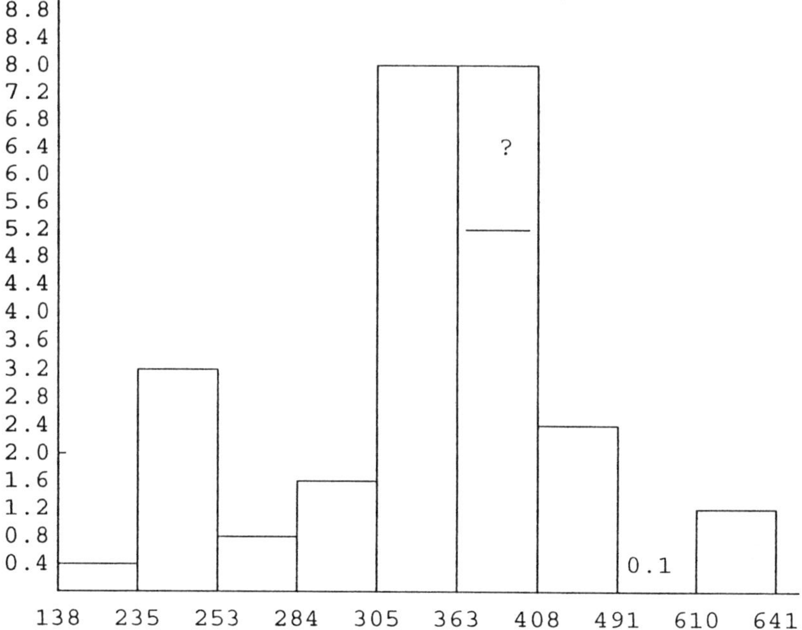

Fig. 36. Quantities of coins in Curium (yearly average)

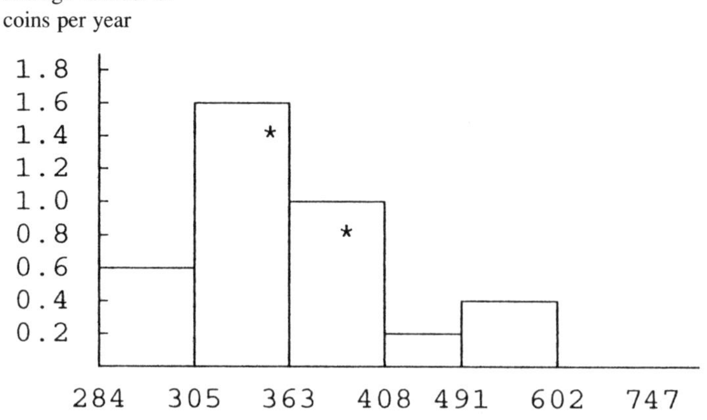

* in addition, there are 4.6 coins per year from the "fourth century"

Fig. 37. Quantities of coins in Memphis (yearly average)

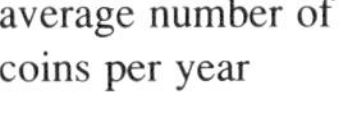

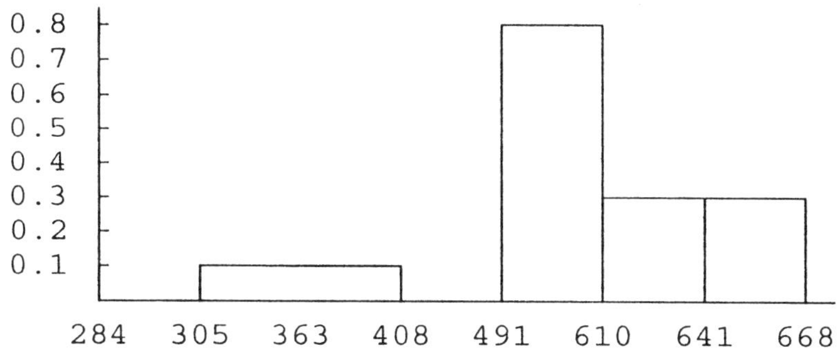

Fig. 38. Quantities of coins in Nessana (yearly average)

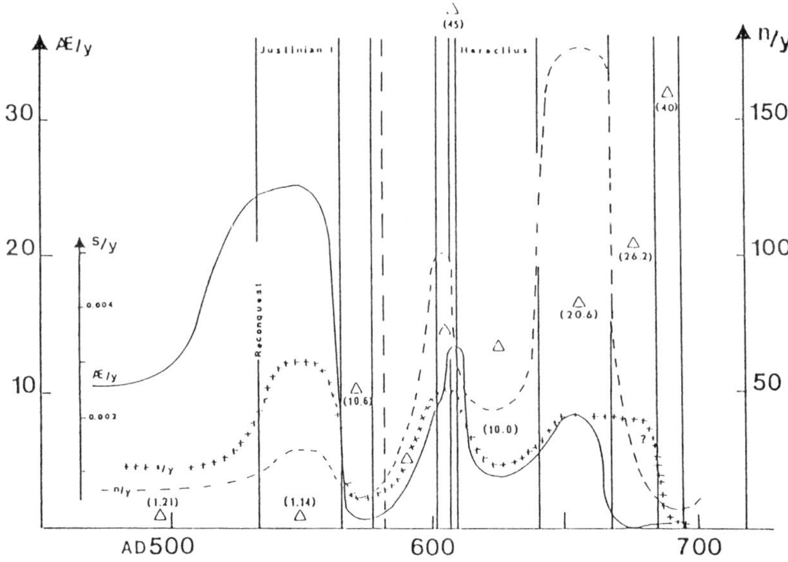

A Annual rate of bronze coins found in Dermech (Michigan) excavations (1975-1979 and 1983). Morrison 1988.

Fig. 39. Quantities of coins in Carthage (yearly average)

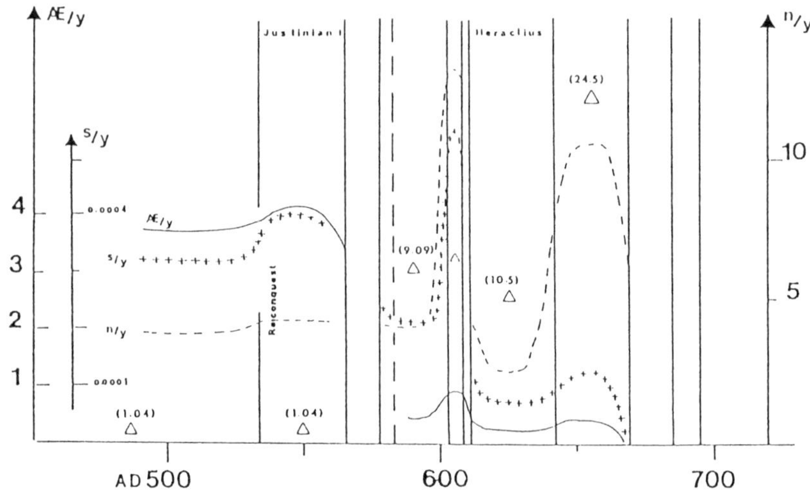

A Annual rate of bronze coins in the Circus (American) excavations (1982-1983). Morrison 1988.

Fig. 40. Quantities of coins in Carthage (yearly average)

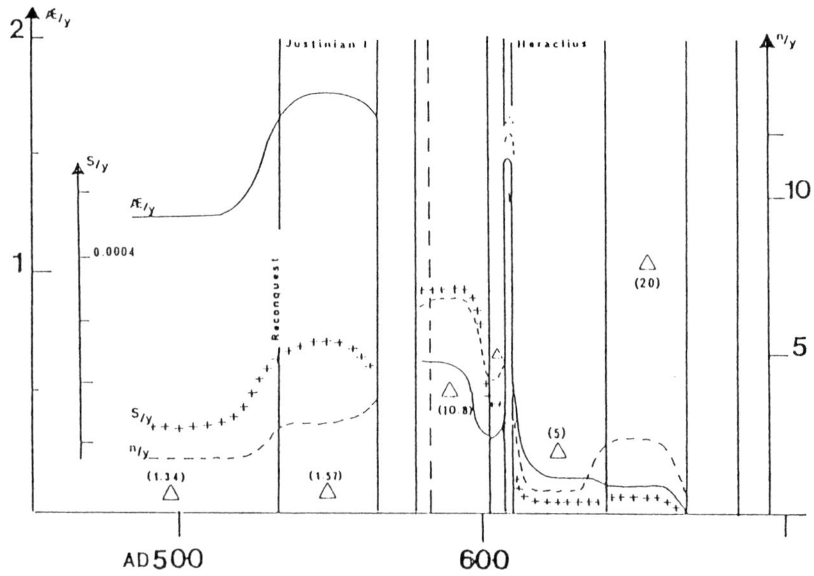

Annual rate of bronze coins found at the British site at Salmmbo. Idem.

Fig. 41. Quantities of coins in Carthage (yearly average)

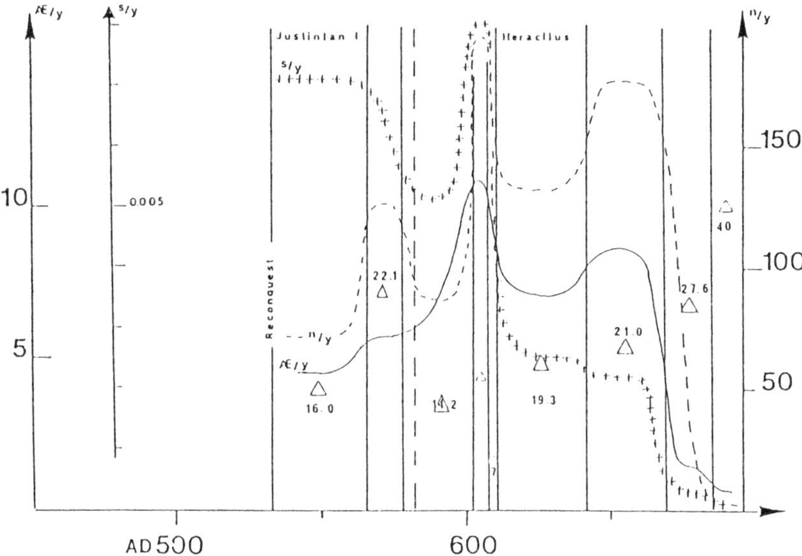

Annual rate of bronze coins preserved in the National Museum at Carthage.

Fig. 42. Quantities of coins in Carthage (yearly average)

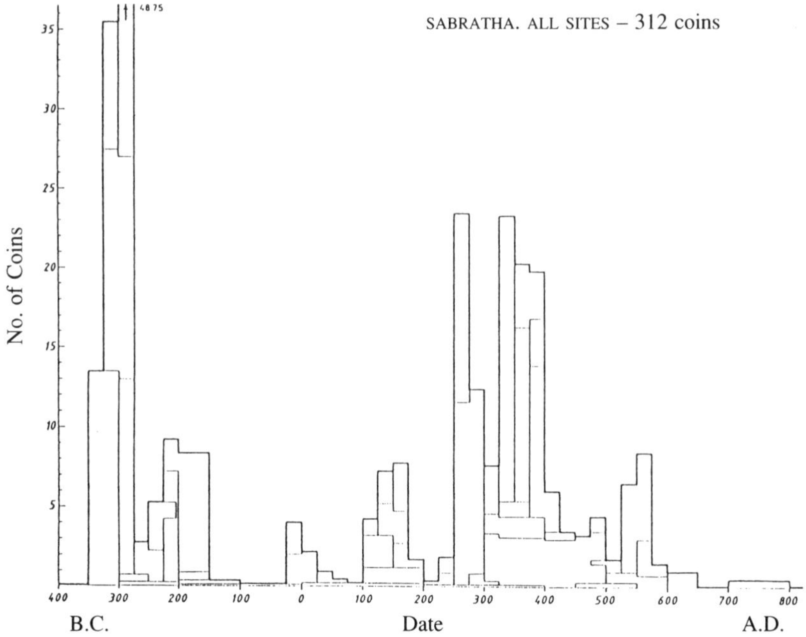

Fig. 43. Quantities of coins in Sabratha (yearly average)

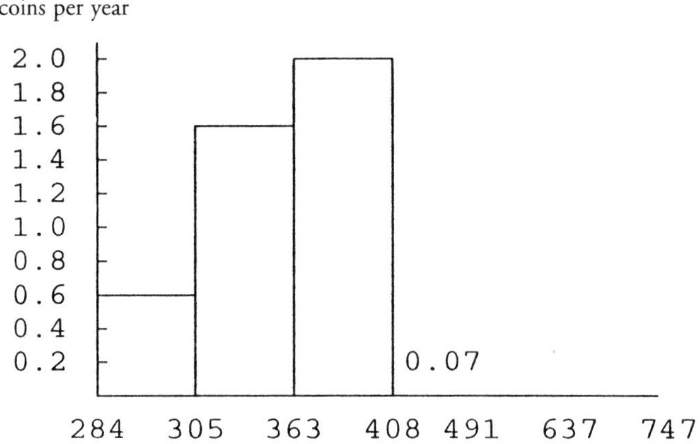

Fig. 44. Quantities of coins in Jalame (yearly average)

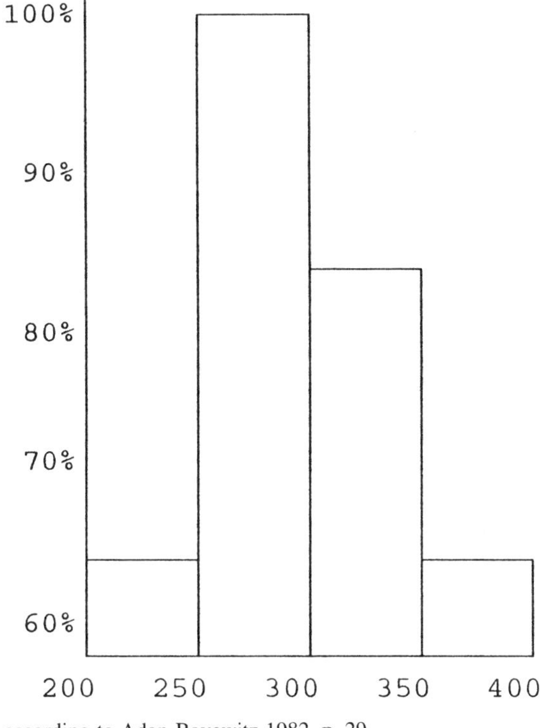

according to Adan-Bayewitz 1982, p. 29.

Fig. 45. Quantities of sherds in'Ammudim

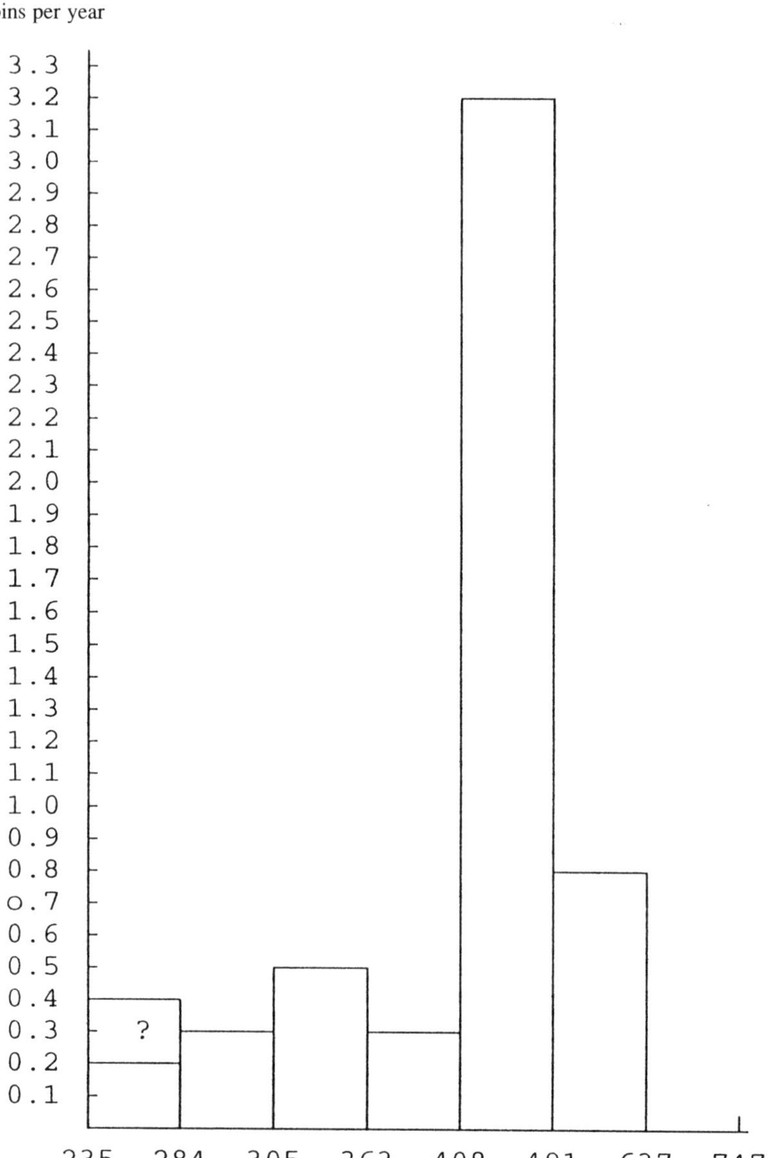

Fig. 46. Quantities of coins in Miron (yearly average)

average number of
coins per year

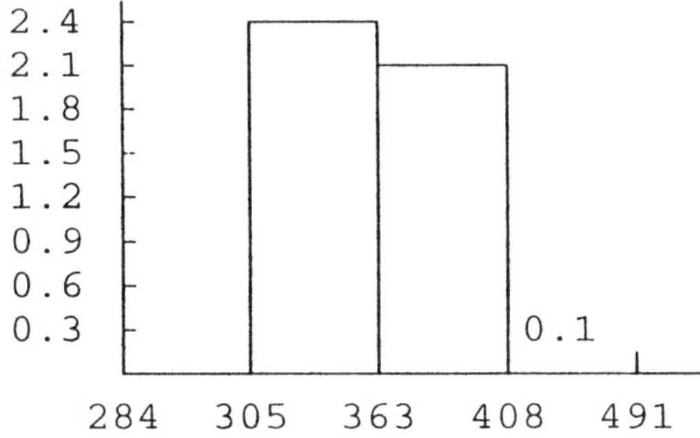

Note: the table is aranged according to the inventory (Reynor and Meshorer 1988, pp. 281-89)

Fig. 43. Quantities of coins in Khirbet Shema' (yearly average)

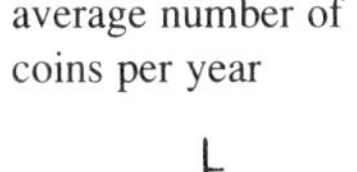

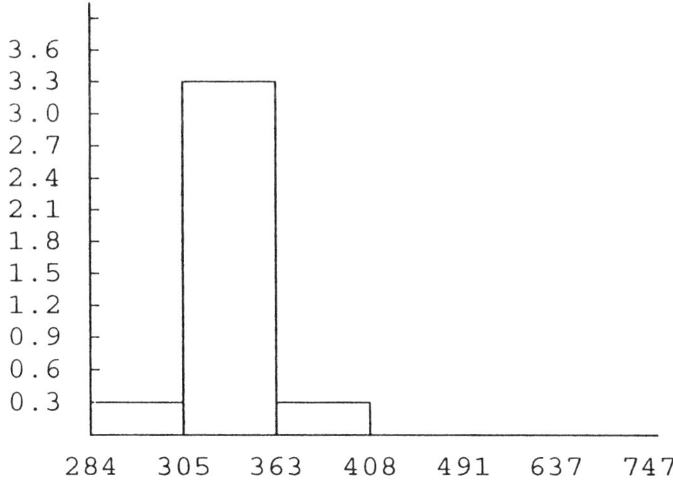

Fig. 48. Quantities of coins in Diocaesarea (yearly average)

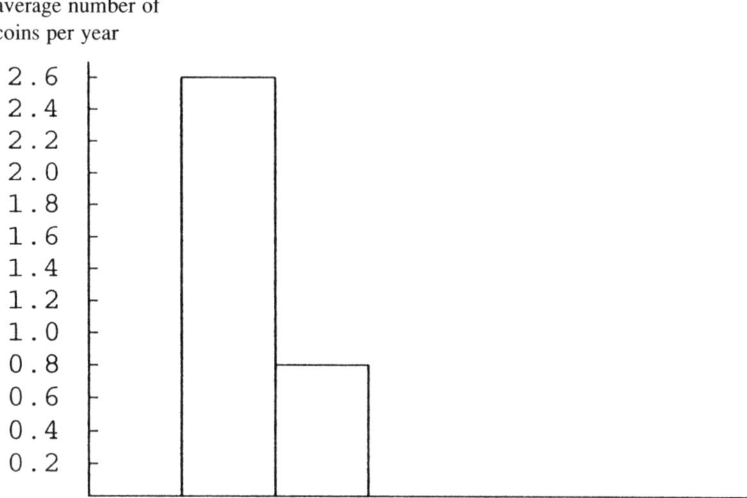

Fig. 49. Quantities of coins in Summaqa (yearly average)

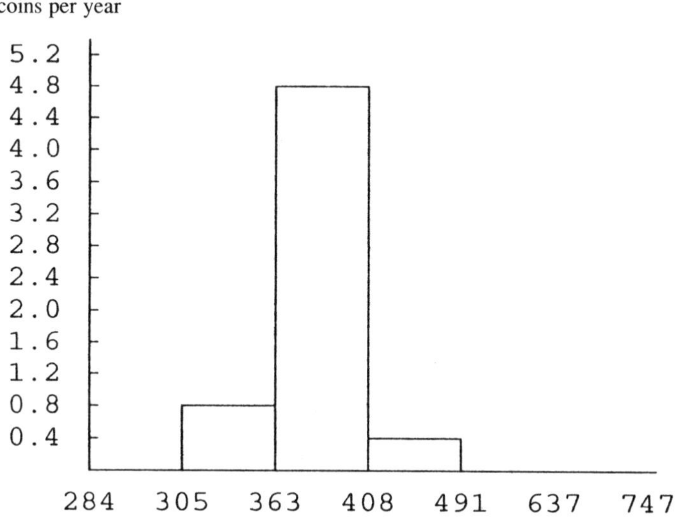

Fig. 50. Quantities of coins in'En Nashut (yearly average)

average number of
coins per year

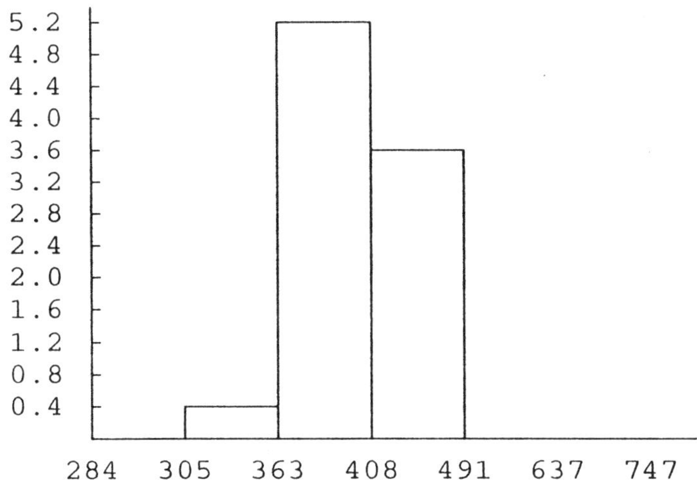

Fig. 51. Quantities of coins in Horvat Kanaf (yearly average)

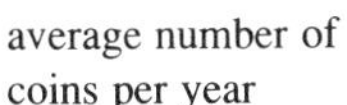

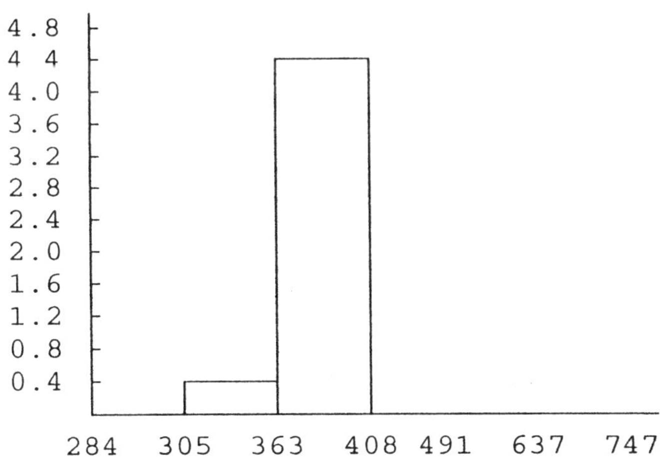

Fig. 52. Quantities of coins in Dabiyye (yearly average)

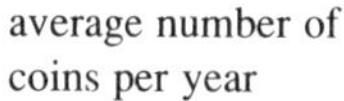

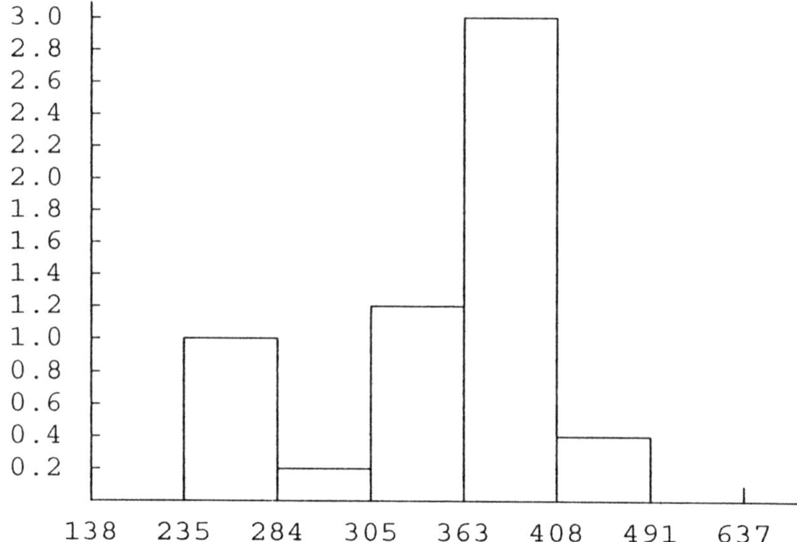

Also found, in addition to these coins, were 2.01 coins per year from the Trier mint in the fourth century. Such a large number of coins from a mint in the western part of the Empire is exceptional, and apparently indiciates a large number of pilgrims from Gaul. For the close religious ties between Christian Palestine and Gaul, which is also known from other sources, see: E.D. Hunt, "Gaul and the Holy Land in the Early fifth Century", in J. Drinkwater and H. Elton (eds.), Fifth Century Gaul: A Crisis of Identity (Cambridge, 1992), pp. 264-274.

Fig. 53. Quantities of coins in Capernaum (yearly average)

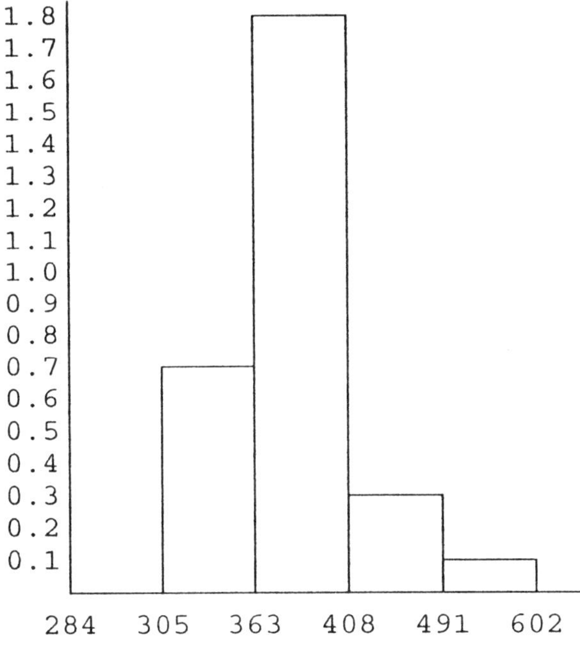

Fig. 54. Quantities of coins in Capernaum (settlement only, the synagogue) (yearly average)

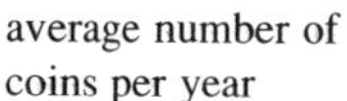

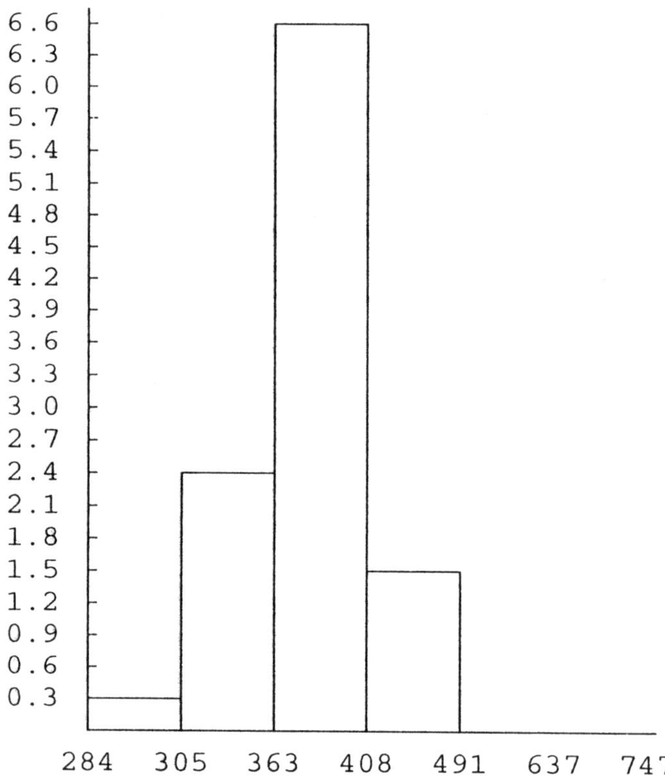

Fig. 55. Quantities of coins in Chorazin (yearly average)

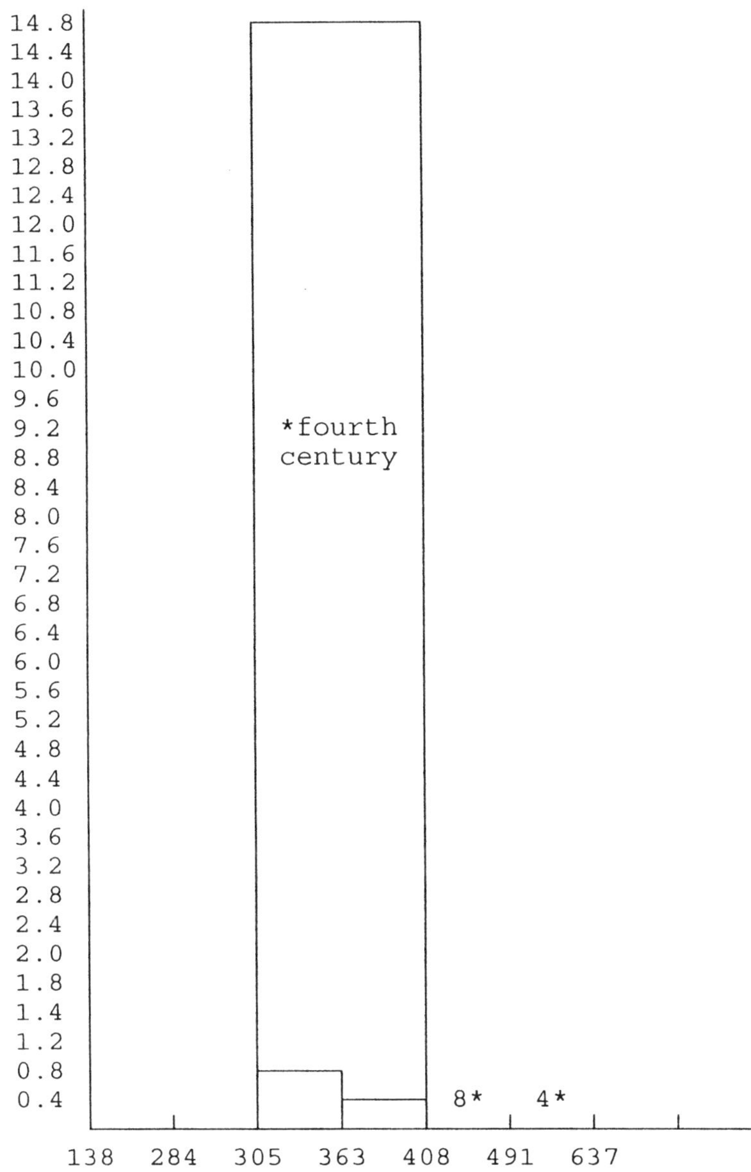

Note: the site contains many fourth-century coins which cannot be identified with precision.

* Nominal number of coins from this century.

Fig. 56. Quantities of coins in Gush Halav (the settlement) (yearly average)

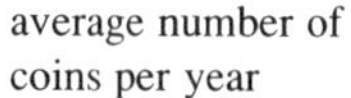

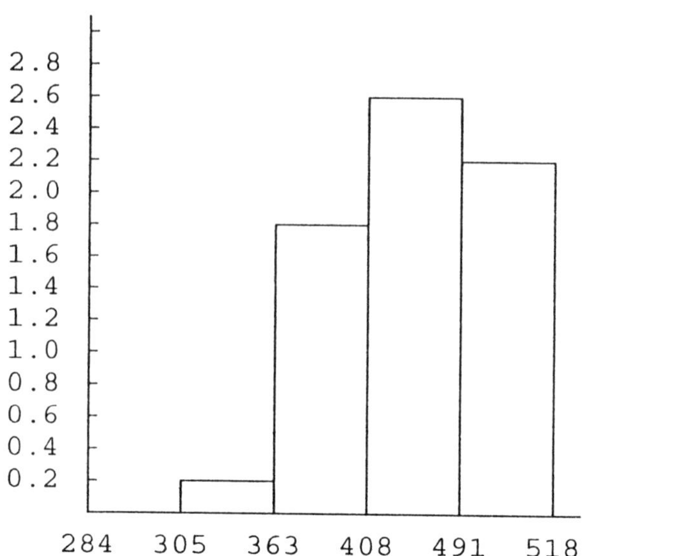

Fig. 57. Quantities of coins in Gush Halav (the hoard) (yearly average)

average number of
coins per year

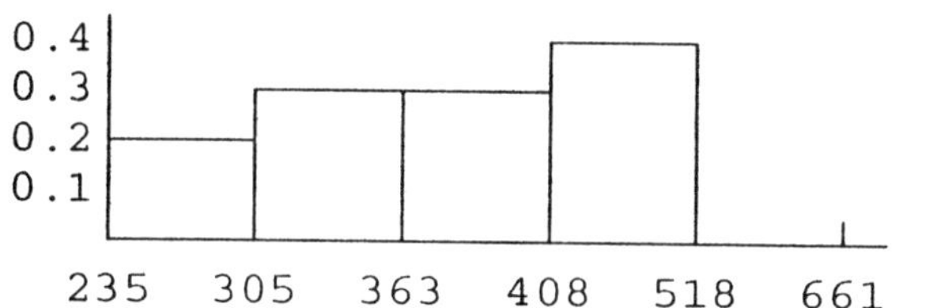

Fig. 58. Quantities of coins in Shiloh (yearly average)

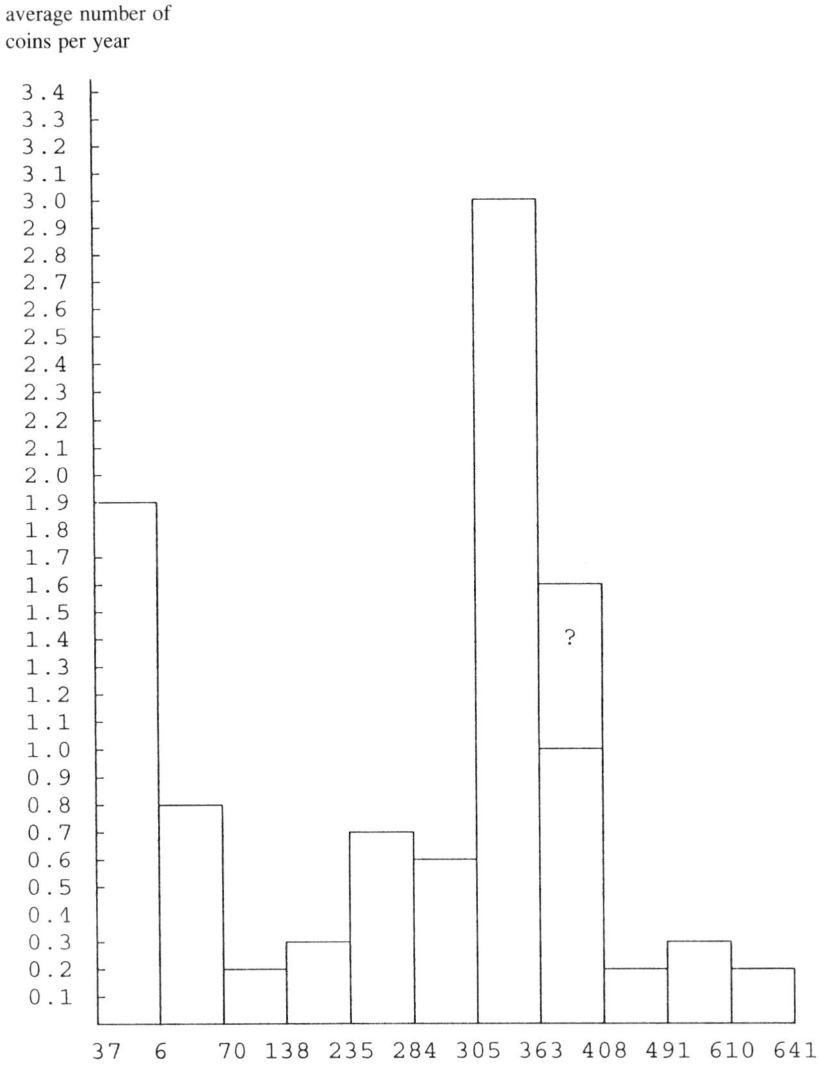

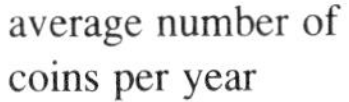

Fig. 59. Quantities of coins in Sebaste (yearly average)

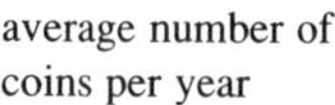

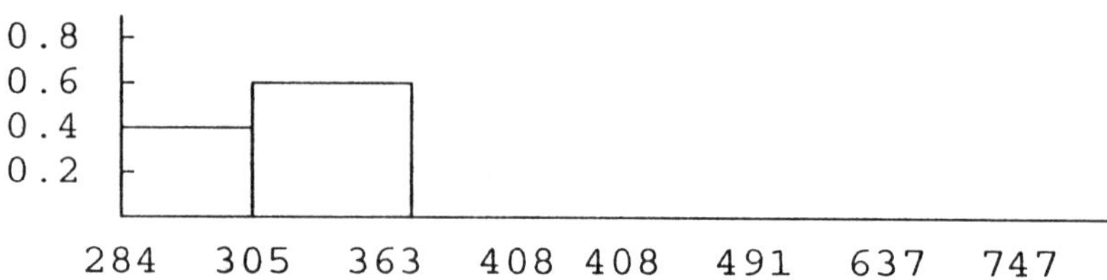

Fig. 60. Quantities of coins in Um Rihan (yearly average)

average number of
coins per year

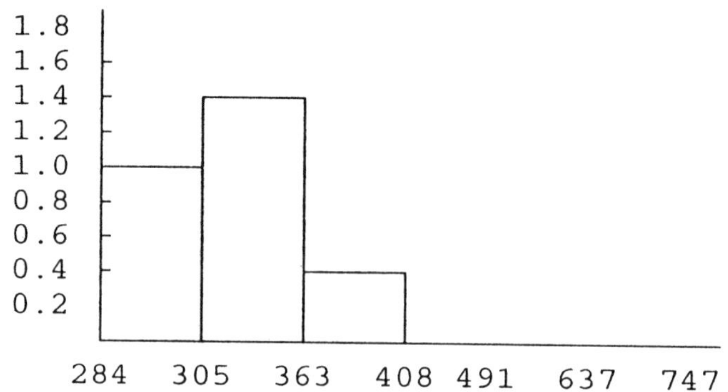

Fig. 61. Quantities of coins in'Emek Hefer (yearly average)

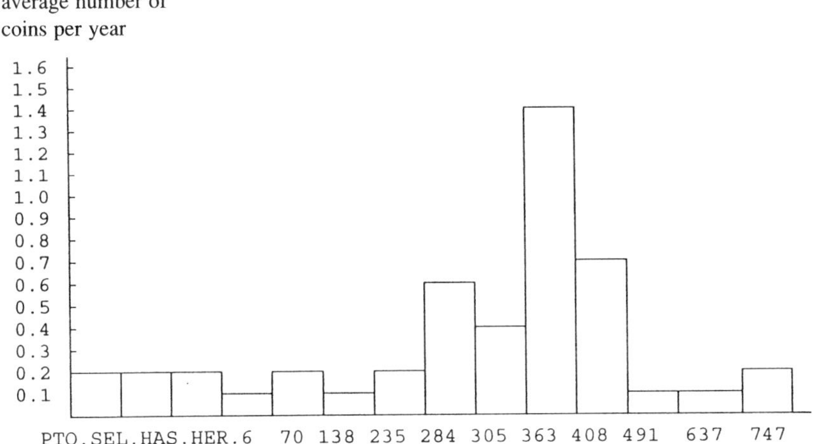

Fig. 62. Quantities of coins in Jamnitarum Portus (yearly average)

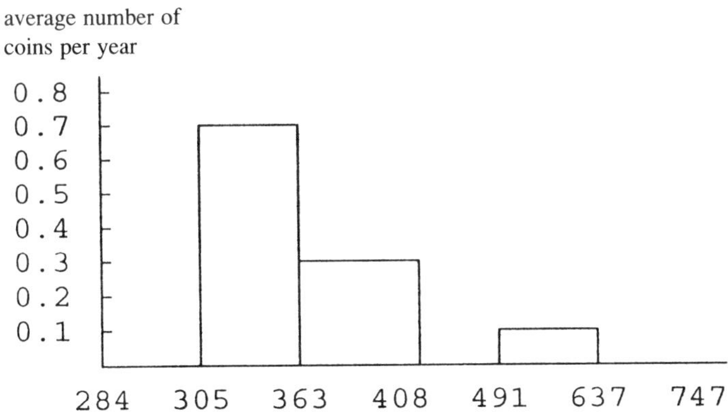

Fig. 63. Quantities of coins in Jaffa (yearly average)

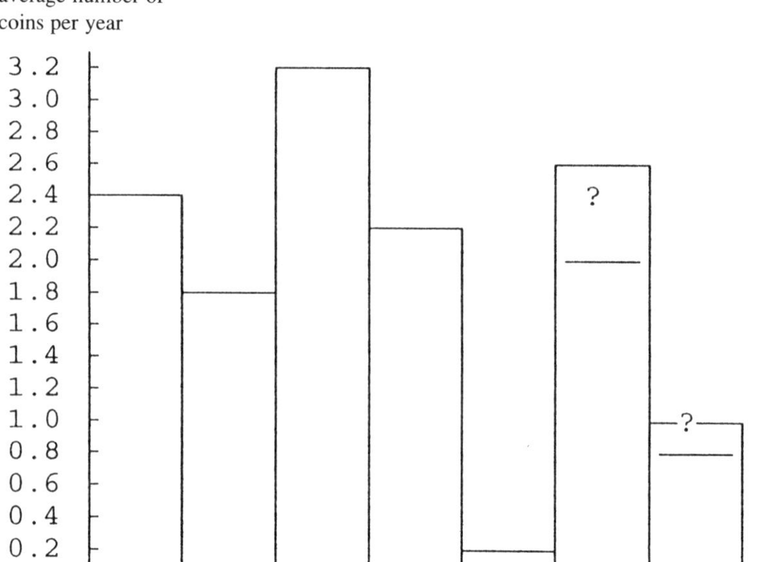

Fig. 64. Quantities of coins in Jerusalem (yearly average)

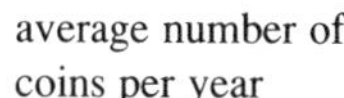

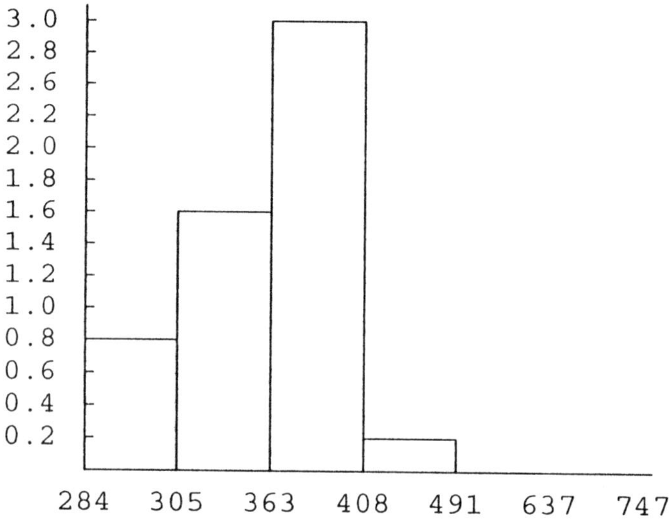

Fig. 65. Quantities of coins in Mambre (yearly average)

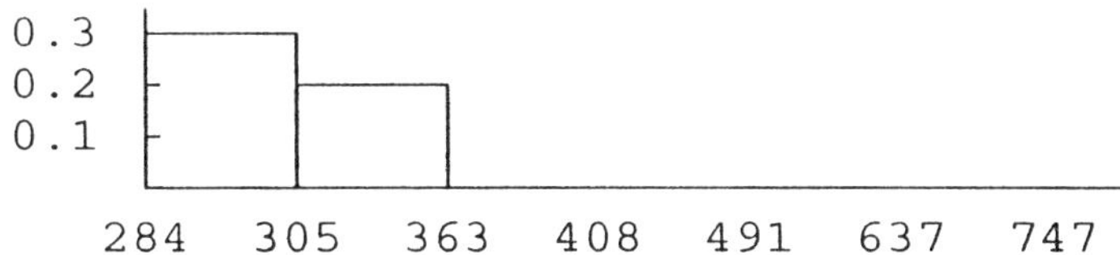

Fig. 66. Quantities of coins in Susiya (yearly average)

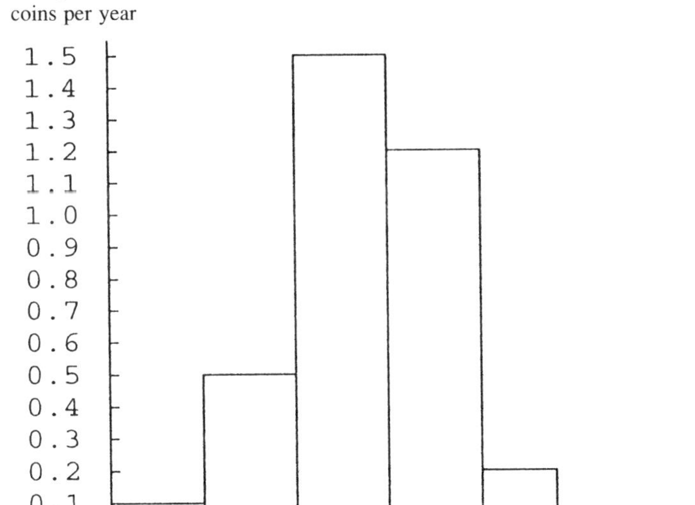

Fig. 67. Quantities of coins in Rimmon (settlement only) (yearly average)

List of Illustrations

42. Quantities of coins in Carthage (yearly average)
43. Quantities of coins in Sabratha (yearly average)
44. Quantities of coins in Jalame (yearly average)
45. Quantities of sherds in'Ammudim
46. Quantities of coins in Miron (yearly average)
43. Quantities of coins in Khirbet Shema' (yearly average)
48. Quantities of coins in Dio Caesarea (yearly average)
49. Quantities of coins in Summaqa (yearly average)
50. Quantities of coins in'En Nashut (yearly average)
51. Quantities of coins in Horvat Kanaf (yearly average)
52. Quantities of coins in Dabiyye (yearly average)
53. Quantities of coins in Capernaum (yearly average)
54. Quantities of coins in Capernaum (settlement only, the synagogue) (yearly average)
55. Quantities of coins in Chorazin (yearly average)
56. Quantities of coins in Gush Halav (the settlement) (yearly average)
57. Quantities of coins in Gush Halav (the hoard) (yearly average)
58. Quantities of coins in Shiloh (yearly average)
59. Quantities of coins in Sebaste (yearly average)
60. Quantities of coins in Um Rihan (yearly average)
61. Quantities of coins in'Emek Hefer (yearly average)
62. Quantities of coins in Jamnitarum Portus (yearly average)
63. Quantities of coins in Jaffa (yearly average)
64. Quantities of coins in Jerusalem (yearly average)
65. Quantities of coins in Mamre (yearly average)
66. Quantities of coins in Susiya (yearly average)
67. Quantities of coins in Rimmon (settlement only) (yearly average)

Selected bibliography

ANCIENT SOURCES

Aeneas of Gaza, *Epistulae* 1950 ed. L.M. Positano, (Rome).
Barsanuphius and Ioannes, 1960, *Biblos (Book)*..., ed. S.N. Schoinas, (Volos).
Cyril of Scythopolis, 1939, *Vitae ss. Euthynii, Sabae* etc. ed. E. Schwartz. TU 49
Epiphanius, *Adversus Haereses*, ed. Holl, K., Gr. Schr., 25, 31-37.
Epiphanius, *De mensuris et ponderibus*, 1935, ed. Dean, J.E. (Chicago — PG, 43, 238-94)
Eusebius, *Ecclesiastical History*, transl. Lake, K.L., and Oulton, J.E.L. (Loeb); PG 27.
Eusebius, Onomastikon, see Klostermann.
Expositio Totius Mundi 1882 (=Totius Oribis Descriptio), ed. Muller, C.W.L., *Geographi Graecis Minores*, 2, (Paris).
Klostermann. E., 1904, *Eusebius — Das Onomastikon der Biblischen Ortsnamen, (*Liepzig).
Marcus Diaconus, 1930, Vita Prophyrii Gazensis, ed. M.A. Kugener, (Paris).
Petrus the Iberian, 1895, *The Life of Petrus by John Rufus*, ed. Raabe. R., *Petrus der Iberer*, (Leipzig).
Procopius of Caesarea, 1905-1913, ed. J. Haury, Leipzig.
Sozomenus, 1960, Historia Ecclesiastica, ed. J. Bidez and G.C. Hanson, Gr. Sch. 50, 1960.

GENERAL BIBLIOGRAPHY

Adan Bayewitz. D., 1993, *Common Pottery in Roman Galilee*, (Ramat Gan).
Albeck, Ch., 1969, *Introduction to the Talmud: Bavli and Yerushalmi,* (Tel Aviv Heb.).
Alon. G., 1977, *Jews, Judaism and the Classical World*, (Jerusalem orig. pub. [Heb.] 1957, 1958).
Ariel, D. T., 1982, "A Survey of Coin Finds in Jerusalem," *LA* 32, pp. 273-326.
Arif, S., 1986, *A Treasury of Classical and Islamic Coins*, (London).
Avi-Yonah, M., 1966, *The Holy Land*, (Jerusalem).
Bagatti. B., 1971, *The Church from the Gentiles in Palestine*, (Jerusalem)
Bagnall, R.S., 1985, "Agricultural Productivity and Taxation in the Later Roman Empire," *TAPA* 115, pp. 289-308.
Barag, D., 1982-3, "Tyrian Currency in Galilee," *INJ* 6-7, pp. 7-13.
Baras Z. et al, 1982, eds, *Eretz Israel from the Destruction of the Second Temple to the Muslim Conquest*, (Jerusalem Heb.)
Bell, H. W., 1916, *Sardis XI. Coins, 1910-1914,* (Leiden).
Bellinger, A.R., 1961, *Troy. The Coins,* (Princeton).

Bellinger. A.D., 1938, *Coins, in Kraeling, C.H., Geraasa city of the Decapolis,* (New Haven).

Bellinger. A.D., 1949, *The Excavations at Dura Europus*, VI (The Coins) (New Haven).

Bennet. M.A., 1972, *Byzantine and Islamic Ceramics from Hebron (El Khalil), the Common Wares*, (Ann Arbor Michigen).

Briend. J., 1980, et al., *Tell Keisan (1971-1976),* (Paris).

Brock, S. P. 1977, "A Letter Attributed to Cyril of Jerusalem on the Rebuilding of the Temple," *BSOAS* 40, pp. 267-86.

Buttrey T. V., et al., *1981, Greek, Roman and Islamic Coins from Sardis,* (Cambridge, Mass).

Callu, J.-P., 1979, *Les Monnaies Romaines* (Brussels).

Chehab, M. H., 1986, *Fouilles De Tyr. La Necropole IV* (Paris).

Clayton, P.A., 1967, "The Coins from Tell Rifa'at," *Iraq* 29, pp. 143-54.

Crawford, M. H., 1970, "Money and Exchange in the Roman World," *JRS* 60, pp. 40-48.

Crowfoot, J.W., et al., 1957, *The Objects from Samaria*, (London).

Dan, Y. 1976, "*Social Life in Eretz Israel in Byzantine Period*," Ph.D. diss., Hebrew University, Jerusalem, (Heb.).

Dar, S., 1988, Archaeological Evidence on the Samaritan Revolts of the Byzantine Period," in Jacoby, D. Tsafrir, Y., eds. *Jews, Samaritans and Christians*, (Jerusalem), pp. 228-38 (Heb.).

Dar, S., 1993, *Settlements and Cult Sites on Mount Hermon, Israel: Ituraean Culture in the Hellenistic and Roman Periods,* (Oxford).

Dunand, M. and Duru, R., 1962, *Oumm el-'Amed — Une Ville de l'Epoque Hellenistique aux Echelles de Tyr* ,(Paris).

Duncan-Jones, R., 1990, *Structure and Scale in the Roman Economy,* (Cambridge).

Ephrathi, J. E., 1973, *The Sevoraic Period and its Literature in Babylonia and in Eretz Israel (500-684),* (Petah Tikvah, Heb.)

Finkelstein, I., 1988-9, "The Land of Ephraim Survey," *Tel-Aviv* 15-16 . pp. 117-183.

Foss, C. , 1975, "The Persians in Asia Minor and the End of Antiquity," *EHR* 90 pp. 721-747.

Foss, C., 1990, *History and Archaeology of Byzantine Asia Minor,* (Variorum).

Fulco. W.J., Zayadin. F.,1981, "Coins from Samaria Sebaste", *ADAJ*, 25 pp. 197-225.

Fulford, M. G., 1980, "Carthage: Overseas Trade and the Political Economy, c. A.D. 400-700," *Reading Medieval Studies* 6, pp. 68-70;

Fulford, M. G., 1984, "The Long Distance Trade and Communication of Carthage, c. A.D. 400 to c. A.D. 650," in *Excavations at Carthage: The British Mission I, 2,* eds. M. G. Fulford and D. P. S. Peacock (Sheffield), pp. 255-61

Goffart, W., 1974, "*Caput and Colonate: Towards a History of Late Roman Taxation*", (Toronto).

Goicoechea, E.O., 1986, *Excavationes en el Agora de Gerasaa en 1983,* (Madrid).

Goldman, H., 1950, *Excavations at Goezlue Kule, Tarsus,* (Princeton).

Grierson, P., 1959, "Commerce in the Dark Ages: a Critique of the Evidence," *Transactions of the Royal Historical Society* Fifth Series, 9, pp. 123-40.

Haatvedt, R. A. et al., *1964, Coins from Karanis* (Michigan).

Haiman, *A.* M.. 1990, *Shepherds and Farmers in the Kadesh Barne'a Region* (Sde Boker, Heb.)

Haldon, J., 1985 "Some Considerations of Byzantine Society and Economy in the Seventh Century," *Byzantinische Forschungen,* 10, pp. 75-112.

Haldon, J., 1994, *Money and Government in the Roman Empire,* (Cambridge).

Hanson, *R., 1980, Tyrian Influence in the Upper Galilee,* (Cambridge, Mass.).

Hartal, M., 1989, *The Northern Golan,* (Katzrin Heb.).

Hayes, J. W., 1972, *Late Roman Pottery,* (London).

Hayes, J. W., 1980, *Supp.* (London).

Hendy, F. M., 1985, *Studies in the Byzantine Monetary Economy c. 300-1450,* (Cambridge).

Hendy, M. F., 1986, "The Coins," in *Excavations at Sarachane in Istanbul,* I, R. M. Harrison, ed., (Princeton).

Herr, M. D., 1978, "Hellenistic Influences in the Jewish City in Eretz-Israel in the Fourth and Sixth Centuries C.E.", *Cathedra* 8, pp. 90-94 (Heb.).

Hodges R., Whitehouse, *D., 1983, Mohammed, Charlemagne and the Origins of Europe: Archaeology and the Pirenne Thesis, (Ithaca, N.Y.).*

Hohlfelder, R. L., 1984, "Caesarea Maritima in Late Antiquity," in W. Heckel and R. Sullivan , (eds.) *Ancient Coins of the Greco-Roman World*, eds. (Ontario), pp. 186-261.

Hopkins, K., 1980, "Taxes and Trade in the Roman Empire (200 B.C. — A.D. 400)," *JRS* 70, pp. 101-125.

Howgego, C. 1992,"The Supply and Use of Money in the Roman World 200 B.C. to A.D. 300," *JRS* 82, pp. 1-31.

Ilan, Z., 1991, *Ancient Synagogues in Israel* (Tel Aviv Heb.).

Jones, A. H. M. , 1958,"The Roman Colonate," *Past and Present* 13, pp. 1-13.

Jones, A. H. M., 1964, *The Later Roman Empire*, 284-602, Oxford.

Jones, A.H. M., 1974, *The Roman Economy*, (Oxford).

Kennedy, F., 1986, "The Towns of Bilad al-Sham and the Arab Conquest," in *Bilad al-Sham during the Byzantine Period*, eds. M. A. Bakhit and M. Asfour (Amman), pp. 88-99.

Kennedy, F., 1985, "The Last Century of Byzantine Syria. A Reinterpretation," *Byzantinische Forschungen* 10, pp. 141-183;

Kirkbride, A. S. 1939,"Currencies in Transjordan," *PEF* 72, pp. 152-61

Kloner. A., Mindel. T., 1981, Two Byzantine Hoards from Ancient Synagogue of Horvat Rimmon, *INJ,* 5, pp. 60-61.

Lamerle, P. 1979, *The Agrarian History of Byzantium from the Origins to the Twelfth Century,* (Galway Ireland).

Lenzen, C.J., 1983, *The Byzantine-Islamic Occupation at Caesarea Maritima as Evidenced through the Pottery,* (Ann Arbor Michigen).

Lewin, B. M., 1929, "Ma'asim le-bne Erez Israel (Palestinian Halachic Practice)," *Tarbiz* 1, no. 1 pp 79-101.

Liebeschuetz, J. H. G. W., 1990, "*From Diocletian to the Arab Conquest: Change in the Late Roman Empire,*" (Variorum).

Lopez, R. S., 1943, "Mohammed and Charlemagne: A Revision," *Speculum* 18, pp. 14-38.

MacMullen, R. 1988, *Corruption and the Decline of Rome* (New Haven).

Mader, E., 1957, *Mambre* (Freiburg im Breisgau).

Mann, J., 1930, "Sefer ha-Ma'asim le-bne Erez Israel (Book of Palestinian Halachic Practice)," Tarbiz 1, no. 3, pp. 1-14.

Margoliot, M., 1973 *Palestinian Halakhot from the Genizah* (Jerusalem Heb.).

McNicoll, A., 1982, et al., *Pella in Jordan, I* (Canberra)..

McNicoll, A., 1992, *Pella in Jordan, II,2* (Sydney).

Meimaris. Y.E., 1986, *Sacred Names, Saints, Martyrs, Church officials ...* (Athens).

Meyers, E. M. and C. L. eds., 1990, *Meiron Excavations Project 5. Excavations at the Ancient Synagogue of Gush Halav,* (Winona Lake).

Meyers, E. M. et al., 1976, *Ancient Synagogue Excavations at Khirbet Shema', Upper Galilee, Israel 1970-1972,* (Durham).

Meyers, E.M., et al., 1981, *Excavations at Ancient Meiron, Upper Galilee, Israel, 1971-1972, 1974-75, 1977* (Cambridge Mass.).

Milne, J. G., 1922, "The Coins from Oxyrhynchus," *Journal of Egyptian Archaeology* 8 (1922), pp. 158-63.

Mor, M., 1989, *"The* Events of 351-352 in Palestine — the Last Revolt against Rome?" in *The Eastern Frontier of the Roman Empire*, eds. D. H. French C. S. Lightfoot (*BAR* 553), (Oxford) pp. 335-53.

Nathanson, B. G., 1981, *The Fourth Century Jewish Revolt during the Reign of Gallus*, Ph.D. diss., (Ann Arbor Michigen).

Naveh, J., 1978, *On Stone and Mosaic: The Aramaic and Hebrew Inscriptions from Ancient Synagogues* (Jerusalem, Heb.).

Negev, A., 1988, "The Architecture of Mamphis Final Report, II: *The Late Roman and Byzantine Periods*," *Qedem* 27.

Oppenheimer, A., 1991, *Galilee in the Mishnaic Period* (Jerusalem Heb.).

Ovadiah A., 1970, *Corpus of the Byzantine Churches in the Holy Land*, (Bonn).

Ovadiah A., and de Silva, C. G. , 1981, "Supplement to the Corpus of the Byzantine Churches in the Holy Land Part I. Newly Discovered Churches," *Levant* 13 pp. 200-61; Ovadiah A., and de Silva, C. G. , 1982, "Supplement ...Part II," *Levant* 14, pp. 129-65.

Pirenne, H., 1939, *Mohammed and Charlemagne*, trans. B. Miall (London).

Portugali, Y., 1986, "The Settlement Pattern in the Western Jezreel Valley from the 6th Century B.C.E. to the Arab Conquest," in *Man and Land in Eretz-Israel*, ed. A Kasher, et al, (Jerusalem), pp. 7-19 (Heb.).

Portugali. J. A., 1982, "Field Methodology for Regional Archaeology (the Iezreel Valley Survey 1981)", *Tel Aviv*, 9 pp. 170-188 .

Pritchard, J.B., 1971, "The Roman Port at Sarafand (Sarepata). Preliminary Report on the Seasons of 1969 and 1970," *Bulletin de Musee de Beyrouth* 24.

Regling, K., 1912, "Die Stadt," in *Altertuemer von Pergamon* I,2: *Stadt und Landschaft* (Berlin), pp. 355-63.

Regling, K., 1927, Die Münzen von Priene, (Berlin).

Reisner. G.A., et al.,1924, *Harvard Excavations at Samaria* (Cambridge).

Riley. J.A., 1975, The Pottery from the first Season of Excavations in the Caesarea Hippodrome, *BASAOR,* 218, pp.25-36.

Rubin, Z., 1986, "The Mediterranean and the Dilemma of the Roman Empire in Late Antiquity," *Mediterranean Historical Review* 1, pp. 13-62.

Safrai, Z., 1985, *The Jewish Community in the Talmudic Period* (Jerusalem Heb.).

Safrai, Z., 1994, *The Economy of Roman Palestine*, (London).

Safrai. Z., 1992, The Roman Army in Galilee, in: Levine, I.L., ed., *The Galilee in Late Antiquity*, Camb. Mass. pp. 103-114.

Saller, S.J., 1941, *The Memorial of Moses on Mount Nebo,*. (Jerusalem).

Shahid, I., 1989, *Byzantium and the Arabs in the Fifth Century,* (Washington, D.C.).

Smith, R. H. and Day, L. P., 1992, *Pella of the Decapolis*, vol. 2 (Wooster).

Sperber, D., 1978, *Roman Palestine 200-400: The Land. Crisis and Change in Agrarian Society as Reflected in Rabbinic Sources,* (Ramat Gan).

Spijkerman, A., 1975, *Cafarnao III Catalogo Della Monete della Citta,* (Jerusalem).

Stemberger, G., 1994. *Juden und Christen*, (München).

Tsaferis, V., 1989, *Excavations at Capernaum, I 1978-1982,* (Winona Lake).

Van Dam, P., 1992, "The Pirenne Thesis and Fifth-Century Gaul," *in Fifth Century Gaul: A Crisis of Identity*, ed. J. Drinkwater H. Elton, eds. (Cambridge), pp. 321-33.

Ward-Perkins, J. B. 1984, *From Classical Antiquity to the Middle Ages: Urban Public Building in Northern and Central Italy, A.D. 300-850,* (Oxford).

Weinberg, G.D., 1988, ed. *Excavations at Jalame and Their Chronological Implications* (Columbia, Miss.).

West, L. C. Johnson, A. C., 1944, *Currency in Roman and Byzantine Egypt,* (Princeton).

Wilkinson, J., 1977, *Jerusalem Pilgrims before the Crusades* (Jerusalem).

Zayadine, E., 1986, ed. *Jerash Archaeological Project 1981-83,* (Amman).

Zayadine, F., 1977-8, "Excavations on the Upper Citadel of Amman Area A," *ADAJ* 22, pp. 38-40.

Index

Subjects

PRINTED ON PERMANENT PAPER • IMPRIME SUR PAPIER PERMANENT • GEDRUKT OP DUURZAAM PAPIER - ISO 9706
ORIENTALISTE, KLEIN DALENSTRAAT 42, B-3020 HERENT